T0380395

New Reflections on
The Revolution of Our Time

PHRONESIS

A new series from Verso edited by
Ernesto Laclau and Chantal Mouffe

There is today wide agreement that the left-wing
project is in crisis. New antagonisms have emerged
— not only in advanced capitalist societies but also
in the Eastern bloc and in the Third World — that
require the reformulation of the socialist ideal in
terms of an extension and deepening of democracy.
However, serious disagreements exist as to the
theoretical strategy needed to carry out such a task.
There are those for whom the current critique of
rationalism and universalism puts into jeopardy the
very basis of the democratic project. Others argue
that the critique of essentialism — a point of
convergence of the most important trends in
contemporary theory: post-structuralism, philosophy of language after the later Wittgenstein, post-
Heideggerian hermeneutics — is the necessary
condition for understanding the widening of the
field of social struggles characteristic of the present
stage of democratic politics. *Phronesis* clearly locates
itself among the latter. Our objective is to establish
a dialogue between these theoretical developments
and left-wing politics. We believe that an anti-
essentialist theoretical stand is the sine qua non of
a new vision for the Left conceived in terms of a
radical and plural democracy.

New Reflections on
The Revolution of Our Time

ERNESTO LACLAU

VERSO

London · New York

First published by Verso 1990
© Ernesto Laclau 1990
Translation © individual translators 1990
All rights reserved

Verso
UK: 6 Meard Street, London W1V 3HR
USA: 29 West 35th Street, New York, NY 10001-2291

Verso is the imprint of New Left Books

British Library Cataloguing in Publication Data
Laclau, Ernesto
New reflections on the revolution of our time.
1. Socialism
I. Title II. Series
335

ISBN 978-0-86091-919-3

US Library of Congress Cataloging-in-Publication Data
Laclau, Ernesto.
New reflections on the revolution of our time / Ernesto Laclau
p. cm. — (Phronesis)

1. Revolutions and socialism. I. Title.
II. Series: Phronesis
(London, England)
HX550.R48L33 1990   90-43438
321.09′4—dc20   CIP

Typeset in Bembo by Leaper & Gard, Bristol, England
Printed in Finland by Werner Söderström Osakeyhtiö

To Viamonte 430,
where everything began

Contents

Acknowledgements

'New Reflections on the Revolution of Our Time' was translated for this volume by Jon Barnes; 'The Impossibility of Society' first appeared in the *Canadian Journal of Political and Social Theory* (vol. 7, nos 1 & 2, Hiver-Printemps 1983); 'Psychoanalysis and Marxism' first appeared in *Critical Inquiry* (vol. 13, no. 2, Winter 1986), and is translated by Amy G. Reiter-McIntosh; 'Post-Marxism without Apologies' first appeared in *New Left Review* (no. 166, November-December 1987); 'Letter to Ernesto' and 'Letter to Aletta' appear here for the first time; 'Building a New Left' was first published in *Strategies* (no. 1, Fall 1988), Laclau's responses are translated by Maria Silvia Olmedo; 'Theory, Democracy and Socialism' is published here for the first time, Laclau's responses are translated by Jon Barnes; 'Beyond Discourse-Analysis' was written in English and appears here for the first time.

Preface

I

This preface was written in February 1990 in a very different historical context from when the volume was originally planned at the start of 1988. The last two years have seen the most important epochal mutation that the world has experienced since the end of the Second World War. Its epicentre has been the transformations currently in progress in Eastern Europe and the Soviet Union. The cycle of events which opened with the Russian Revolution has definitively closed, both as a force of irradiation in the collective imaginary of the international left, and also in terms of its ability to hegemonize the social and political forces of the societies in which Leninism, in any of its forms, constituted a state doctrine. The corpse of Leninism, stripped of all the trappings of power, now reveals its pathetic and deplorable reality. Without any doubt, ideologies bearing a historical transformation always exercise a violence on the contingent and limited reality that must embody them. There is in fact a certain distance or gap that is inevitable in any process of embodiment. But the *dimensions* of that gap are what finally counts, and the rule is clear: the more 'universal' the idea to be embodied is, the greater the distance from the historical limitations of the social agents intended as its bearers will be; and the more likely it is that the result will be a monstrous symbiosis. Hegel said that Napoleon was the Absolute Spirit on a white horse. It would be too optimistic to suppose, now that the Absolute Spirit has left the mortal body of Leninism, that what we are left with is a white horse.

There is no point in minimizing the depth of the revisions now needed in the assumptions on which the traditional discourse of the left has been based. Only such a critique and revisions can provide a new start that is fresh and sound. And above all else there must be no wishful thinking in terms of a hypothetical Marx whose discourse has been left intact by the subsequent deformations of 'Marxism'. As Gareth Stedman Jones asserted recently:

> Marx was far more successful in evoking the power of capitalism than in demonstrating in any conclusive fashion why it had to come to an end. It was eloquence rather than science which established the association between the end of capitalism and the destiny of the working class. His conviction of a future society based upon a higher notion of freedom amounted to no more than a few cryptic utterances, unsubstantiated either by evidence or logic. Finally, despite the claims of his followers, he never succeeded in establishing a coherent theory of the connections between property relations and political forms. As a result, his refusal to accept that capitalism might be controlled by political reform and collective pressure was ultimately a dogmatic assertion.[1]

The post-Marxist perspective of which this volume forms part is therefore much more than a mere theoretical choice: it is an inevitable decision for anyone aiming to reformulate a political programme for the left in the historical circumstances prevailing in the last decade of the twentieth century.

II

The title of this volume takes its inspiration from Harold Laski. It is worth dwelling on this point briefly, as the theoretical and political practice we are offering distances itself not just from Marxism and Communism, but from classical forms of social democracy as well. Published in 1943 — the year that represented the turning point in the Second World War — Laski's *Reflections on the Revolution of Our Time* take on the retrospective status of a manifesto for the subsequent experience of the Labour government in the immediate post-war period, formulating as they did the project of a 'planned democracy'. The radicalization of Laski's thought in the 1930s took the form of a growing sympathy for the Soviet experience in that it was based on a system of central planning (although he deplored the dictatorial excesses of Stalinism, the true dimensions of which were not known at the time). Laski recommended these achievements of a system of state planning for the West, affirming at the same time that they might be made compatible with the basic political values of a democratic society. Both communists and social democrats of the time, then, shared a common faith in the centralized state as the instrument capable of guaranteeing economic growth and the advent of more just, free and egalitarian societies.

Such confidence in the transforming capacities of the state make these analyses look dated. Centralized planning is discredited in communist societies and any prospect of future economic growth is referred to the reintroduction — in many cases the introduction *tout court* — of market economic mechanisms. And in the capitalist societies of the West the welfare state was discredited by the bureaucratic forms accompanying its implementation in the twenty years following the war, leading to the expansion of neo-conservatism and free-market ideologies in the 1980s.

Does this mean that we must give up any conscious regulation of the economic process and trust entirely in market mechanisms, as advised with a considerable dose of cynicism by our conservatives in the West, and with a considerable dose of utopianism by the emergent political elites in Eastern Europe? Of course not, because, among other reasons, the automatism of market mechanisms is largely a myth — indeed, state intervention in the regulation of the economy has been greater under neo-conservative regimes than during the period of the welfare state; and also because the results of such automatism, in the cases where it has operated freely, have been anything but beneficial for society as a whole. But this is exactly where the formulation of a new politics of the left must begin: with the deconstruction of the exclusive alternative between market and social regulation as its point of departure. For it must be remembered that the very notion of '*social* regulation of the production process' is dialectically linked to its opposition to market regulation conceived as wholly based on the *individual* pursuit of profit. It is only on the basis of the total and exclusive nature of this antithesis that 'socialism' can be seen as the radical elimination of private ownership of the means of production.

This is precisely where the problem arises. For if the notion of *social* underlying the idea of social regulation of the production process acquires content exclusively through its opposition to *individual*, then the homogeneous and indivisible nature of community must be automatically accepted. This social homogeneity, which assumed the function of giving concrete embodiment to universality in Marxist discourse, was guaranteed by sociological hypotheses such as the growing proletarianization of society and the progressive simplification of class structure under capitalism. But if this simplification does not occur, the homogeneity of the 'social' assumed by socialist discourse as the agent of planning will be necessarily absent: planning will not be carried out for the benefit of a supposed 'universal community' — a non-existent entity — but for the particular constellation of forces exercising control of the state (ranging from a bureaucratic class, as in Eastern Europe, to a political party in alliance with the trade unions, as in the case of British Labour governments).

The conclusion to be drawn from this is not negative, however. If the word of God can no longer be heard, we can start giving our own voices a new dignity. If our actions no longer have to be justified before a tribunal external to ourselves — History, Doctrine, the Party — we can begin to come to terms with the limitations from which we think and act, and even respect our own mistakes. Tolerance is not a marginal virtue: as the point at which recognition of our human condition can begin, it has an ontological function. This has three crucial implications for the left. The first is that if there is no 'objective' historical tendency for the social to emerge as a homogeneous subject that would coincide with the empty universality of the opposite to the 'individual', then any 'social' management will be by historically limited social actors. As a result, the radicality of a politics will not result from the emergence of a subject that can embody the universal, but from the expansion and multiplication of fragmentary, partial and limited subjects who enter the collective decision-making process. It is in this sense that Chantal Mouffe and I have attempted to redefine the project of the left as the construction of a radical and plural democracy. Secondly, the deconstruction of the 'social' in the market/social regulation dichotomy does not mean that its other pole becomes automatically valid, since it is the dichotomy itself, rather than either of the two poles in isolation, that has been deconstructed. In terms of the social pole, this involves a dispersion and dislocation of power. It is worth recalling in this respect that certain, apparently libertarian, forms of alternative to bureaucratic planning — like social management by direct producers — continue an authoritarian course in an inverted fashion; for unless society is homogenized in such a way that every member is a direct producer, such management can only mean a dictatorship over consumers and other strata of the population affected by the consequences of the production process. A radical and plural democracy involves the multiplication of those constituencies by which the social management of production is determined. The various identities arising from the fragmentation of the labour process, the different categories of workers, social and racial differences — as well as those produced by the effects of environmental exploitation on the whole of the population — all have a stake, and must therefore participate, in the global management of society. *Social* regulation is thus linked to an essential instability and incompletion of the constituencies defining it, and cannot be reduced to the 'statism' peculiar to both communism and social democracy. It is important to point out, however, that the notion of 'regulation through the market' does not remain unaffected by this deconstruction either. The free play of market forces is just as incapable as bureaucratic planning of producing a 'society effect'. In practice this means that social regulation will be a complex and pragmatic process in which state intervention and market mechanisms will combine according to forms that are irreducible to any aprioristic principle. As a result, just as the element of conscious state intervention does not find a teleological principle of explanation in a supposed immanent tendency to establish total state control over economic life, likewise there is no essential teleological link between the presence of market mechanisms and their total subordination to the goal of individual profit.

In that case, however — and this is the third consequence — the degree to which a radical democracy is being reached cannot be measured in terms of the level of state intervention in economic life. Socialism is no longer a blueprint for society, and comes to be part of a radical democratization of social organization. And this principle of democratization is of course compatible with a wide variety of concrete social arrangements that depend on circumstances, problems and traditions. It is in the multiplication of 'public spaces' and their constituencies beyond those accepted by classical liberalism that the base for the construction of a radical democratic alternative lies. There is nothing utopian in the proposition of these alternatives, given the growing fragmentation of social sectors and the proliferation of new identities and antagonisms in the societies in which we live.

III

Rethinking a radical democratic alternative for the twenty-first century requires countless discursive interventions, ranging from politics — in the current sense of the term — to economics, and from aesthetics to philosophy. This can only be the work of a whole generation, carried out over a number of years. A preliminary task, however, consists of exploring the intellectual assumptions of the prejudices that must be questioned, effecting a displacement that would allow a new viewpoint to be formed. The first essay in this volume is a contribution to this task where the reader will find an attempt to construct a viewpoint from which to think politics rather than a detailed discussion of concrete political problems.

The second part comprises a series of articles and discursive interventions published during the 1980s, and the third comprises two interviews I have given in recent years. The most recent and longest of these interviews, organized by Verso, is being published for the first time. Given the nature of this material and the extremely polemical climate in which such interventions took place – dominated by a number of reiterated political alternatives and questionings – a certain amount of overlap and repetition has been inevitable. I have nevertheless decided to gather all this material together in a single volume because the reiteration of an argument in different discursive contexts can contribute to its clarification.

I cannot do justice to all those who have contributed in one way or another to making this book possible – the list would be too long. But there are a few cases in which I want to make explicit my debt of thanks. To Robin Blackburn, with whom I originally planned the volume, and who has been a most patient publisher, accepting with resignation and good humour my continual transgression of deadlines. To Chantal Mouffe, whose personal and intellectual encouragement has accompanied me in this venture as it has on so many other occasions. To Slavoj Žižek, who enthusiastically welcomed the theoretical approach of *Hegemony and Socialist Strategy* and contributed an incisive critique of our treatment of the question of the subject. Its impact on my thought can be seen in the first piece of the book. I also want to thank Frank Cunningham and Zoltan Szankay for their commentaries on some of the contributions in this book. And last but not least, to my PhD students in the Department of Government at the University of Essex who have given me the opportunity to discuss many of these ideas in the context of one of the most demanding and intellectually creative seminars I have ever taken part in.[2]

Notes

1. Gareth Stedman Jones, 'Marx after Marxism', *Marxism Today*, February 1990, p. 3.

2. My special thanks to Aletta J. Norval and Anna-Marie Smith for their contributions to this volume.

PART I

1

New Reflections
on the Revolution of Our Time

1. Every age adopts an image of itself — a certain horizon, however blurred and imprecise, which somehow unifies its whole experience. The rediscovery of a past which gave access to the natural order of the world for the Renaissance; the imminence of the advent of Reason for the Enlightenment; the inexorable advance of science for positivism: all were such unifying images. In each case, the different stages of what has become known as 'modernity' were conceived as moments of transition towards higher forms of consciousness and social organization, holding the promise of a limitless future.

The intellectual climate of recent decades, on the other hand, has been dominated by a new, growing and generalized awareness of limits. Firstly, limits of reason, as has been pointed out from very different intellectual quarters — from epistemology and the philosophy of science to post-analytical philosophy, pragmatism, phenomenology and post-structuralism. Secondly, limits, or rather slow erosion of the values and ideals of radical transformation, which had given meaning to the political experience of successive generations. And finally, limits arising from the crisis of the very notion of 'cultural vanguard' which marked the different moments and stages of modernity. After decades, possibly centuries, of announcing the arrival of 'the new', it is as if we have reached a point of exhaustion, and mistrust the outcome of all experimentation.

An initial reaction to this new intellectual climate has been to become entrenched in the defence of 'reason' and attempt to relaunch the project of 'modernity' in opposition to those tendencies considered 'nihilistic'. The work of Habermas is perhaps the most representative of this attitude. Our position, however, is exactly the opposite: far from perceiving in the 'crisis of reason' a nihilism which leads to the abandonment of any eman-

3

cipatory project, we see the former as opening unprecedented opportunities for a radical critique of all forms of domination, as well as for the formulation of liberation projects hitherto restrained by the rationalist 'dictatorship' of the Enlightenment. The grounds for this position will become clear in the course of this essay.

2.   This whole debate has profound political consequences for the formulation of a democratic and socialist politics, since socialism, more than any other political orientation, is based on a radical critique of the existing social order and the assertion that the latter can be transcended. To uphold the limits of reason, to relativize the ethical, political and intellectual values of modernity, is this not to dismantle the ground on which a radical and progressive politics could be built?

The answer to this question is a clear 'No' for reasons that will be elaborated later. My explanation will be based on demonstrating the following: that negativity is part of any identity and that the rationalist project to determine the ultimate objective or positive meaning of social processes was consequently doomed to failure; that the contingent and precarious nature of any objectivity has only become fully apparent with contemporary capitalism and its associated dislocatory effects which show the historicity of being; and that this recognition of the historicity of being — and thus of the purely human and discursive nature of truth — opens new opportunities for a radical politics. Such opportunities stem from the new liberty gained in relation to the object and from an understanding of the socially constructed nature of any objectivity.

3.   Some of the themes in this essay have already been dealt with in *Hegemony and Socialist Strategy*,[1] written in collaboration with Chantal Mouffe. The structures and aims of the two works, however, are different.

In *Hegemony and Socialist Strategy* the project of a radical democracy was presented through a deconstruction of the history of Marxism as its starting point, hence its emphasis on the subversive nature and growing centrality of 'hegemony' in Marxist discourse. Here the argument is presented positively as a logical sequence of its categories. Its three parts — 'Dislocation and Antagonism', 'Dislocation and Capitalism' and 'Social Imaginary and Democratic Revolution' — are aimed at depicting the following: the intrinsic negativity of all antagonism, which prevents us from fixing it a priori in any positive theorization about the 'objectivity' of social agents (such as the class struggle, for example); the historical terrain on which conflicts in contemporary societies proliferate; and the new projects linked to the political reconstruction of social identities.

Two final observations are in order. Firstly, that the aim of this essay, which is something of an introduction and something of a manifesto, is to present the reader with a clear and logically structured theoretical and political argument. Quotations and concepts not defined by the text itself have been kept to a minimum. That is to say that the discursive areas on which our text draws, ranging from linguistics to psychoanalysis and from metaphysics to political theory, have undergone a constant translation into a uniform (though hopefully not oversimplified) theoretical language.

The second observation is that such a standardization is an impossible operation — the idea of a neutral, self-defining language flies in the face of everything I believe about language. My only excuses for this are that the construction of society is also an impossible task, of which human beings never tire, however; and also that if the reader understands by the end of this essay why its aim is impossible, then it will have been useful in any case. As Wittgenstein said: 'My propositions serve as elucidations in the following way: anyone who understands me eventually recognizes them as non-sensical, when he has used them — as steps — to climb beyond them. (He must, so to speak, throw away the ladder after he has climbed up it.)'[2]

Dislocation and Antagonism

4.   Let us begin by quoting one of the most classic Marxist texts:

In the social production of their existence, men inevitably enter into definite relations, which are independent of their will, namely relations of production appropriate to a given stage in the development of their material forces of production. The totality of these relations of production constitutes the economic structure of society, the real foundation on which arises a legal and political superstructure and to which correspond definite forms of social consciousness. The mode of production of material life conditions the general process of social, political and intellectual life. It is not the consciousness of men that determines their existence, but their social existence that determines their consciousness. At a certain stage of development, the material productive forces of society come into conflict with the existing relations of production or — this expresses the same thing in legal terms — with the property relations within the framework of which they have operated hitherto. From forms of development of the productive forces these relations turn into their fetters. Then begins an era of social revolution. The changes in the economic foundation lead sooner or later to the transformation of the whole immense superstructure. In studying such transformations it is always necessary to distinguish between the material transformation of the economic conditions of production, which can be determined with the precision of natural science, and the legal, political, religious, artistic and philosophic — in short ideological forms in which men become conscious of this conflict and fight it out. Just as one does not judge an individual by what he thinks about himself, so one cannot judge such a period of transformation by its consciousness but, on the contrary, this consciousness must be explained from the contradictions of material life, from the conflict existing between the social forces of production and the relations of production.[3]

If we compare this passage with that of another famous Marxist text, the *Communist Manifesto*, a profound difference springs to view. While the latter asserts that 'The history of all hitherto existing societies is the history of the class struggle',[4] in the Preface to the *Contribution to the Critique of Political Economy* class struggle is completely absent. History, in its ultimate determining level, is explained exclusively in terms of the contradiction between productive forces and relations of production. How can these two moments be logically articulated — on the one hand, the contradiction between productive forces and relations of production and, on the other, class struggle (which, according to Marx, takes in bourgeois society the simplified form of a confrontation between wage labour and capital)?

Firstly, it should be noted that the structure of the two contradictions is not identical. In the first case, there is a contradiction in the strict sense of the term: the continued expansion of the productive forces beyond a certain point within a particular system of relations of production is *logically* impossible. It would lead in the short or long term to the mechanical collapse of the system. Marx says so himself in the quote above: 'The material transformation of the economic conditions of production ... can be determined with the precision of natural science.' But this is a contradiction *without antagonism*. The fact that it is impossible for an economic system to expand indefinitely does not *necessarily* mean that its collapse must take the form of a confrontation between groups. The *Preface* presupposes a period of social revolution, as well as the antagonistic nature of relations of production under capitalism and before; but it does not make such antagonistic moments — on which the class struggle is based — a logically integral part of the model of historic change presented by the contradiction between productive forces and relations of production. As we shall see shortly, the problem is that if the contradiction between productive forces and relations of production is a contradiction without antagonism, class struggle, for its part, is an antagonism without contradiction.

5. It is clear, however, that whatever form of logical articulation may exist between 'class struggle' and 'contradictions emerging from the expansion of productive forces', it is the latter which ultimately determine social change for Marx. On the one hand, the class struggle is based on relations of production which can only be overcome when they have become a brake on any further development of the productive forces; on the other, 'the ground on which men become conscious of this conflict and fight it out' is that of superstructures. But in that case, the possibility of fusing the contradictions emerging from the expansion of the productive forces with class struggle depends on whether the latter can be reduced to an internal moment in the endogenous development of the former.

Let us dwell briefly on the sequence of these structural moments. If the relationship between productive forces and relations of production, as well as between wage labour and capital, are conceived as *contradictory*, and if the fundamental dynamics of social change lie in the first rather than the second, then the latter must be an internal moment in the dialectical development of the former. The reasons are clear: if the two contradictions were independent of each other, it would mean that the dialectical unity of history would be placed in doubt; and more important still, that the relationship between the two would no longer be fixed down a priori in a general theory of history, but would become *contingent* and based on *power*. (As the contradiction between productive forces and relations of production would cease to be the *foundation* of history, it would always have something constitutively external to itself, and the assertion that the development of the productive forces will *necessarily* predominate in the long run would become an arbitrary dogma. Indeed, relations of production could be structured in such a way as to hold back any further development of the productive forces indefinitely.)

Everything depends, then, on being able to show that the intrinsic antagonism of the relations of production (the conflict between wage labour and capital, for example) is a contradiction; and that the antagonism is inherent to the *relations* of production. It should be noted why the two are *sine qua non* conditions. Firstly, because it is only the dialectical form of the contradiction that ensures that antagonism should be conceived as an internal movement of the concept, rather than as a contingent power relationship between its two poles. For history to be grasped conceptually as a rational and coherent process, antagonism must be reduced to a contradiction. Secondly, assuming for a moment that relations of production *necessarily* correspond to a stage in the development of the productive forces, it is only if this relationship is *in itself* antagonistic (that is to say contradictory in this approach) that the 'rational' form of the historical process lacks something external to itself and can thus be reduced to the manifestations of its endogenous development.

Let us analyse the capitalist–worker relationship. Is it a contradictory relation? The sense of this question should be noted. Accepting for the moment that the relationship *is* antagonistic, the problem is to determine whether this antagonism can be seen as a contradiction. But it only needs a few moments' thought to realize that here there is no contradiction at all. The relationship between productive forces and relations of production could be considered contradictory if we accepted that history is unified by the *necessary* development of the productive forces; and that a particular system of relations of production becomes a break on any further development of the productive forces when it reaches a certain stage. But it is a very different situation with the antagonism between wage labour and capital: the fact that there is an antagonism between the two poles of the relationship — over the appropriation of surplus value, for example — does not mean that the relationship is *contradictory* in itself. Antagonism does not necessarily mean contradiction. Nevertheless, there is a vital difference between an antagonism regarded as non-contradictory and a contradiction *sensu stricto* as conceived by Hegel. In the case of the latter, the dialectical (and thus internal) movement of the concept predetermines its subsequent forms, while in the case of the antagonism without contradiction, that internal connection is absent. The resolution (or non-resolution) of the antagonism depends entirely on a factual and contingent history.

6.   There is, however, perhaps another way of overcoming this impasse: by showing that antagonism is inherent to the *form* of relations of production. For while antagonism cannot lead by itself to the abolition of capitalist relations of production (assuming that the latter correspond to a certain phase in the development of the productive forces), it may do so once the development of the productive forces has rendered a parti-

cular system of relations of production obsolete. This, in general terms, is how the Marxism of the Second International construed the imbrication between automatic collapse of capitalism and the conscious action of the working class in its overthrow.

But such a demonstration is impossible. Conceived as a form, capitalist relations of production are not intrinsically antagonistic. It should be remembered that capitalist relations of production consist of a relationship between *economic categories*, of which social actors only form part insofar as they are *Träger* (bearers) of them. The wage worker does not count as a concrete person, of flesh and blood, but as a seller of labour power. To show that capitalist relations of production are *intrinsically* antagonistic would therefore mean demonstrating that the antagonism stems *logically* from the relationship between the buyer and seller of labour power. But this is exactly what cannot be done. Could it be argued that the relationship is intrinsically antagonistic because it is based on unequal exchange and because the capitalist extracts surplus value from the worker? The answer to this point is 'No' because it is only if the worker *resists* such an extraction that the relationship becomes antagonistic; and there is nothing in the category of 'seller of labour power' to suggest such resistance is a *logical* conclusion.

In denying that capitalist relations of production are intrinsically antagonistic, it is important to draw attention to exactly what is being rejected; and also to point out the consequences for the model of historical development presented by Marx in the Preface. It is obviously not being denied that conflicts exist between workers and entrepreneurs, but merely that they spring from the logical analysis of the wage-labour/capital relationship. It should not be forgotten, however, that the theoretical foundations of this relationship had been based on the reduction of concrete social agents to the economic categories of buyer and seller of labour power. Once these categories are reintegrated into the social totalities forming the agents that are their bearers, we can easily imagine a multitude of antagonisms arising between those concrete social agents and the relations of production in which they participate. For example, a decent standard of living is impossible when wages fall below a certain level; and fluctuations in the labour market affect housing conditions or the worker's access to consumer goods. In this case, however, the conflict is not internal to capitalist relations of production (in which the worker counts merely as a seller of labour power), but takes place between the relations of production and the worker's identity outside of them. As we shall see, this *constitutive outside* is inherent to *any* antagonistic relationship.[5]

To understand the pattern and nature of social antagonisms under capitalism (or social antagonisms *tout court*), a conceptual clarification is therefore needed, both in terms of what is meant by an inside–outside relationship and in terms of the identity of social agents. Before dealing with this point, however, we must return to the consequences of this 'outside' for the historic model of the *Preface*.

Let us recall the various steps of our argument which asserts: (1) that in the *Preface* Marx presents, on the one hand, a theory of history based on the contradiction between productive forces and relations of production – a contradiction *without* antagonism, and on the other, a description which *presupposes* the antagonistic nature of relations of production in class societies; (2) that the logical coherence of his schema therefore depends on theoretically reintegrating antagonism into his more general theory of historical change; (3) that an initial solution might be to reduce antagonism to a contradiction, since it would be logically integrated into the dynamics of the conceptual interaction between productive forces and relations of production; but that this reduction is impossible; (4) that another means of conceptual recovery would be to show that antagonism, while not contradictory, is nevertheless an intrinsic part of the relations of production themselves and would therefore be subject to the laws of movement governing the latter's transformation. However, as we have seen, antagonism cannot be reintegrated in this way: on the contrary, it establishes the conditions for a permanent 'outside'. But if, in this case, history is faced with a permanent outside, the outcome of its different moments depends on contingent power relations between forces that cannot be reduced to any kind of unified logic. In this way the rationalism of the Preface and its attempt to reduce the historical process to an ultimately intelligible structure are dissolved.

7.   There is perhaps another way of defending the historical schema of the *Preface*, albeit reducing its eschatological ambitions. Let us assume we accept the irreducible presence of an 'outside', but that this 'outside' can be conceptualized in precise terms. In that case, its relations with the 'inside' constituted by the main line of historical development could also be rationally conceptualized. It would have been a case of a false 'outside' after all. Let us attempt briefly to move in this direction.

The most obvious path would be to introduce *one* supplementary hypothesis concerning the subjectivity of the agent, such as the *homo oeconomicus* of classical economics. This assumption, of course, does not have a logical or necessary link with the category of 'seller of labour power'. But if it is added as *just one more assumption*, we can assert that antagonism is inherent to relations of production since the former would have become a zero-sum game between the worker and the capitalist. This, however, presents two insurmountable problems.

The first is the implicit affirmation that the worker is as much a profit maximizer as the capitalist. This is largely why such a solution has been rejected by the majority of Marxist theorists — and for good reasons. Apart from going against the most elementary historical and social evidence, it forgets that the maximization of profits on which capitalist accumulation is based — the M-C-M' process — is an objective process which is independent of the motivations of the agents. To suppose that workers are profit maximizers in the same way as capitalists would be to remove all objective ground for any kind of link, whether automatically or hegemonically constructed, between the working class and socialism.

The second and most important reason for rejecting the universalization of profit maximization as the driving force of social agents is that the model of individual market competition is not one of antagonistic relations — it does not have an 'outside'. The market is a system of rules in which both the laws of movement and the individual moves of the participants are internal to the system. If I produce or buy more than I owe and go bust, I only have myself, or rather my misjudgement, to blame. There is therefore no antagonism: my identity as an economic agent is not denied. But there is indeed an antagonism if someone attacks and tries to rob me at home: my identity is denied and no shared system of rules exists between the latter and my aggressor. This is why the classic liberal misrepresentation of the worker–capitalist relationship reduces the latter to its legal form — the contract between free economic agents; and also why criticism of this misrepresentation points out how worker and capitalist *enter* into relations of production from an unequal starting point, and transform the relationship into one of conflict. To repeat: antagonism is established between the relations of production and something external to them, not within the relations of production themselves. (More generally, this is the limitation of all efforts to interpret social antagonisms in terms of game theory. The latter entails a system of rules which sets down the possible moves of the players and consequently establishes their identity. But with antagonism, rules and identities are *violated*: the antagonist is not a player, but a cheat.)

We have so far established that, unless antagonism is either reintegrated into the forces and relations of production schema or conceptually neutralized by a theory of subjectivity which deliberately establishes determinate relations with the latter, the theory of history based on the necessary development of the productive forces is faced with an 'outside' which strips it of any ultimate rational coherence. We have seen that the reduction of social agents to profit maximizers does not provide that neutralization, since it eliminates antagonism instead of explaining it.

Another possible solution would be to abandon the homogeneous and individualistic universe of the market and endow the productive forces with a subjectivity. In Hegelian fashion, their scope would be the installation of a progressive rationality in history, while the role of successive ruling classes would be to personify the global interests of humanity throughout time. In this way, the constitutive, 'outside' nature of antagonism would be apparently eliminated: its reintegration would be confirmed by splitting the historical subject into a rational 'humanity', conceived as the indefinite development of the productive forces, and its relations of correspondence (or non-correspondence) with the classes dominant at each phase of the productive forces' development. All antagonism would thus be reduced to the contradiction between productive forces and relations of production.

Such an endeavour characterizes, among others, the work of G.A. Cohen,[6] who states his case bluntly: 'With focus on the development of the productive forces, history becomes a coherent story. Perhaps history is not really coherent, but Marx thought it was, and he said the development of material power made it so.'[7] Cohen agrees with Marx and sets out to defend this thesis. His argument is as follows:

> A measure of acceptance of the development thesis may be motivated by reflection on three facts:
> (c) Men are, in a respect to be specified, somewhat rational.
> (d) This historical situation of men is one of scarcity.
> (e) Men possess intelligence of a kind and degree which enables them to improve their situation ...
> Given their rationality [(c)] and their inclement situation [(b)], when knowledge provides the opportunity of expanding productive power they will tend to take it, for not to do so would be irrational. In short, we put it as a reason for affirming the development thesis that its falsehood would offend human rationality.[8]

Productive forces and their development have therefore come to constitute a subject: 'human rationality'. Long live the Absolute Spirit! As to the problem that there is always 'some shadow (sic) between what reason suggests and what society does', Cohen reassures us that 'the shadow is not unduly long': 'Historical materialism fills the gulf between the demands of reason and the actual tendency of history by maintaining ... a rough correspondence of interests between ruling class and humanity at large.'[9] As can easily be imagined, any 'outside' has been removed from this picture: Cohen relegates any data which calls into question the development of the productive forces to the abnormalities typical of a 'historical pathology' in which we have the joint discussion of earthquakes, kidney diseases ... and the fall of the Roman Empire! Needless to say, class struggle has a totally secondary role in his analysis, and is reduced to a determination of its position in relation to the general interests of humanity (that is to say, the productive forces).

Nevertheless, it is important to dwell briefly on this argument since, in less crude forms, it underlies numerous theoretical and political formulations. It is based on a hypostatization of the abstract. A set of features allowing the comparison of very different social realities are abstracted from the latter and transformed into an actually existent entity with its own laws of movement — in this case 'human rationality'.

The review of Cohen's book by Andrew Levine and Erik Olin Wright[10] is instructive in this regard. They show how his whole model of historical change, with its emphasis on the productive forces, is based on a systematic evacuation of concrete social relations. Moreover, for them, the individualism characterizing classical contractualism underlies not only the vision of Cohen, but also that of Marx in the *Preface* of 1859. The automatism of working class capacities, resulting from the development of the productive forces under capitalism, is dogmatically assumed by Cohen, who ignores the disintegrative tendencies of those 'class capacities' arising from capitalist development. Finally, the thesis that the productive forces are fettered under capitalism is based on nothing more than an assertion that 'because capitalism is production for exchange rather than use, capitalist relations of production have a built-in bias for using progress in productive forces to expand output rather than to expand leisure time (where leisure is defined as release from burdensome toil.)'[11] In this way, captialist irrationality is not inherent to the rationality of a particular social system. Rather, 'relations of production become irrational with respect to a general notion of improving the human condition.'[12] The key concepts of 'scarcity' and 'rationality' must therefore be defined independently of any concrete social relationship.

Levine and Wright, on the other hand, correctly attempt to shift Cohen's abstract discussion of 'scarcity' and 'rationality' to the field of specific social relations. The 'scarcity' affecting feudal lords in their military rivalry for particular lands, for example, which drove them to develop technology and extract a growing surplus from the peasants, 'came not ... from a rational desire to augment productive capacity in the face of natural scarcity, but as an indirect effect of feudal relations of production'.[13] Any form of rationality occurs within — and thus presupposes — a certain system of relations of production. Moreover, it cannot be deduced that 'class capacities', defined as 'those organizational, ideological and material resources available to classes in struggle', will automatically emerge from the very process which forms 'class interests'.

It is this point, however, which reveals a clear insufficiency in Levine and Wright's analysis, making it vulnerable to the same criticisms that they level against Cohen. It is undoubtedly true that, in any historical situation, there will always be a relatively wide gap between any group's 'interests' and its ability to achieve them. But the key question is this: how are interests established? The following passage is revealing:

> The rational peasant (and other subordinate direct producers) in feudal society would probably have preferred a society without feudal lords and military competition; a society where there was nothing 'rational' about the way in which feudalism allowed for the development of the productive forces. But peasants as a subordinate class, separated from the means of repression, lacked the capacity to translate their rational interests into collective actions. Therefore the rationality and scarcity of the ruling class was imposed on them by the relations of production.[14]

This does not look at all like a historical reflection on how medieval peasants perceived their interests. Rather, it is the application of a universal model of rationality to a concrete case — the 'would *probably* have preferred' (my emphasis) is merely a euphemism. It is *only* if the peasants had not needed the lord's protection in a climate of violence and private power; had not seen their identity as part of a divine plan establishing a universal hierarchy; had possessed the intellectual tools to distinguish between economic interests, political ties and religious duties; in short, it is only if the Middle Ages had never existed and the peasants had been Levine, Wright or nineteenth-century Manchester entrepreneurs, that they could have seen that it was in their 'interest' to get rid of the lord and appropriate all the surplus for themselves. The 'rationality' presupposed here is a rationality without history, that is to say without origins or conditions of possibility. In this vision, interests are not formed, but recognized. Given a set of positions in the social structure, we simply proceed to allocate interests according to *our* criteria of rationality and then judge the degree of rationality of the different social agents in terms of whether they adapt to them or not. If Levine and Wright have historicized 'class *capacities*', their conception of 'class *interests*' remains as abstract and rationalist as that of Cohen. But whereas the latter bases his rationalism on the thesis of the primacy of productive forces, Levine and Wright have undermined such a foundation, thus rendering their rationalism doubly dogmatic and groundless.

8.   Let us draw out the consequences of our analysis. It is like an ascent in which the eschatological and rationalist pretensions of the original schema have been brought increasingly into question. We found the extreme form of the schema in the *Preface* where the development of the productive forces is the rational ground of history, the class struggle merely intervening as a *deus ex machina* which does not appear to be *logically* integrated into the argument. From there we set out the conditions under which a full logical integration might take place — the contradictory nature of antagonism and its inherence to the relations of production themselves — and observed that the first was not fulfilled. A new, albeit weakened, form of the schema of the *Preface* could have been maintained, had it been possible to show that antagonism is inherent to the relations of production themselves and that at some point the latter come into conflict with any further development of the productive forces. But as we saw, antagonism does not occur *within* the relations of production, but between the latter and the social agent's identity outside them. A third line of defence, therefore, is to attempt to incorporate into the argument, as a constant value, the 'outside' formed by the subjectivity of the agent. Unfortunately, however, as has been shown, neither the *homo oeconomicus* nor a 'human rationality' *à la* Cohen can do the trick. For their part, eclectic solutions — which we have exemplified with the case of Levine and Wright — are historically and descriptively more correct; but paradoxically, they are all the more inconsistent *for that very reason*.

This last point is important. The more the dogmatic rationalism of the primacy of the productive forces is abandoned and the more the conduct and abilities of the social agents become dependent on concrete circumstances and contexts which they have not determined, the more the effort to determine rational identifiable 'interests' outside of those circumstances and contexts ends up being inconsistent. We are faced here with the problem of the paradoxical forms that the recognition of new pieces of evidence questioning deep-seated prejudices assumes: this very questioning, when linked to the refusal to abandon such prejudices, leads to various efforts to make both compatible. Thus the first forms of discursive presence of the new evidence coexist with the most extreme reaffirmation of the principles concealing it — that is with the moment in which the latter attempt to hegemonize the former.

It only remains to be added that a final form of dependency regarding a rationalist version of history is to accept its limitations fully, but without drawing all the conclusions from such an admission. But these conclusions are so fundamental and demand such critical distance from the intrinsic prejudices of current forms of viewing the socio-historical field, that they should be specified at some length.

9.   If our argument was limited to rejecting the primacy of the productive forces and to upholding that of the relations of production instead, the modifications thereby introduced in the historical schema of the *Preface* would be relatively minor. History would not be unified as a 'coherent story' and the *objective* and *positive* nature of social relations would not be placed in question. But as we have seen, relations of production are not *intrinsically* antagonistic. Thus, to assert their primacy does not automatically mean privileging class struggle. In this new approach, the element of *antagonism*, of *struggle* would continue to be as unthought out as in the version of history of the *Preface*.

Let us return to our previous example. Insofar as an antagonism exists between a worker and a capitalist, such antagonism is not inherent to the relations of production themselves, but occurs between the latter and the identity of the agent outside. A fall in a worker's wage, for example, denies his identity as a consumer. There is therefore a 'social objectivity' — the logic of profit — which denies another objectivity — the consumer's identity. But the denial of an identity means preventing its constitution as an objectivity. This throws up two alternatives: either the element of negativity is reabsorbed by a positivity of a higher order which reduces it to mere appearance; or the negation is irreducible to any objectivity, which means that it becomes *constitutive* and therefore indicates the impossibility of establishing the social as an objective order.

As is known, the philosophies of history were oriented in the first direction. A concept such as the 'cunning of reason' in Hegel can only assert the rationality of the real at the expense of reducing antagonism, negativity, to an appearance through which a higher form of rationality and positivity works. It is therefore clear why class struggle had to be excluded from the *Preface*: to affirm its preeminence would have meant questioning the ultimate coherence and rationality of history. It is characteristic of Hegelian and Marxist visions of history that, at the very point of opening up to a deeper understanding of the role of struggle and negativity in the construction of the social, they immediately step back and attempt to integrate this understanding into a most traditional kind of theory of the positivity of the social — a theory based, of course, on what Heidegger and Derrida have termed the 'metaphysics of presence'.

On the other hand, the constitutive nature of the negative — our second alternative — 'works' within Marxist texts, disarticulating here and there the supposed coherence of their basic categories. As we pointed out in *Hegemony and Socialist Strategy*, the political and intellectual history of Marxism has largely been the history of this internal tension. My aim here, however, is different. It is to depict the nature and depth of the changes in our social and historical outlook which stem from privileging the moment of negativity, since the abstract acceptance of an argument does not imply automatic comprehension of all the dimensions in which it operates.

10.   The crucial point is that antagonism is the *limit of all objectivity*. This should be understood in its most literal sense: as the assertion that antagonism does not have an objective meaning, but is that which prevents the constitution of objectivity itself. The Hegelian conception of contradiction subsumed within it both social antagonisms and the processes of natural change. This was possible insofar as contradiction was conceived as an internal moment of the concept; the rationality of the real was the rationality of the system, with any 'outside' excluded by definition. In our conception of antagonism, on the other hand, we are faced with a 'constitutive outside'. It is an 'outside' which blocks the identity of the 'inside' (and is, nonetheless, the prerequisite for its constitution at the same time). With antagonism, denial does not originate from the 'inside' of identity itself but, in its most radical sense, *from outside*; it is thus pure facticity which cannot be referred back to any underlying rationality.

This can be seen more clearly if we compare antagonisms with the processes of change in nature which do not have an 'outside'. In a world of 'real' objects, there are continual processes of transformation, but not negativity. A stone's identity is expressed by remaining immutable or by breaking, depending on whether its physical environment changes or stays the same. If the stone broke, it would obviously be absurd to say that its identity had been 'denied'. 'Transformation' means precisely the opposite: it is a wholly positive process that *explains itself* in terms of the identity of its constituent elements. With antagonism, however, it is an entirely different matter: it is not my identity which is expressed, but the impossibility of its constitution. The antagonizing force *denies* my identity in the strictest sense of the term. Here we find ourselves again with the alternative referred to earlier. Either we can describe the development and outcome of an antagonistic process in terms of causal or dialectical 'transformation'. In that case the unity and positivity of the process must be assumed, thus requiring the negativity experienced by social agents to be reduced to the mere appearance of an 'objective meaning' which escapes them. Or we can make negativity constitutive and foundational, with the result that the uniqueness and rationality of history must be abandoned. But in the second case it is easy to see, as objectivity presupposes the positivity of all its elements, that the presence of the inherent negativity of a 'constitutive outside' means that the social never manages to fully constitute itself as an objective order.

The 'outside' is thus a *radical* outside, without a common measure with the 'inside'. Our next task, then, is to explore the various dimensions and related logics of an 'outside' that is constitutive, making them the starting point for a new inquiry concerning the social.

11.   An initial definition of the 'outside' characteristic of antagonism can be established through the exploration of the notion of 'contingency'. Our thesis is that antagonism has a revelatory function, in that it shows the ultimately contingent nature of all objectivity. We will begin this discussion by locating the specificity of the 'contingent' within the general field of the 'accidental'.

The notion of 'accident' comes from Aristotle's *Metaphysics* where it is defined as follows: '"Accident" [or "attribute"] means that which applies to something and is truly stated, but neither necessarily nor usually: as if, for example, while digging a hole for a plant one found a treasure'.[15] Aristotle then goes on to introduce a second example:

> Nor is there any definite cause for an accident, but only a chance; i.e. indefinite cause. It was by accident that X went to Aegina if he arrived there, not because he intended to go there but because he was carried out of his course by a storm, or captured by pirates. The accident has happened or exists, but in virtue not of itself but of something else; for it is the storm which was the cause of his coming to a place for which he was not sailing — i.e. Aegina.[16]

These two examples are fundamentally different. Finding a treasure while digging a hole does not interfere with the purposive action of digging, whereas in the case of being carried out of one's way in a storm, it is the purposive action which is affected. Moreover, it should be added that, for Aristotle, all permanent characteristics of an entity which do not form part of its essence are also accidents (for example, it is an accident that I may be tall or short, while being a rational animal is part of my human essence). It is clear, however, why Aristotle could put all these cases on the same level and subsume them under the general category of 'accident': because his main objective was to show the impossibility of attributing a definite cause to the form's 'outside' constituted by the 'accidental', that is, the impossibility of making it a determinate and knowable part of the first instance of being. It was therefore a question of establishing a strict limit between the *eidos* and what is outside it — between knowable form and unknowable matter. From this perspective, Aristotle was fully justified in subsuming his various examples under the same label of 'accidental'. But the very generality of this label shows us that, while the 'outside' characteristic of an antagonistic relationship could be included in the general field of the 'accidental', the generality of the latter is not enough to define the specificity of the former.

Christianity takes the concept of 'accident' in a new direction with the notion of 'contingency'. Contingent is that being whose essence does not entail its existence. Thus, the only necessary being whose essence and existence coincide is God. This leads to two fundamental modifications vis-à-vis classical philosophy. Firstly, that while a rigid boundary exists for the latter between form and matter, for Christianity the affirmation of the original act of Creation means that the form itself becomes contingent. Secondly, the fact that the act of Creation is conceived as a strict *creatio ex nihilo* on the part of a being that keeps an infinite distance from the created — which is therefore not, unlike Aristotle's God, an ingredient of the cosmos — means that the *ens creatum* is also susceptible to a radical annihilation and essentially vulnerable as a result. The identity of finite beings is a threatened identity. In this way, a dimension of negativity penetrates and is latent in any objectivity.

To assert that something is radically contingent, and that its essence does not imply its existence, therefore amounts to saying that the conditions of existence of an entity are exterior to it. Only in the case of a strictly necessary being does a perfect coincidence between essence and existence occur. Where are the conditions of existence of a finite and contingent being located? In Christian thought, the answer is clear: in the original act of creation. To ground the contingent being on its conditions of existence is thus to refer it to a foundation or origin which maintains an infinite distance from it. The infinite nature of that distance is the condition of contingency as such. In response to this, the alternative exists of referring finite beings back to conditions of existence which are necessary, but which are conceived not in terms of an infinite distance from them, but rather as the ground for a self-generating and self-regulating totality. From Spinoza to Marx, this is the line of modern thought. In this case, however, contingency is eliminated and radically absorbed by the necessary. It is in this sense that Hegel proclaims the identity between the rational and the real.

This point allows us to glimpse why a conception which aims to assert the *constitutive* nature of the dimension of negativity characterizing antagonism is strictly incompatible with an objectivist and positive conception of the social. There can be nothing contingent in the latter if there is identity between the rational and the real. However, if antagonism *threatens* my existence, it shows, in the strictest sense of the term, my radical contingency. And at this point, as we said, the alternative is clear: either antagonism is the mere appearance of a deeper rationality *through* which the latter is realized, in which case both its two poles and its denouement can be referred back to *necessary* conditions of existence; or, if negativity is radical and the outcome of the struggle not predetermined, the contingency of the identity of the two antagonistic forces is also radical and the conditions of existence of both must be themselves contingent.

This can be seen even more clearly if it is considered from the point of view of the relational or non-relational character of the identities. The *eidos* of classical philosophy was an identity that could be fully understood independently of accidents and therefore maintained a link of exteriority with them. It was of course possible, as in the case of modern rationalist philosophies, to establish the existence of relations of logical implication between identities so that they all referred back to an intelligible totality in which each constitutes an internal moment. But even in this case, their location within that totality is entirely determinate and thinkable. With merely contingent identities, however, this boundary between essence and accident is impossible to maintain and the accidents themselves come to form part of the identities. Contingency does not therefore mean a set of merely external and aleatory relations between identities, but the impossibility of fixing with any precision — that is, in terms of a necessary ground — either the relations *or the identities*.

In this case, then, what one gets is a field of simply relational identities which never manage to constitute themselves fully, since relations do not form a closed system. This has two important consequences. The first is that the identities and their conditions of existence form an inseparable whole. In the case of Christian thought, there was an infinite distance between the two; in that of rationalism, an essential unity, but which was simply the necessary unity of the whole of the real; in our case, there is a more subtle dialectic between necessity and contingency: as identity depends entirely on conditions of existence which are contingent, its relationship with them is absolutely necessary. What we find, then, is a relationship of complete imbrication between both: essence is nothing outside its accidents. But this means — and this is the second consequence — that the antagonizing force fulfils two crucial and contradictory roles at the same time. On the one hand, it 'blocks' the full constitution of the identity to which it is opposed and thus shows its contingency. But on the other hand, given that this latter identity, like all identities, is merely relational and would therefore not be what it is outside the relationship with the force antagonizing it, the latter is also part of the conditions of existence of that identity. As Saint-Just said: 'What constitutes the unity of the Republic is the total destruction of what is opposed to it.'[17] This link between the blocking and simultaneous affirmation of an identity is what we call 'contingency', which introduces an element of radical undecidability into the structure of objectivity.

This point makes it fully visible why the two explanations of the logic of history offered by Marxism — one founded on the contradiction between forces and relations of production, the other on the centrality of class struggle — proved difficult to integrate. The reason was clearly because one presupposes the rationality of the real and thus the radical objectivity of history and society, while the other assumes the constitutive nature of antagonism. Depending on which perspective is adopted, the questioning of the social will be of a fundamentally different kind. In the first case, the questioning will refer to the *objective meaning* of historical processes and the *positive logics* in the constitution of the social. The analysis will aim to reveal, beyond the awareness of social actors and the phenomenal forms that their actions take, a rationality which is established at the level of essences. Behind the empirical and contingent variation of concrete situations, there is an essential objectivity whose laws of movement rule historical transformation.

Understanding history, then, consists of an operation of recognition in which essential actors, whose fundamental identity is known in advance, are identified in the empirical actors personifying them. Here we find ourselves at the antipodes of Wittgenstein's 'language games'. While the rules of the latter only exist in the practical instances of their application — and are consequently modified and deformed by them — in the first case it is the opposite; the practical instances of a concrete empiricity are *accidents* that merely affect details of a history which takes place in all its essential movements, according to rules known a priori. The *eidos* dominates exclusively and history is therefore a history without 'outside'. Let us consider, for example, a question of the following kind: is the English Revolution of the seventeenth century *the* bourgeois-democratic revolution? Here the theoretical object of 'bourgeois-democratic revolution' is not built on an empirical and contingent history but pre-exists it; its advent is required by another kind of temporality, an essential temporality which is wholly objective and necessary.

On the other hand, if the constitutive nature of antagonism is taken for granted, the mode of questioning of the social is completely modified, since contingency radically penetrates the very identity of the social agents. The two antagonistic forces are not the expression of a deeper objective movement that would include both of them; and the course of history cannot be explained in terms of the essential 'objectivity' of either. The latter is always an objectivity threatened by a constitutive outside. But as we know, this implies that the conditions of existence of any objectivity that might exist must be sought at the level of a factual history. Moreover, as this objectivity has a merely relational identity with its conditions of existence, it means that the 'essential identity' of the entity in question will always be transgressed and redefined. The 'bourgeois-democratic revolution', far from being an object to be identified in different latitudes (France, England, Italy) — an object that would therefore establish relations of exteriority with its specific conditions of existence in different contexts — would instead be an object that is deformed and redefined by each of its contingent contexts. There would merely be 'family resemblances' between the different 'bourgeois-democratic revolutions'. This allows the formulation of questions such as: how bourgeois was the democratic revolution in country X?; or rather, how democratic was the bourgeoisie in context Y? There is thus a historicization of the categories of social analysis which, on linking the unity between the components of an object to contingent and specific conditions of existence, introduces an essential instability into the relations between such components. While the first — objectivist — kind of questioning of the social looks for essential characters behind historical specificity, the second moves in the opposite direction; weakening the boundary of essence through the radical contextualization of any object.

In practice, Marxist historical analysis has constantly mixed both types of questioning and this has led to unstable equilibria between opposing discursive movements. Take the debate about the relationship between capitalism and racism in South Africa, for example. The liberal school has sustained that there is an essential incompatibility between them; apartheid is a relic of the past that would be eliminated by capitalist modernization. In response, the so-called neo-Marxist school has cogently argued that apartheid, far from being incompatible, is an essential part of capitalist accumulation, since its various regulations and forms of discrimination allow the rate of exploitation to be increased. This can be interpreted from an economistic point of view: the logic of capitalist accumulation is the ultimate rationale of politics, with the South African state and racism representing a superstructure that is functionally integrated into that logic. But the argument could be turned on its head: if racism is a functional requirement of the form of capitalist accumulation existing in South Africa, does this not mean that racism is a condition of existence of such accumulation? In that case — and given that the fluctuations in racist politics are determined by a number of processes (struggles and divisions in the dominant elite, international pressure etc.) which are not directly linked to the endogenous logic of capital accumulation — does this not mean that the economy has a constitutive 'outside' and that the abstract logic of capital, far from dictating the laws of movement in every area of social development, is itself contingent, since it depends on processes and transformations which escape its control? The same can, of course, be said of racism or any other aspect of South African society.

At stake here is the questioning of any 'superhard' transcendentality[18] showing the factual conditions of existence on which any concrete objectivity depends. Arguments against economistic forms of Marxism have generally been presented as a critique of a *direct* determination of the superstructural processes by the economy, and as a defence of the relative autonomy of the other levels. For a number of reasons that we have analysed elsewhere, we believe these various anti-economistic efforts are theoretically inconsistent. But apart from such inconsistencies, the real difficulty is that these efforts do not address the fundamental question. For what is at stake is not the degree of effectiveness of a fully constituted object — the economy — on the rest of social development, but to determine the extent to which the economy is constituted as an autonomous object, separated by a boundary of essence from its factual conditions of existence. And here we can fully apply what we established earlier: if a set of socio-political configurations such as apartheid, for example, are conditions of existence of the economy and capitalist accumulation, then the economy cannot be constituted as an object separate from those conditions since we know that the conditions of existence of any contingent identity are internal to the latter. What we find, then, is not an interaction or determination between fully constituted areas of the social, but a field of relational semi-identities in which 'political', 'economic' and 'ideological' elements will enter into unstable relations of imbrication without ever managing to constitute themselves as separate objects. The boundary of essence between the latter will be permanently displaced. The combinatorial games between hypostatized entities — the 'economic', the 'political' and the 'ideological' — remind one most of those economic abstractions which Marx described as 'an enchanted, perverted, topsy-turvy world in which *Monsieur le Capital* and *Madame la Terre*, who are social characters as well as mere things, do their *danse macabre*'.[19] This does not mean, of course, that an area of the social cannot become autonomous and establish, to a greater or lesser degree, a separate identity. But this separation and autonomization, like everything else, has specific conditions of existence which establish their limits at the same time. What is not possible is to begin by accepting this separate identity as an unconditional assumption and then go on to explain its interaction and articulation with other identities on that basis.

This argument on the contextual nature of identities must be maintained without restriction. Claude Lefort, for example, has shown how a category like 'worker' does not designate a suprahistorical essence, since its condition of existence is the separation of the direct producer from the community and the land, and this required the genesis of capitalism. Lefort asserts: 'To say that human beings do not have the status of "labourer" is to say that they are not differentiated, in their activity, from the environment in which they work, that the land which serves as dwelling place, as raw material, and as a source of implement is not external to them.'[20] And having cited Marx's assertion that the *clan community*, the natural community appears, not as a *result* of, but as a *presupposition for the communal appropriation* (temporary) *and utilization of the land*, Lefort adds:

> But anyone who thinks that Marx is referring here only to the *representation* of the community would be on the wrong track. The community appears to human beings as it really *is*. 'Communality of blood, language, customs':

such is the primordial condition of all appropriation, just as the land does not merely *seem* to be but actually 'is the great workshop, the arsenal which furnishes both means and material labour, as well as the seat, the *base* of the community'.[21]

Naturally, knowing what a 'labourer' is in our world, we can project this category towards the past and subsume all direct producers under it. This is not an illegitimate exercise to the extent that it is recognized for what it is: a history of the referent which *constitutes* an object which only has validity, for a number of comparative purposes, as part of a historian's discourse. But from there, an illegitimate transition is just a step away: to conceive the 'labourer' as a transcendental a priori category representing the essence of every direct producer, whose historically differentiated forms in relation to the conditions of production would merely constitute empirical variations.

In his analysis, Marx referred the conditions for the emergence of capitalism back to two fundamental processes: the existence of free labour and its sale in the labour market, and the separation of free labour from the means and material of labour. In so doing, he admitted that some of the conditions of existence of capitalism were provided by extra-economic forces, hence his analysis of the process of original accumulation. From this point onwards, however, he tended to believe (and with him the bulk of the Marxist tradition of the Second International) that the process of capitalist accumulation was driven by its own laws — that is to say that it generated its own conditions of existence. But this is the point where Marxist analysis becomes unacceptable. If, as we have seen, the very antagonism between worker and capitalist is not internal to the relations of production, but is established between the relations of production and an identity *external* to them, then the modes of relation with that 'outside' cannot be an automatic effect of the logic of accumulation. The conditions of existence of capitalist accumulation are provided by a set of factors which correspond to complex balances of forces — partly economic, of course, but also political, institutional and ideological. None of them can therefore be conceptualized as a 'superstructure'. In other words, the 'structural' effectiveness of the extra-economic factors does not just operate at the moment of original accumulation, but is a condition of existence of *all* stages of capitalist accumulation. In that case, the myth of a separate and definable 'economic instance' must be abandoned. What exists is not an essentially homogeneous entity — the capitalist system — which merely allows for empirical and accidental variations in different historical and geographical contexts. Instead, there are global configurations – historical blocs, in the Gramscian sense – in which the 'ideological', 'economic', 'political' and other elements are inextricably fused and can only be separated for analytical purposes. There is therefore no 'capitalism', but rather different forms of capitalist relations which form part of highly diverse structural complexes.

12.   We must now go on to explore the other implications for our argument stemming from the assertion of the constitutive nature of antagonism and the consequent radical contingency of all objectivity. First, however, a number of clarifications must be made regarding the notions of 'negativity' and 'contingency' that we have been using here.

Firstly, the notion of negativity on which our analysis is based is not negativity in the dialectical sense of the term. The Hegelian notion of negativity is that of a *necessary* negativity and as such was conceived as *determinate* negation. That is to say that the negative is a moment in the internal unfolding of the concept which is destined to be reabsorbed in an *Aufhebung*, or higher unity. It is not even necessary here, as has been occasionally claimed, for the final term of the dialectical movement to be positive; even if the system is conceived as a successive movement between positivity and negativity, the latter is always internal to it. Contingency itself is absorbed as a moment in the self-unfolding of the necessary. While the outside that we have attempted to define is a radical and constitutive outside, dialectical negativity is not a true outside since it is merely present to be recovered by the inside. But if the negativity of which we are speaking reveals the contingent nature of all objectivity, if it is truly constitutive, then it cannot be recovered through any *Aufhebung*. It is something which simply shows the limits of the constitution of objectivity and cannot be dialecticized.

On the other hand, to assert the radically contingent nature of all objectivity, does this not mean inverting the essentialist logic of necessity and replacing it with its 'other'? The truth is that if the assertion of the contingent nature of all objectivity merely implied the absence of any necessity, we would just be faced with an empty totality, since the discourse of contingency would simply be the negative reverse of that of necessity and would not be able to transcend the latter's limits. In a universe from which necessity had evaporated, we would thus find nothing but indeterminacy and the impossibility of any coherent discourse. But this is obviously not what we mean. We are dealing not with a *head-on negation* of necessity (which as such would leave it conceptually unchanged), but with its *subversion*. Let us consider the threat to an identity (and thus to an objectivity) that antagonism presupposes. For antagonism to be able to *show* the contingent nature of an identity, that identity must be there in the first place. The structure of any relation of threat presupposes positing and questioning an identity at the same time. Seen from the perspective of the antagonized force, the possession of a full identity would presuppose the entirely sutured objectivity of the latter, that is its necessary character. But this is precisely what the antagonizing force deprives it of. Without the coexistence of these two moments — the completeness of an objectivity and its impossibility — no threat would exist at all. And this very duality is also present if we consider the threat from the point of view of the antagonizing force: it is not possible to threaten the existence of something without simultaneously affirming it. In this sense, it is the contingent which subverts the necessary: contingency is not the negative other side of necessity, but the element of impurity which deforms and hinders its full constitution.

Just to say that everything is contingent, then, is an assertion that would only make sense for an inhabitant of Mars. It is true that in the *final instance* no objectivity can be referred back to an absolute ground; but no important conclusion can be drawn from this, since the social agents never act in that final instance. They are therefore never in the position of the absolute chooser who, faced with the contingency of all possible courses of action, would have no reason to choose. On the contrary, what we always find is a limited and given situation in which objectivity is *partially* constituted and also *partially* threatened; and in which the boundaries between the contingent and the necessary are constantly displaced. Moreover, this interplay of mutual subversion between the contingent and the necessary is a more primary ground, ontologically, than that of a pure objectivity or total contingency. To assert, as we have, the constitutive nature of antagonism does not therefore mean referring all objectivity back to a negativity that would replace the metaphysics of presence in its role as an absolute ground, since that negativity is only conceivable within such a very framework. What it does mean is asserting that the moment of undecidability between the contingent and the necessary is *constitutive* and thus that antagonism is too.

13.   In *Hegemony and Socialist Strategy* we presented the history of Marxism as the process of a progressive incorporation of the various

areas of the social into the operative field of the articulatory logics of hegemony, and as the consequent withdrawal from the field of 'historic necessity'. But it is important not to transfer to the category of 'hegemony' the totalizing effects that have been displaced from the field of 'objective structures'. In this regard, we can point to three levels of theoretical radicalization of the category of 'hegemony', which also imply three levels of analysis of the necessity—contingency relationship.

(1) A first approach would operate at the level of what we might call the articulation of 'floating signifiers'. For example, a signifier like 'democracy' is essentially ambiguous by dint of its widespread political circulation: it acquires one possible meaning when articulated with 'anti-fascism' and a completely different one when articulated with 'anti-communism'. To 'hegemonize' a content would therefore amount to *fixing* its meaning around a nodal point. The field of the social could thus be regarded as a trench war in which different political projects strive to articulate a greater number of social signifiers around themselves. The open nature of the social would stem from the impossibility of managing a total fixity. The 'necessity' and 'objectivity' of the social would depend on the establishment of a stable hegemony, with the periods of 'organic crisis' characterized as those in which the basic hegemonic articulations weaken and an increasing number of social elements assume the character of floating signifiers. Although this approach certainly captures part of the process of the hegemonic—discursive construction of the social, its limitations are also more than evident. They stem from what could be termed the 'transparency of the project' which underlies it. Indeed, for this approach there cannot be a closed totality because it is not empirically possible for a social force to impose its hegemonic supremacy in such a complete way; but it is assumed that if such a supremacy ideally came about, the social would take on the character of a self-regulated and self-generated ensemble. However, this conclusion can only be upheld if, at the same time, it is maintained that the project of the hegemonic force is absolutely self-transparent; in other words, if the ambiguities of the structure do not penetrate the project as such. As can be seen, this leads to a naïve vision of the social agents' homogeneity and self-awareness.

(2) A second approach would attempt to overcome this limitation by partially transferring the ambiguities of the structure to the project. The incomplete and contingent nature of the totality would spring not only from the fact that no hegemonic system can be fully imposed, but also from the intrinsic ambiguities of the hegemonic project itself. The

project would not be external to the structures, but would be the result of a movement generated with them, in an effort to achieve an articulation and fixity that can only be partial. The deconstruction of the exclusive subject–structure duality thus begins. But even this second approach has a basic flaw. It sees the ambiguity of a social signifier as limited by what we might call, to use an Aristotelian term, 'equivocity' – that is, an ambiguity stemming from the fact that a term can be used differently in two separate contexts, but with a clear and unquestionable meaning in each. In our case ambiguity would arise because the clarity of that context has not been achieved and the term does not manage to take on a definite sense as a result. Although ambiguity now penetrates both the 'project' and the 'structure', the latter is an ambiguity which depends entirely on the imperfections of that which is empirically attainable. But the ideal of a pure contextual transparency is not placed in question – it continues dominating as a regulative idea.

(3) A third level of radicalization of the dimension of contingency inherent to any hegemonic articulation is achieved when the ambiguity and incompletion of the structure is conceived, not as the result of the empirical impossibility of its specific coherence being fulfilled, but as something which 'works' within the structure from the beginning. That is to say that, even as a regulative idea, the coherence of the structure must be questioned. Let us take an example inspired by Wittgenstein. If I begin counting the numerical series, 1, 2, 3, 4, and ask someone to continue, the spontaneous answer would be 5, 6, 7, etc. But I can adduce that this is wrong, since the series I have in mind is 1, 2, 3, 4; 9, 10, 11, 12; 17, 18, 19, 20; etc. But if my interlocutor believes that s/he has now understood the rule and tries to follow it by continuing the series in the stated way, I can still adduce that s/he is wrong since my initial enunciation was merely a fragment of a different series – for example, one comprising the numbers 1 to 20, 40 to 60, and 80 to 100 etc. And obviously, I can always change the rule by continuing the series in a different way. As can be seen, the problem here is not that the coherence of a rule can never be fully realized in empirical reality, but that the rule itself is undecidable and can be transformed by each new addition. Everything depends, as Lewis Carroll would say, on who is in command. It is a question of hegemony in the strictest sense of the term. But in this case, if the series is undecidable in terms of its very formal structure, the hegemonic act will not be the *realization* of a rationality preceding it, but an act of radical *construction*.

Let us go on to consider the various dimensions of the hegemonic process that are conceivable on the basis of this third approach. Firstly, if undecidability lies in the structure as such, then any decision developing *one* of its possibilities will be contingent, that is external to the structure, in the sense that it is not determined by that particular structure, even though it may be made possible by it. But secondly, the agent of that contingent decision must be considered, not as an entity *separate* from the structure, but constituted in relation to it. However, if the agent is not entirely internal to the structure, this is because the structure itself is undecidable and cannot be entirely repetitive, since the decisions based upon, but not determined by it, transform and subvert it constantly. This means that the agents themselves transform their own identity in so far as they actualize certain structural potentialities and reject others. Given that any contingent identity is essentially relational in terms of its conditions of existence, it is important to point out that any change in the latter cannot fail to affect the former. For example, if the trade unions' relationship with the political system is drastically transformed by a number of political and economic decisions, we do not have the same identity – the trade unions – in a new situation, but a new identity. As with our example of the numerical series, just as each unit changes with a modification of the rule defining the series, likewise a new hegemonic configuration alters the identity of all social forces present.

Nevertheless, there is a third aspect here which must be thoroughly analysed, as it holds the key to understanding the specificity of the political. It is clear from the above that a decision taken on the basis of an undecidable structure is contingent in relation to it. It is also clear that if, on the one hand, the subject is not external to the structure, on the other it becomes partially autonomous from it to the extent that it constitutes the *locus* of a decision not determined by it. But this means: a) that the subject is nothing but this distance between the undecidable structure and the decision; b) that ontologically speaking, the decision has the character of a ground which is as primary as the structure on which it is based, since it is not determined by the latter; and c) that if the decision is one between structural undecidables, taking a decision can only mean repressing possible alternatives that are not carried out. In other words, that the 'objectivity' arising from a decision is formed, in its most fundamental sense, as a power relationship.

For this relationship of necessary implication between objectivity and power to be fully comprehensible, we must here clarify a number of points. Firstly, the assertion that a decision is 'irrational' if it is based on an 'undecidable' structure must be rejected. The irrational is only the 'other side' or opposite of reason and requires, as in the case of the opposition between the contingent and the necessary, the full constitution of its two poles. What we find here, however, is an undecidability located within reason itself. The decision based on an undecidable structure is not therefore opposed to reason, but is something which attempts to supplement its deficiencies. Thus the fact that a decision may, in the final instance, be arbitrary, merely means that the person taking it cannot establish a necessary link with a *rational* motive. But this does not mean that the decision is not *reasonable* — that is to say that an accumulated set of motives, none of which has the value of an apodictic foundation, make it preferable to other decisions.

But what this principle of structural undecidability does mean is that if two different groups have taken different decisions, the relationship between them will be one of antagonism and power, since no ultimate rational grounds exist for their opting either way. It is in this sense that we assert that all objectivity necessarily presupposes the repression of that which is excluded by its establishment. To talk of repression immediately suggests all kinds of violent images. But this is not necessarily the case. By 'repression' we simply mean the external suppression of a decision, conduct or belief, and the imposition of alternatives which are not in line with them. An act of conversion thus means the repression of previous beliefs. It is also important to point out that repressed possibilities are not all those which prove logically possible in a certain situation — in other words, those which do not violate the principle of contradiction; they are merely those we might call *inchoate* possibilities — that is, those whose actualization was once attempted but were cancelled out of existence.

14. We determined that social relations are always contingent relations. And following the reflections above, we can attribute a second characteristic to them: they are always power relations. This affirmation must nevertheless be given a precise meaning. There are three misconceptions here that should be eliminated. The first is that power is an empirical reality which characterizes relations between social forces, but that the latter's specific identity can be conceived independently of power relations. This is not what we are asserting, however. Our thesis is that the constitution of a social identity is an act of power and that identity as such *is* power. This proposition can be gathered from our reasoning above. As we have seen, asserting the constitutive nature of antagonism entails asserting the contingent nature of all objectivity and this, in turn, means that any objectivity is a threatened objectivity. If, in

spite of this, an objectivity manages to partially affirm itself, it is only by repressing that which threatens it. To study the conditions of existence of a given social identity, then, is to study the power mechanisms making it possible. But there is another point here. It could be thought that objectivity is power in the sense that the former's *existence* depends on its ability to repress that which threatens it, but that its *essence*, or objective identity as such is not placed in question. This is the second misconception. Without power, there would be no objectivity at all. An objective identity is not a homogeneous point but an articulated set of elements. But as this articulation is not a necessary articulation, its characteristic structure, its 'essence' depends entirely on that which it denies. Here the sentence from Saint-Just quoted earlier must be taken in its most literal sense: republican identity, the 'people' are exclusively the denial of the forces opposed to it. Without that opposition, the elements constituting popular unity would disintegrate and its identity would fall apart. Bernstein rightly sustained that the unity of the German working class was simply the result of repression during the period of the anti-socialist laws and that as soon as they were abolished, the demands of the different trade union groups tended to split apart. The existence of the 'working class' as a unified identity became increasingly ill-defined. To give a final example: several recent studies have shown how the 'East' is simply the result of the orientalist discourse of Western academics. The unification of India, China and the Muslim world into a single entity can only be performed by establishing an equivalent relationship between the cultural characteristics of those peoples, a link that is based on the simple negative fact that none of them is Western. But it is important to point out that this unification does not just take place in Western books. Insofar as its overriding discourse is embodied in the forms and institutions that have dominated the course of Western penetration of the Third World, the equivalence imposed by them will end up creating 'oriental' identities that will, at the moment of anti-colonialist rebellion, inevitably turn upside down the hierarchy of Western values.

Derrida has shown how an identity's constitution is always based on excluding something and establishing a violent hierarchy between the two resultant poles — form/matter, essence/accident, black/white, man/woman etc. In linguistics a distinction is made between 'marked' and 'unmarked' terms. The latter convey the principal meaning of a term, while marked terms add a supplement or mark to it. In the word 'dogs', for example, the mark 's' is added to the main meaning provided by the singular. In this respect, we could say that the discursive construction of secondariness is based on a difference between two terms where one maintains its specificity, but where this specificity is simultaneously presented as equivalent to that which is shared by both of them. The word 'man' differentiates the latter from 'woman' but is also equated with 'human being' which is the condition shared by both men and women. What is peculiar to the second term is thus reduced to the function of accident, as opposed to the essentiality of the first. It is the same with the black—white relationship, in which 'white', of course, is equivalent to 'human being'. 'Woman' and 'black' are thus 'marks', in contrast to the unmarked terms of 'man' and 'white'.

At this point, however, we are faced with another problem. The violent hierarchies just mentioned elicit an immediate ethical response which tends not only to turn them upside down, but to suppress them. This is where the third misconception lies. Underlying that response is the assumption that a free society is one from which power has been totally eliminated. But as we saw, if power is the prerequisite of any identity, the radical disappearance of power would amount to the disintegration of the social fabric. As we shall see later, it is this profound contradiction which underlies any project of *global* emancipation. By global emancipation we do not mean specific or even a broad and articulated set of emancipations, but the notion of an emancipation aimed at transforming the very 'root' of the social. A harmonious society is impossible because power is the condition for society to be possible (and, at the same time, impossible, for the reasons adduced earlier). Even in the most radical and democratic projects, social transformation thus means building a new power, not radically eliminating it. Destroying the hierarchies on which sexual or racial discrimination is based will, at some point, always require the construction of other exclusions for collective identities to be able to emerge.

15.   A third characteristic of social relations, closely linked to the previous two, is what could be termed the primacy of the political over the social. A more detailed discussion is in order here. Let us start from an objection that could apparently be made to the thesis that the constitution of any identity is based on the exclusion of that which denies it. Many relations and identities in our world do not seem to entail any denial: the relationship with a postman delivering a letter, buying a ticket in the cinema, having lunch with a friend in a restaurant, going to a concert — where is the moment of exclusion and negativity here? To understand this point, let us begin with the distinction made by Husserl

between sedimentation and reactivation and develop it in a very different direction. For Husserl the practice of any scientific discipline entails a routinization in which the results of previous scientific investigation tend to be taken for granted and reduced to a simple manipulation, with the result that the original intuition which gave rise to them is completely forgotten. At the end of his life, Husserl saw the crisis of European science as the consequence of a growing separation between the ossified practice of the sciences and the vital primary terrain in which the original or constitutive intuitions of those sciences were rooted. The task of transcendental phenomenology consisted of recovering those original intuitions. Husserl called the routinization and forgetting of origins 'sedimentation', and the recovery of the 'constitutive' activity of thought 'reactivation'.

The moment of original institution of the social is the point at which its contingency is *revealed*, since that institution, as we have seen, is only possible through the repression of options that were equally open. To reveal the original meaning of an act, then, is to reveal the moment of its radical contingency — in other words, to reinsert it in the system of real historic options that were discarded — in accordance with our analysis above: by showing the terrain of the original violence, of the power relation through which that instituting act took place. This is where Husserl's distinction can be introduced, with certain modifications. Insofar as an act of institution has been successful, a 'forgetting of the origins' tends to occur; the system of possible alternatives tends to vanish and the traces of the original contingency to fade. In this way, the instituted tends to assume the form of a mere objective presence. This is the moment of sedimentation. It is important to realize that this fading entails a concealment. If objectivity is based on exclusion, the traces of that exclusion will always be somehow present. What happens is that the sedimentation can be so complete, the influence of one of the dichotomous relationships' poles so strong, that the contingent nature of that influence, its *original* dimension of power, do not prove immediately visible. Objectivity is thus constituted merely as presence.

In our case, however, the moment of reactivation cannot consist of a return to the origins, to the historic system of alternative possibilities that were discarded. Let us recall our previous remarks: rejected alternatives do not mean everything that is *logically* possible, but those alternatives which were *in fact* attempted, which thus represented antagonistic alternatives and were suppressed. But in a new situation, the system of those alternatives will be different. Reactivation does not therefore consist of returning to the original situation, but merely of rediscovering, through the emergence of new antagonisms, the contingent nature of so-called 'objectivity'. In turn, however, this rediscovery can reactivate the *historical* understanding of the original acts of institution insofar as stagnant forms that were simply considered as objectivity and taken for granted are now revealed as contingent and project that contingency to the 'origins' themselves.

The sedimented forms of 'objectivity' make up the field of what we will call the 'social'. The moment of antagonism where the undecidable nature of the alternatives and their resolution through power relations becomes fully visible constitutes the field of the 'political'. Two points must be clarified. The first is that social relations are constituted by the very distinction between the social and the political. If, on the one hand, a society from which the political has been completely eliminated is inconceivable — it would mean a closed universe merely reproducing itself through repetitive practices — on the other, an act of unmediated political institution is also impossible: any political construction takes place against the background of a range of sedimented practices. The ultimate instance in which all social reality might be political is one that is not only not feasible but also one which, if reached, would blur any distinction between the social and the political. This is because a *total* political institution of the social can only be the result of an absolute omnipotent will, in which case the contingency of what has been instituted — and hence its political nature — would disappear. The distinction between the social and the political is thus ontologically constitutive of social relations. It could be called, to use a term from Heidegger, an 'existential'. But the boundary of what is social and what is political in society is constantly displaced.

The second point is linked to the consequences stemming from this constitutive nature of the distinction between the social and the political. The most important is that opaqueness will always be an inherent dimension of social relations and that the myth of a reconciled and transparent society is simply that: a myth. We have therefore upheld the contingency of social relations, the ineradicability of power relations, and the impossibility of reaching a harmonious society. Are not these pessimistic conclusions? Everything depends, of course, on the political and social practices that are thinkable with these conclusions as their starting point. Indeed, far from being the cause for pessimism, they are the basis for a radical optimism, as will be explained later. But we can argue the following straight away: if social relations are contingent, it means they can be radically transformed through struggle, instead of that transformation being conceived as a self-transformation of an objective nature; if power is ineradicable, it is because there is radical liberty that is not fettered by any essence; and if opaqueness is constitutive of the social, it is precisely this which makes access to the truth conceived as an unveiling (*alétheia*) possible. We shall return to these themes shortly.

16.   A final characteristic of social relations is their radical historicity. This is clear from the contingent nature of their conditions of existence. There is not what might be called a basic structural objectivity from which history 'flows'; rather, that very structure is historical. Moreover, the being of objects is also historical in that it is socially constructed and structured by systems of meaning. To understand something historically is to refer it back to its contingent conditions of emergence. Far from seeking an objective meaning in history, it is a question of deconstructing all meaning and tracing it back to its original facticity.

17.   On the basis of these four characteristics of social relations — contingency, power, primacy of politics, and historicity — we can now identify the kind of questions characterizing a non-objectivist conception of the social. Following are a few examples.

(a) To what extent is a certain society a society? In other words, to what extent does it manage to conceal the system of exclusions on which it is based? The starting point for analysis must therefore be the determination of those points of negativity that we have termed conditions of possibility and, at the same time, impossibility of social objectivity. The analytical effort is aimed at determining how structural the structure is, and this is only possible by shedding light on what we called the 'conditions of existence' of that structure. But those conditions of existence will only become visible if the objectivity is a threatened objectivity; in other words, if the power system on which objectivity is based is reactivated.

(b) The same possibility—impossibility dialectic constituting the social 'totality' also constitutes the identity of social actors. The crucial question, then, is not who the social agents are, but the extent to which they manage to constitute themselves. The analysis must therefore begin with the explicit 'objective' identities of the social agents — those making up their 'fullness' — and then go on to emphasize the dislocations adulterating that fullness. Secondly, it must refer to both the identities and dislocations operating within those explicit objective identities, and to the contingency of their respective conditions of existence. To illustrate this point, let us examine an attempt to conceive such dislocations in exactly the opposite direction from our own: the category of 'false conscience'. This approach to the problem identifies, without any doubt, a dislocation between the agent's identity and its forms of representation. But it already points out that the agent's real identity can only be essential and that its conditions of existence cannot therefore be contingent. The transition from false conscience to 'conscience for itself' is identified with that of appearance to reality. For that very reason, the conditions of existence of false conscience cannot be contingent either: both its appearance and resolution are inscribed in the internal movement of essence. But if the conditions of existence — both of identities and their dislocations — are wholly contingent, then the very idea of conceiving dislocation in terms of the appearance—reality opposition loses all meaning. Think of the analysis of working class identities: an essentialist approach will attempt to present the causes which *prevent* the development of a full class consciousness — e.g. the embourgeoisement arising from imperialist exploitation, the subsistence of peasant features in a recently developed proletariat, the action of forces such as the media and trade union bureaucracies or the influence of religion, etc. But this analysis assumes that a full consciousness (in the Marxist sense of the term) would become spontaneously developed if none of these countervailing forces was at work. On the other hand, if the notion of an essential identity is abandoned, it means that the absence of a revolutionary class awareness cannot be explained in terms of the factors blocking its emergence, since such an awareness is merely *one* of the working class identities that might develop and depends on precise historical conditions that cannot be teleologically conceived. For that very reason the '*class* struggle' cannot be taken for granted as the form that social conflicts will necessarily take. Indeed, the fundamental question is this: to what extent are social agents formed as classes by the collective struggles forging the unity of their positions as subjects? The answer will obviously differ in each specific case.

(c) Finally, the possibility—impossibility dialectic also operates within the fundamental categories of socio-political analysis. Take the concepts of 'autonomy' and 'representation'. In the case of autonomy, it refers to the locus of an insoluble tension. If an entity was *totally* autonomous, it would mean that it was totally self-determined. But in that case the concept of autonomy would be completely redundant (what, exactly, would it be autonomous from?) On the other hand, if autonomy was *totally* inexistent, the social entity in question would be completely determined. It would not, however, be something separate from that which determines it and the unsplittable ensemble of the determinant and the determined would obviously be self-determined. As can be seen, the notions of total determination and total autonomy are absolute equivalents. The concept of autonomy is only useful — or rather, meaningful — when neither of the two extremes (equivalents) is achieved. For if an external intervention is experienced as an interference in the development of a certain activity, we can indeed propose the need to autonomize that activity in terms of the intervention interfering in its development. The determination by the interfering force is clearly an *external* intervention in this case, since it is resisted by the person on whom it is practised. Without interference, then, autonomy does not exist. The degree of autonomy may vary, but the concept of total autonomy is devoid of all meaning. In this sense, autonomy will always be relative, since if one force has the power to interfere and the other the power to resist, the two will be partially effective and neither will manage to predominate exclusively. The field of relative autonomy is therefore a war of position in which neither of the two participant forces can achieve absolute victory. This once again confirms what our whole analysis has asserted: that the field of social identities is not one of full identities, but of their ultimate failure to be constituted. A realistic analysis of socio-political processes must therefore abandon the objectivist prejudice that social forces are something, and start from an examination of what they do not manage to be.

It is the same with the category of representation. In its literal sense, representation presupposes the presence of someone in a place from which they are actually absent. It is therefore a *fictio iuris*. But this is precisely where the difficulties begin, as the terrain on which representation takes place is different from that on which the identity of the person represented is constituted. In this sense, representation cannot simply be the transmission belt of a will that has already been constituted, but must involve the construction of something new. There is thus a double process: on the one hand, to exist as such, a representation cannot operate completely behind the back of the person represented; and on the other, to be a representation at all requires the articulation of something new which is not just provided by the identity of what is being represented. At this point, we find ourselves in the same situation as with autonomy: absolute representation, the total transparency between the representative and the represented, means the extinction of the relationship of representation. If the representative and the represented constitute the same and single will, the 're-' of representation disappears since the same will is present in two different places. Representation can therefore only exist to the extent that the transparency entailed by the concept is never achieved; and that a permanent dislocation exists between the representative and the represented. This opaqueness of the relationship of representation can vary to a greater or lesser degree, but it must always be present if the representation is to take place.

18.   The whole argument developed above leads to the growing centrality of the category of 'dislocation'. As we saw, every identity is dislocated insofar as it depends on an outside which both denies that identity and provides its condition of possibility at the same time. But this in itself means that the effects of dislocation must be contradictory. If on the one hand, they threaten identities, on the other, they are the foundation on which new identities are constituted. Let us consider the dislocatory effects of emerging capitalism on the lives of workers. They are well known: the destruction of traditional communities, the brutal and exhausting discipline of the factory, low wages and insecurity of work. But this is only one side of the effects, for the workers' response to the dislocation of their lives by capitalism was not to submit passively, but to break machines, organize trade unions, and go on strike. In this process new skills and abilities were inevitably born, which might not have been the case otherwise. The uncontrolled dislocatory rhythm of capitalism meant that the elementary conditions of survival – once apparently guaranteed in a stable society where the direct producer was not separated from either the land or the means of production (and where the world thus appeared as guaranteed by a divine or natural order) – were now secured as a result of victory in struggle. Society appeared more and more like an order constructed by men.

This means that the generalization of dislocatory relations has a triple effect, giving rise not only to negative consequences but also to new possibilities of historical action. Firstly, the accelerated tempo of social transformation and the continual rearticulatory interventions the latter demands lead to a higher awareness of historicity. The rapid change in discursive sequences organizing and constituting objects leads to a clearer awareness of the constitutive contingency of those discourses. The historicity of being of objects is thus shown more clearly.

This has a second effect. We maintained earlier that the subject is merely the distance between the undecidable structure and the decision. This means that the more dislocated a structure is, the more the field of decisions not determined by it will expand. The recompositions and rearticulations will thus operate at increasingly deeper structural levels, thereby leading to an increase in the role of the 'subject' and to history becoming less and less repetitive.

Finally, the third effect is what might be called unevenness of power relations. A dislocated structure can clearly not have a centre and is therefore constitutively decentred. But it must be understood what a decentred structure is. The dislocation we are referring to is not one of a machine that has broken down because of the maladjustment of one of its components. We are dealing with a very specific dislocation: one that stems from the presence of antagonistic forces. Social dislocation is therefore coterminous with the construction of power centres. But given that the possibility of resistance to that power means that the latter is not a total power, the vision of the social emerging from this description is that of a plurality of power centres, each with different capacity to irradiate and structure. That is what is meant by a decentred structure: not just the *absence* of a centre but the *practice of decentring* through antagonism. Strictly speaking, the points we have repeatedly been making can be applied here: centres can exist only because the structure is decentred. If the structure was *totally* closed, each of its constitutive elements would have a merely relational identity with the others and none would be able to assume the character of a centre as a result. But in as far as the structure is dislocated, the possibility of *centres* emerges: the response to the dislocation of the structure will be its recomposition around particular nodal points of articulation by the various antagonistic forces. Centring — the action of 'centring' — is therefore only possible through dislocation and unevenness. To repeat: dislocation is both the condition of possibility and impossibility of a centre at the same time. This clearly shows why the response to the essentialism of those who affirm the presence of a single structural power centre cannot be pluralism, as the term is understood in American political science: the diffusion of power is merely the symmetrical reverse of the 'ruling class' theory, and the dimension of unevenness that is essential to all dislocation is as absent in one case as it is in the other.

We thus have a set of new possibilities for historical action which are the direct result of structural dislocation. The world is less 'given' and must be increasingly constructed. But this is not just a construction of the world, but of social agents who transform themselves and forge new identities as a result. At this point let us consider the differences between our approach and that of the classical Marxist tradition. In both cases there is an insistence on the maladjustments and dislocations generated by capitalism. But the differences are also clearly visible. The main difference is that dislocations have an objective meaning for classical Marxism and are part of a process whose direction is predetermined. The *subject* of change is therefore internal to that process and is determined by it. The subject is completely absorbed by the structure. In our analysis, on the other hand, the location of the subject is that of dislocation. Thus, far from being a moment of the structure, the subject is the result of the impossibility of constituting the structure as such — that is as a self-sufficient object. Hence also our different conception of the socialist project. For classical Marxism, the possibility of transcending capitalist society depended on the simplification of social structure and the emergence of a privileged agent of social change, while for us, the possibility of a democratic transformation of society depends on a proliferation of new subjects of change. This is only possible if there is something in contemporary capitalism which really tends to multiply dislocations and thus create a plurality of new antagonisms. It is these tendencies of contemporary capitalism that we must now go on to analyse.

Dislocation and Capitalism

19.   Let us begin by identifying three dimensions of the relationship of dislocation that are crucial to our analysis. The first is that dislocation is the very form of temporality. And temporality must be conceived as the exact opposite of space. The 'spatialization' of an event consists of eliminating its temporality. Let us consider the case of Freud's *Fort/Da* game. Through the game the child symbolizes the absence of the mother, which is a traumatic event. If the child comes to terms with that absence in this way, it is because absence is no longer *just* absence but becomes a moment of the presence—absence succession. Symbolization means that the total succession is present in each of its moments. This synchronicity of the successive means that the succession is in fact a total *structure*, a space for symbolic representation and constitution. The spatialization of the event's temporality takes place through repetition, through the reduction of its variation to an invariable nucleus which is an internal moment of the pre-given structure. And note that when we refer to space, we do not do so in a metaphorical sense, out of analogy with physical space. There is no metaphor here. Any repetition that is governed by a structural law of successions is space. If physical space is

also space, it is because it participates in this general form of spatiality. The representation of time as a cyclical succession, common in peasant communities, is in this sense a reduction of time to space. Any teleological conception of change is therefore also essentially spatialist. It is important to note that we are not dealing with the synchrony/diachrony opposition here. Diachrony, insofar as it is subject to rules and attempts to capture the *sense* of a succession, is also synchronic in our terms. But this means that only the dislocation of the structure, only a maladjustment which is spatially unrepresentable, is an event. Through dislocation time is overcome by space. But while we can speak of the hegemonization of time by space (through repetition), it must be emphasized that the opposite is not possible: time cannot hegemonize anything, since it is a pure effect of dislocation. The ultimate failure of all hegemonization, then, means that the real — including physical space — is in the ultimate instance temporal.

The second dimension is that dislocation is the very form of possibility. To understand this, let us again return to Aristotle. Movement (in the broad sense of change in general) is defined in the *Metaphysics* as the actuality of the possible as possible. Let us imagine the case of a white object which becomes black. At moment 'A' the object is white as actuality and black as potentiality; at moment 'B' it is actually black. But what about the specific moment of change, or the ontological status of 'blackening'? At that point the object is no longer white, but nor is it yet black. The Aristotelian formula of 'actuality of the possible as possible' tries to grasp this situation conceptually: what the change reveals is the *possibility* of the object becoming black. The Aristotelian possibility, however, is a single possibility because the process of change is conceived as *development* and thus appears dominated by the *telos* of the transition from potentiality to actuality. In this sense, it is a spurious possibility, one for our eyes alone. It is not the possibility we are referring to when we assert that a situation 'opens possibilities', for example. Possibility appears completely 'spatialized' in the sense we mentioned earlier. But with dislocation there is no *telos* which governs change; possibility therefore becomes an authentic possibility, a possibility in the radical sense of the term. This means that there must be *other* possibilities, since the idea of a single possibility denies what is involved in the very concept of possibility. As we have seen, because structural dislocation is constitutive, the dislocated structure cannot provide the principle of its transformations. The dislocated structure thus opens possibilities of multiple and indeterminate rearticulations for those freed from its coercive force and who are consequently outside it. And the very possibility of this dislocation reveals the character of *mere possibility* of the articulatory ensemble forming the structure before dislocation. The pure form of temporality and the pure form of possibility thus coincide. Just as, in the final instance, time always overcomes space, we can also say that the character of mere possibility of any kind of arrangement imposes itself, in the long term, on all structural necessity. To avoid any misunderstanding, we must once again emphasize that the dislocation of a structure does not mean that *everything* becomes possible or that *all* symbolic frameworks disappear, since no dislocation could take place in that psychotic universe: a structure must be there for it to be dislocated. The situation of dislocation is that of a lack which involves a structural reference. There is a temporalization of spaces or a widening of the field of the possible, but this takes place in a *determinate* situation: that is, one in which there is always a relative structuration.

The third dimension is that dislocation is the very form of freedom. Freedom is the absence of determination. Whoever is *causa sui* is free. Let us consider various possibilities on this basis. One is the Spinozan formula: any individual entity is merely a link in a chain of determinations surpassing it. As a result, freedom can only be attributed to the totality of the existent (*Deus sine Natura*); or in its structuralist version: it is not me who is speaking, but the structures which are speaking through me. Total freedom and total determination coincide and freedom comes from the 'self' of self-determination. This identity between freedom and self-determination persists when we move to a second possibility: that each individual identity in the universe teleologically tends towards the purpose fixed in advance by its nature. The alternative, then, is either a total liberty — if that purpose is guaranteed by a pre-established harmony assuring the absence of interaction with other entities — or that that interaction is inevitable, in which case freedom can only be relative. In contrast with these two variants of the notion of freedom conceived as self-determination, we have a third possibility, which is the existentialist conception of freedom. Man is condemned to be free; he is transformed into an absolute chooser by the absence of any predetermined nature; but he is a chooser who no longer has any reason to choose.

At this point, however, a different possibility opens up. Let us assume we fully accept the structuralist vision: I am a product of structures; there is nothing in me with a separate substantiality from the discourses making me up; a total determinism governs my actions. Very well, let us concede the whole argument. But the question immediately arises: what happens if the structure I am determined by does not manage to constitute itself, if a *radical* outside — which does not share a common measure or foundation with the inside of the structure — dislocates it? The structure will obviously not be able to determine me, not because I have an *essence* independent from the structure, but because the structure has failed to constitute itself fully and thus to constitute me as a subject as well. There is nothing in me which was oppressed by the structure or is freed by its dislocation; I am simply *thrown up* in my condition as a subject because I have not achieved constitution as an object. The freedom thus won in relation to the structure is therefore a traumatic fact initially: I am *condemned* to be free, not because I have no structural identity as the existentialists assert, but because I have a *failed* structural identity. This means that the subject is partially self-determined. However, as this self-determination is not the expression of what the subject *already* is but the result of its lack of being instead, self-determination can only proceed through processes of *identification.* As can be gathered, the greater the structural indetermination, the freer a society will be. We shall come back to this point.

These three dimensions of the relationship of dislocation — temporality, possibility and freedom — are mutually involved. If temporality was not radical, in other words if the event was not essentially exterior to the structure, it could be inscribed as an internal moment of the latter. This would mean that the possibilities would be those *of* the structure and not those emerging *from* structural dislocation. In that case there would be no self-determination, and thus no freedom either. Once again we find the paradox dominating the whole of social action: freedom exists because society does not achieve constitution as a structural objective order; but any social action tends towards the constitution of that impossible object, and thus towards the elimination of the conditions of liberty itself. This paradox has no solution; if it did, we would have simply returned to the sociological objectivism we are taking issue with in this essay. It is because it is insoluble that dislocation is the primary ontological level of constitution of the social. To understand social reality, then, is not to understand what society *is*, but what *prevents it from being.* However, if what we have argued previously is true, in that case there is no common measure between the paradox as such and the possibilities of historic action — the language games — that it opens up. Such possibilities are therefore not a necessary structural development of the paradox, but can be taken advantage of by someone outside it. It is to this set of possibilities that we must now turn our attention. As a result of our previous argument, we will divide the discussion in two parts. In the first, to which the rest of this section will be dedicated, we will analyse the dislocatory tendencies operating in contemporary capitalism and the new possibilities of political intervention it opens up. In the section that follows, we will discuss the question of agency — that is the new forms of political subjectivity that are constructed on the basis of those possibilities (and which, as we said, are not *determined* by the dislocated structures). Our basic thesis is that the *possibility* of a radical democracy is directly linked to the level and extension of structural dislocations operating in contemporary capitalism.

20.   It is important to remember that reflection on dislocation and its possible political fruitfulness does have a tradition within Marxism: it is a feature of the group of phenomena linked to 'permanent revolution' and 'uneven and combined development'. As has been pointed out, the concept of 'bourgeois-democratic revolution' which was to become the cornerstone of the stagist Marxism of the Second International, was never explicitly formalized in the works of Marx and Engels and both had growing doubts about its possible generalization as a historical category. The concept was clearly linked to the historic experience of the French Revolution and combined the bourgeois objectives of the Revolution with its character of mobilization 'from below'. But it was precisely this combination that later developments in Europe placed in question. The bourgeoisie was increasingly able to achieve its objectives through non-revolutionary means. In his introduction to Marx's *Class Struggles in France* in 1895, Engels concluded that the cycle of bourgeois revolutions from below had closed after the experiences under Napoleon III and Bismarck and that a period of revolutions from above was beginning. But the other side of the situation was that if bourgeois revolution appeared less and less linked to democracy, democratic revolution was assuming an increasingly less bourgeois character. Hence Marx's texts on permanent revolution which go back to the very beginning of his work and coexist with those upholding economistic stagism. Take the following well known passage, for example: 'The Communists turn their attention chiefly to Germany, because that country is on the eve of a bourgeois revolution that is bound to be carried out under more advanced conditions of European civilization, and with a much more developed proletariat than that of England was in the seventeenth, and of France in the eighteenth century, and because the bourgeois revolution in Germany will be the prelude to an immediately following proletarian revolution.'[22]

It is easy to note that, in this text, it is structural dislocation which creates the revolutionary juncture. The internal laws of the structure, which would have required a full introduction of capitalist relations of production until they became incompatible with any further development of the productive forces, are interrupted here by a dislocation that creates a new political possibility. The late development of capitalism in Germany (which would fall under what Trotsky called 'the privilege of backwardness') gives a political strength to the proletariat that bears no relation to the level of development of German capitalism. It should be noted that it is not a case of replacing one conception of structural laws with another here. On the contrary, it is the *dislocation* of structural laws which creates the *possibility* of a revolutionary politics. Here we find the seed of a vision of history that is different from economistic stagism: a succession of dislocatory junctures that may or may not be taken advantage of.

This different vision of history is insinuated in several of Marx's texts. Take the famous letter to Vera Zasulich in 1881, for example.

> Russia finds itself in a modern historical environment. It is contemporaneous with a superior civilization, it is tied to a world market in which capitalist production predominates. By appropriating the positive results of this mode of production, it is in a position to develop and transform the yet archaic form of its village community, instead of destroying it.[23]

The key issue lies in determining whether this 'appropriation' is a contingent historical *possibility* arising from the unevenness — and thus dislocation — of the development of capitalism in Russia, or whether it is the result of a necessary structural law. Marx's whole argument on the issue moves in the first direction. In his prologue with Engels for the Russian edition of the *Manifesto* (1882), for example, the interrelationship between a revolution in Russia and a proletarian revolution in the West is affirmed and the possible maintenance of the Russian peasant community is made a condition for that revolution. We are not dealing at all with a process that is dominated by necessary infrastructural laws, but with a body of contingent articulations that have been made possible by junctures depending on the uneven development of world capitalism.

It is important to note that by dislocation and unevenness we do not mean 'contradiction' in the classical Hegelian-Marxist sense of the term. Contradiction is a necessary moment of the structure and is therefore internal to it. Contradiction has a theoretical *space* of representation. As

we saw, however, dislocation is not a necessary moment in the self-transformation of the structure but is its failure to achieve constitution and is
mere temporality in this sense. For that reason it opens different *possibilities* and expands the area of *freedom* of the historical subjects.

This tendency to make structural dislocation the very crux of political
strategy is later accentuated in the work of Trotsky where it develops
much of its potential richness. For Trotsky, the very possibility of revolutionary action depends on structural unevenness. Let us consider, first of
all, the formulation of the permanent revolution perspective in his writings on the revolution of 1905. Trotsky borrowed from Parvus the idea
that the capitalist system should be seen as a global totality and that the
prospects for revolution should be viewed in terms of the dislocations
experienced by that total structure. Hence his well-known description of
the peculiarities of Russian history: the hypertrophied development of
the state as a military centre to contain Asian invasions; the consequent
preponderance of the state with respect to civil society; the bureaucratic
nature of cities which, unlike those of Western Europe, did not develop
primarily as centres of craft and trade. To this must be added the late
development of capitalism in Russia and its main feature: that its
predominant sources of finance were investments by foreign capital. As a
result, the local bourgeoisie was weak and, given the high concentration
of capital invested in Russia, the working class gained increasingly in
social and political influence. This structural imbalance between bourgeoisie and proletariat was at the heart of the bourgeoisie's inability to
lead the democratic revolution. The democratic revolution was hegemonized by the proletariat and, according to Trotsky's conception of the
revolution, this involved the need to go beyond democratic tasks and to
move in a socialist direction.

As can be seen, in this schema the *totality* of the revolutionary strategy
appears based on a succession of dislocations. In the first place, the dislocation of the relation between base and superstructure: the military-
bureaucratized state of tsarism inverts the 'normal' relations between
state and civil society. In the second place, the dislocation of the relation
between democratic revolution and the bourgeoisie as the agent to carry
it through: the break in the relation between the two, which had already
been predicated incipiently by Marx in connection with the countries of
Central and Western Europe, is even more the case in Russia. And
finally, the dislocation of the relation between democracy and socialism,
which should have been a relation of succession but which now becomes
a relation of articulation. The possibility of revolution does not spring

from underlying and positive structural laws dominating the whole of the historical process, but from the latter's dislocations which determine an unevenness that cannot be grasped by any structure. The schema is so daunting, however, that Trotsky himself hesitates; it is the point where he does not dare — at this stage of his theoretical evolution, at least — to step outside and draw the conclusions that can be logically deduced from his own analysis. While the revolution begun in Russia must move in a socialist direction to achieve consolidation, Trotsky does not believe — and nor do any of the Russian Social Democratic leaders either — that it can be consolidated without the triumph of a proletarian revolution in the West. Stagism still dominates the vision of 'world history' and the unevenness of the historical process merely intervenes to explain the dynamics of the seizure of power in a specific case.

It is at the end of the 1920s and the beginning of the 1930s that Trotsky's theoretical vision broadens and that the permanent revolution logic comes to hegemonize his global view of contemporary history. The global dimension of capitalism as a world system and its uneven character tend to overlap.

> Capitalism ... prepares and in a certain sense realizes the universality and permanence of man's development. By this a repetition of the forms of development by different nations is ruled out. Although compelled to follow after the advanced countries, a backward country does not take things in the same order.... Unevenness, the most general law of the historic process, reveals itself most sharply and complexly in the destiny of the backward countries. Under the whip of external necessity, their backward culture is compelled to make leaps. From the universal law of unevenness thus derives another law which, for the lack of a better name, we may call the law of *combined development* — by which we mean a drawing together of the different stages of the journey, combining of separate steps, an amalgam of archaic with more contemporary forms.[24]

Referring to the previous passages, Michel Löwy aptly comments:

> Thus the amalgam of backward and advanced socio-economic conditions becomes the structural foundation for the fusion or combination of democratic and socialist tasks in a process of permanent revolution. Or, to put it differently, one of the most important political consequences of combined and uneven development is the unavoidable persistence of unresolved *democratic tasks* in the peripheral capitalist countries. Despite the claims of his critics, Trotsky never denies the democratic dimension of revolution in

backward countries nor did he ever pretend that the revolution would be 'purely socialist'; what he did repudiate, however, was the dogma of bourgeois–democratic revolution as a *separate historical stage* that has to be completed before the proletarian struggle for power can commence.[25]

In this generalization of the theory it is important to observe that the two terms of Trotsky's formula – unevenness and combination – are strictly incompatible with each other. For if unevenness is the 'most general law of the historic process', then the 'drawing together of the different stages of the journey' which characterizes combination loses all meaning. If unevenness is *absolutely* radical (and must be if it is the most general law of history), then the elements of combination cannot be assigned to stages established a priori. On the contrary, what we have are elements whose combination depends on contingent hegemonic articulations and not on any structurally necessary stage. Either there is uneven development – in which case the element of combination disappears – or the combination of different stages is a superficial historical phenomenon which necessarily refers to a deeper structural stratum in which the dominance of stagism is unchallenged – in which case unevenness cannot have the function of a ground attributed to it by Trotsky's text.

Trotsky does not perceive the problem and the conclusions he draws from his own lucid analysis are limited as a result. In fact, the very unity of Trotsky's text depends entirely on maintaining that hidden inconsistency: only at that price can he simultaneously introduce the possibility of absolutely original political articulations in relation to the Marxist tradition and maintain a conception of social agency which is characteristic of the most traditional Marxism. But in order to draw completely new political and theoretical conclusions, let us fully accept his thesis of the primacy of unevenness (in other words, dislocation) and take to the limit its concomitant deconstructive effects on stagism.

Firstly, an uneven structure cannot have objective and positive laws of movement: the action of each of the uneven elements will collide with the others and limit their action. Moreover, if unevenness really does have the character of a ground, such collisions and limitations cannot be reduced to a supergame whose rules would 'spatialize' them.

Secondly, the very fact that the notion of 'structural stage' has dissolved, means that the unevenness in question cannot result from the synchronic presentation of elements that should have appeared as a succession, but must be thought differently. As far as the combination of stages is concerned, one structural arrangement is as possible as another.

But if we are faced with elements that, considered in isolation, are indifferent to the various structural ensembles with which they can be articulated, where is the unevenness? The solution is suggested by Trotsky's own examples. As we saw, he proclaims, speaking of the backward countries, that 'under the whip of *external* necessity, their backward culture is *compelled* to make leaps' (our emphasis). This reference to compulsion and externality is fundamental, because it clearly implies that the unevenness results from the *disruption* of a structure by forces operating *outside* it. This is exactly what we have called dislocation. The unevenness of development is the result of the dislocation of an articulated structure, not the combination of elements which essentially belong to different 'stages'.

Thirdly, the structural dislocation particular to unevenness and the external nature of that dislocation mean that the structure does not have in itself the conditions for its possible future re-articulation. And the very fact that the dislocated elements are not endowed with any kind of essential unity outside their contingent forms of articulation means that a dislocated structure is an open structure in which the crisis can be resolved in the most varied of directions. It is strict *possibility* in the sense we defined earlier. As a result, the structural rearticulation will be an eminently *political* rearticulation. The field of unevenness is, in the strict sense of the term, the field of politics. Moreover, the more points of dislocation a structure has, the greater the expansion of the field of politics will be.

Fourthly, the subjects constructing hegemonic articulations on the basis of dislocation are not internal but external to the dislocated structure. As we stated above, they are condemned to be subjects by the very fact of dislocation. In this sense, however, efforts to rearticulate and reconstruct the structure also entail the constitution of the agents' identity and subjectivity. It is this point which clearly shows the limits of Trotsky's 'permanentist' approach. For Trotsky, the identity of social agents — classes — remains unaltered throughout the whole process. It is to make that result possible that stagism, while shaken, had to be maintained. But if the constitutive nature of unevenness makes any fixing of identities impossible in terms of stages, it means that the elements articulated by social agents come to form part of the latter's identity. It is not a question of whether the *same* subject — the working class — can take on democratic tasks or not, but of whether, having assumed them, a new subject is constituted on the basis of articulating working class identity and democratic identity. And this articulation changes the meaning of both identities. As we have argued elsewhere, this decisive step is not taken by Trotsky or by the Leninist tradition considered as a whole. It is only with the Gramscian notion of 'collective will' that the barrier of class essentialism begins to dissolve.

Fifthly, the greater the dislocation of a structure is, the more indeterminate the political construction emerging from it will be. In this sense, Leninism represented an advance from the orthodox Marxism of the Second International, in spite of its limitations. No wonder the International's most representative leaders hurled accusations of 'voluntarism' and 'adventurism' against Leninist political practice. To base political intervention on the opportunities opened up by the *indetermination* of a historical juncture went right against a vision of politics which saw the latter as lacking all autonomy, since it was merely the result of an *entirely* determined process. Once again, it is only by radicalizing this dimension of indetermination that the field of politics can be extended, and this requires a deepening of the dialectic implicit in the dislocation—possibility relationship.

21.   Let us examine this relationship in a case which has been traditionally put forward as an example of capitalism's growing control of social relations: the phenomenon of commodification. In its most frequent description, capitalism has an inherent tendency to dissolve previous social relations and to transform all objects of private life previously outside its control into commodities. The human beings produced by this growing expansion of the market would be completely dominated by capitalism. Their very needs would be created by the market and through the manipulation of public opinion by the mass media controlled by capital. We would thus be moving in the direction of increasingly regimented societies dominated by the major centres of economic power. Given that the working class would be increasingly incorporated into the system at the same time, no radically anti-capitalist sector would exist and future prospects would appear more and more bleak. Hence the deep pessimism of an Adorno. But this picture does not at all correspond with reality. It is without doubt true that the phenomenon of commodification is at the heart of the multiple dislocations of traditional social relations. But this does not mean that the only prospect thrown up by such dislocations is the growing passive conformity of all aspects of life to the laws of the market.

The response to the negative effects of the commodification process can be a whole variety of struggles which attempt to subject the activities of the market to social regulation. This does not necessarily have to be state regulation; numerous forms of local and national organization — consumer organizations, for example — can be given the power to participate. Only a nostalgia for traditional social relations can maintain an exclusively pessimistic vision of this process. And it is worth remembering that the world broken up by capitalist expansion was far from idyllic and was the source of many relations of subordination. More crucially still, a world organized round traditional social relations is one in which the possibilities of variation and transformation are strictly limited: human beings cannot choose and build their own life because it has already been organized for them by a pre-existent social system. The dislocation of social relations, on the other hand — generated by a phenomenon such as commodification — provokes acts of resistance which launch new social actors into the historical arena; and the new actors, precisely because they are moving on a dislocated terrain, must constantly reinvent their own social forms.

The pessimism of the Frankfurt School stems from the fact that in its approach two central assumptions of Marxist theory remain unchanged: a) that the capitalist system constitutes a self-regulating totality and b) that the transformation of the system, as in any self-regulating totality, can only take place as a result of the development of the internal logic of the system itself. Since this vision accepts that the internal logic of the system does not lead to the emergence of an agent capable of overthrowing it, the only thing left intact is the system's character as a self-regulating totality, as a result of which it can now expand limitlessly. But it is with this conception of a self-regulating totality that the dislocation-possibility dialectic breaks. Since the dislocation is radical, the movements of the system cannot just be internally determined. Among other things, this means that there is no system in the strong sense of the term. As a result of this externality, and to the very extent that it prevents the social from closing into a systematic whole, the prospects created by a historical juncture expand. In this way, I believe a much more optimistic vision is gained of the prospects opening up for contemporary social struggles. The latter start from the reality of the commodification phenomenon and attempt to control it socially, not to wage a merely defensive struggle against an apparently self-regulating and inexorable structure. The problem, then, is how to articulate the presence and functioning of the market with a democratic and socialist society. But this requires a break, both with a vision of socialism as an absolutely planned society in which all market mechanisms have been suppressed, and with a conception of the market's functioning in which it is presented as having an internal logic that leads automatically to capitalism.

22. We can refer to the problem of the growing bureaucratic unification and control of social relations in contemporary societies in the same way. The obligatory reference here, of course, is Max Weber. Unlike traditional societies in which social relations appear dominated by customary practices, under modern conditions there is a growing rationalization of social endeavour by bureaucratic power. Just a step away is the assertion that we are moving increasingly towards regimented societies in which the concentration of administrative power is becoming almost total. But what this vision ignores, on the one hand, is that the administrative standardization in a single power centre is increasingly questioned by the internationalization of political and economic relations, and, on the other, that bureaucratization produces resistance by those suffering its effects. The Weberian theory of bureaucracy was elaborated in an age which believed firmly in the ability of the centralized national state to regulate economic activity and to intervene effectively in the management of social and political relations. Not in vain was the theory of 'organized capitalism' (organized within the framework of the national state, that is) formulated at that time. But the rapid internationalization of political and economic relations in recent decades have rendered the national framework obsolete — or rather, have transformed it into just one of the forces to be taken into account in the determination of any structural change. The conditions for bureaucratic efficiency and rationality thus appear constantly placed in question.

The phenomenon of bureaucratization thus gives rise to a double liberating effect. On the one hand, bureaucratic rationalization dislocates the old structural power relations. In this sense, the first *positive* effect of bureaucratization (even if it presents itself in an 'alienated' form) is that it constitutes a victory for conscious political intervention in the sedimented practices of tradition. The 'alienated' character of the bureaucratic decision stems from its origin in a 'universal class' (Hegel) — that is, an absolute power that springs from society, but at the same time takes a controlling distance from it. But inasmuch as that absolute power is resisted by antagonistic social forces and limited by the international framework in which the bureaucratic state is operating, the omnipotent nature of bureaucracy is questioned and demystified. Bureaucratic power is thus revealed as *one more* power along with the rest. But in that case — and this is the second liberating effect — it is not possible to return to the traditional social relations prior to bureaucratic rationalization. The struggle between bureaucracy and the social forces opposing it takes place entirely in the field opened by the bureaucratic transformation. The latter is confronted, not with a return to customary repetitive practices, but with a range of alternative forms of rationalization. These rationalizations will not now start from a single power centre, but from a multiplicity of power centres; and they will be more democratic in that the decisions adopted will come through negotiation between those multiple powers. But in any case, such democratic planning would have been impossible without a) the dislocation of traditional social structure by bureaucratic power and b) the historical agents' new awareness of their capacity to transform their social relations, also conferred by bureaucratic intervention. In this way bureaucracy — the opposite of democracy — is the historical condition for it. Let us recall de Tocqueville's thesis on the symmetry between the *ancien régime* and the Revolution: the Revolution was only possible on the basis and as a continuation of the administrative unification and rationalization carried through by the *ancien régime*. As with commodification, the result of bureaucracy would just be a totally administrated society if it was guaranteed an absolute a priori power: but if that is not the case, the prospects opened by the bureaucratic revolution are much broader than anything it can control in terms of its own logic.

23.   Finally, it is the same if we go on to consider the organization of the production process itself. Marx has pointed to the radical revolutionary nature of the transition from manufacture to large-scale industry: while in the first the worker found, in spite of having to concentrate all his labour effort in a partial task, that his body and skill still imposed limits on and determined technical progress, in the second these limits are broken. Referring to such an analysis by Marx, Lefort comments:

> Of what does the radical newness of the era of large-scale industry consist? From now on, the production process becomes autonomous; the mode of the division of labour obeys the technical necessities of mechanical fabrication such as they are made known by the natural sciences, instead of remaining bound to the range of individual aptitudes. In the language of Marx, the subjective principle of the division of labour is substituted by an objective principle. In manufacturing, the worker certainly had to adapt himself to a specific operation before entering the production process; but

the operation was accommodated in advance to the worker. In other words, the organic constitution of the worker determined the division and combination of gestures required for a given production process. A corporeal schema continued to determine how the workshop was structured. In mechanical production, by contrast, the principle of the division of labour ceases to be subjective.[26]

In other words, while the limits of technical transformation possible under manufacture were set by the worker's body and skill, in the case of large-scale industry they were transgressed by a process completely dominated by the internal logic of technical change. And here we find ourselves in the same situation as with commodification and bureaucracy. On the one hand, the existing situation of large-scale industry could be described in terms of alienation, as the direct producer ceases to be the centre of reference and meaning of the production process. But on the other, the situation can be seen in exactly the opposite way: with large-scale industry the limits are no longer biologically determined and the organization of the production process is freed from any dependence on the direct producer. If this is not fully visible from the way the problem is dealt with by Marx, it is because of the contrast he makes between the division of labour in manufacture — where it is a subjective principle — and in large-scale industry — where it is an objective principle. Behind this conception of the objective nature of the organizational and technological transformation of large-scale industry, of course, is the naturalist vision of the economic process as a self-generating process, subject to the same necessary laws as nature. But if we abandon this objectivist outlook, we are offered a completely new vision. Hidden behind the apparent objectivity of the changes in the division of labour are the decisions of the capitalist, which are no longer subject to the constraints imposed by the 'organic constitution' of the worker. And in the event of the economic process passing from private capitalist ownership to some form of social management, the capitalist's liberation from the limitations of direct production is transferred to the community as a whole. What the direct producer loses in individual autonomy, s/he more than gains as a member of a community.

24.   In one sense, our analysis keeps within the field of Marxism and attempts to reinforce what has been one of its virtues: the full acceptance of the transformations entailed by capitalism and the construction of an alternative project that is *based on* the ground created by those

transformations, not on *opposition to* them. Commodification, bureaucratization, and the increasing dominance of scientific and technological
planning over the division of labour should not necessarily be resisted.
Rather, one should work within these processes so as to develop the
prospects they create for a non-capitalist alternative. In another sense,
however, our analysis departs from Marxism. From a Marxist perspective,
the development of social alternatives to capitalism is a process which fully
accepts the historical ground it has created, but which must nevertheless be
conceived as the internal development of the contradictions belonging to
capitalist forms themselves. We are thus dealing with a process whose
basic dimensions are entirely predetermined and where the question of
power as a political construction is removed. For if the analysis assumes
that any non-capitalist alternative is merely the result of the *internal*
contradictions of capitalism, then the question of the power that capitalism could have to impose its *diktats* in a given juncture is eliminated.
Not in vain can politics only be a superstructure in this approach. In our
analysis, on the other hand, the problem of the resolution of power
relations is never taken for granted. Any transformation of capitalism
opens up a range of possibilities that are not just determined by the
endogenous logic of capitalist forms, but also by the latter's constitutive
outside and by the whole historical situation in which those logics
operate. Inasmuch as capitalism always had a constitutive outside, its
domination can never be merely imposed through the internal development of its logic, but must be imposed through the hegemonization of
something radically exterior to itself. In which case, capitalism must be
seen, in terms of its most fundamental and constitutive features, as a
system of power. And to this we must add something that can be
deduced from our analysis above. The more dislocated is the ground on
which capitalism operates, the less it can rely on a framework of stable
social and political relations and the more central this political moment
of hegemonic construction will be; but for that very reason, the more
extensive the range of alternative political possibilities opposed to capitalist hegemonization will also be.

Let us consider the crucial breaking points of the vision of capitalism
as a force generating its transformation from its own internal logic. The
peak moment of this image corresponds to the age of so-called liberal
capitalism. The processes of accumulation at the level of civil society are
considered sufficient to guarantee the self-reproduction of the system as
a whole. This autonomy was largely a myth, of course, but one which did
have a certain historical foundation: insofar as social reproduction

appeared as immanent in traditional social relations, the idea of it being consciously regulated was completely unthinkable. In such circumstances the image of the self-regulating market — and of capitalist accumulation, which was only the extension of market relations to the field of production — was imposed as an alternative to traditional society but nevertheless retained one of the latter's essential features. The objective nature of the laws of the market, their operation outside the will and awareness of the producers, constituted an intelligible principle of social functioning (which made the existence of political economy possible as a science), but one which, like all pre-capitalist mechanisms of social reproduction, escaped the conscious intervention of the agents and did not therefore give space for alternative possibilities.

It is with the transition to what Hilferding dubbed 'organized capitalism' that the element of conscious regulation — and thus an eminently political regulation — begins to take on a new centrality. The characteristics of organized capitalism are well known: the rapid concentration and centralization of industrial, commercial and finance capital; the growing dependency of industries on bank credit; the growing separation between ownership and control of enterprises and the consequent expansion of managerial bureaucracies; imperialist expansion; the growing interrelation between the state and capitalist monopolies; the corporatization of economic and social power based on a tripartite agreement between the state, a few monopolistic enterprises and national trade union organizations; the concentration of industry in a few cities and in particular regions of the world; the growth in the number of employees in large-scale enterprises and the parallel growth of the big cities, etc.

It is worth concentrating a moment on the most conspicuous features of the organized capitalism theory. Firstly, it recognizes that regulation by the market is not enough to guarantee the conditions of capitalist reproduction. It must be supplemented by the conscious regulation imposed by monopolistic agreements, banking control, state intervention and corporatist agreements. This conscious intervention thus allows the regulation of the increasingly dislocated reality of the market. But secondly, if the element of conscious intervention becomes autonomous from the blind mechanisms of the market, then there is no logic for the latter to be necessarily imposed on the former. In this sense, conscious intervention can be oriented in various directions, and this means that the system of possible alternatives arising at a given juncture expands. Take the various forms of 'planism' that proliferated in the 1920s and

1930s, or later, the project of a welfare state as a redistributive effort within the framework of a corporatist agreement. Whether planning takes one direction or another, then, appears to be an eminently political decision that depends on existing power relations. Thirdly, the theory of organized capitalism assumes, both in its left-wing and right-wing forms, that the national state constitutes the framework of all economic planning. The conception of state power as the locus and source of all economic decisions and planning is one of the cornerstones of the welfare state.

This second mode of capitalist operation — between the theory and practice of which there are profound differences, of course — has gone into crisis in recent decades. We have entered what some authors have called 'disorganized capitalism'.[27] Lasch and Urry characterize its main features as follows: the internationalization of capital has led to nationally based enterprises having less control over domestic markets. There has been a deconcentration of capital and a general decline in cartels. A growing separation has also occurred between financial and industrial capital. The number of manual workers in manufacturing industry has dropped in absolute and relative terms; and a shift has taken place from Taylorism to more flexible forms of organization which no longer involve the concentration of the workforce in large plants. In industrial relations, this has led to a decline in collective bargaining at the national level, while the growing independence of the monopolies from the state has reduced the importance of corporatist agreements. In terms of social structure, there has been a rapid development in the services sector, in particular, and thus of the professional class. Such transformations have been accompanied by a new international division of labour: the Third World countries have seen successive investments in basic extractive and manufacturing industries and this has produced a change in the occupational structure in the First World, where employment is now oriented towards the service occupations. Finally, the new spatial division of labour has weakened the regional concentration of industry, and accentuated the export of labour-intensive industries to the Third World. At the same time, it has led to the emergence of rural spaces in the metropolitan countries, as well as to a decline in towns and cities, both in terms of size and their domination of the surrounding area.

As can be seen, we are faced with an absolute and relative decline in the decision-making power of the national state as a centre of regulation of economic life. This decline, however, is just that: a decline. We are not facing a collapse in which a once absolute power has suddenly been transferred *in toto* to the multinational corporations. A break must be made with the simplistic vision of an ultimate, conclusive instance of power. The myth of liberal capitalism was that of a totally self-regulating market from which state intervention was completely absent. The myth of organized capitalism was that of a regulatory instance whose power was disproportionately excessive and led to all kinds of wild expectations. And now we run the risk of creating a new myth: that of the monopoly corporations' limitless capacity for decision-making. There is an obvious symmetry in all three cases: one instance — be it the immanent laws of the economy, the state or monopoly power — is presented as if it did not have conditions of existence, as if it did not have a constitutive outside. The power of this instance does not therefore need to be hegemonically and pragmatically constituted since it has the character of a ground.

On the other hand, if we abandon this metaphysical hypothesis of the ultimate instance and accept, according to our previous analysis, that all power is contingent and depends on conditions of existence that are contingent themselves, then the problem of power is decisively displaced: the construction of a popular power does not mean transferring an absolute power from one instance to another, but taking advantage of the opportunities offered by the new dislocations characterizing disorganized capitalism to create new forms of social control. The response to the decline in the regulatory capacity of the national state cannot therefore be to abandon political struggle with a sense of impotency, nor to call up the myth of an impossible autarchy, but to open up new spaces for popular struggle on the real ground on which economic regulation will have to take place in an era of disorganized capitalism: that of supranational communities (the European Community, for example).

The novelty of the present situation, then, lies in the fact that the nodal point around which the intelligibility of the social is articulated does not now tend to be displaced from one instance to another in society, but to dissolve. The plurality of dislocations generates a plurality of centres of relative power, and the expansion of all social logic thus takes place on a terrain that is increasingly dominated by elements external to it. Accordingly, articulation is constitutive of all social practice. But in that case, to the very extent that dislocations increasingly dominate the terrain of an absent structural determination, the problem of *who* articulates comes to occupy a more central position. It is this problem of who the subjects of historical transformations are — or, more fundamentally, what being a subject entails — that we must now consider.

Social Imaginary and Democratic Revolution

25. Our approach to the problem of the social agent/structure alternative can be clearly gathered from the development of our argument above. Let us recapitulate the main points. (1) The opposition between a society that is completely determined in structural terms and another that is entirely the creation of social agents is not an opposition between different conceptions of the social, but is inscribed in social reality itself. As we said earlier, the subject exists because of dislocations in the structure. (2) Dislocation is the source of freedom. But this is not the freedom of a subject with a *positive* identity – in which case it would just be a structural locus; rather it is merely the freedom of a structural fault which can only construct an identity through acts of *identification*. (3) But as these acts of identification – or of decision – are based on a radical structural undecidability, any decision presupposes an act of power. Any power is nevertheless ambiguous: to repress something entails the *capacity* to repress, which involves power; but it also entails the *need* to repress, which involves limitation of power. This means that power is merely the trace of contingency, the point at which objectivity reveals the radical alienation which defines it. In this sense, objectivity – the being of objects – is nothing but the sedimented form of power, in other words a power whose traces have been erased. (4) However, since there is no original *fiat* of power, no moment of radical foundation at which something beyond any objectivity is constituted as the absolute ground on which the being of objects is based, the relationship between power and objectivity cannot be that of the creator and the *ens creatum*. The creator has already been partially created through his or her forms of identification with a structure into which s/he has been thrown. But as this structure is dislocated, the identification never reaches the point of a full identity: any act is an act of reconstruction, which is to say that the creator will search in vain for the seventh day of rest. And as the creator is not omniscient, and has to create within an open range of possibilities that reveal the radical contingency of any decision, power and objectivity become synonymous. (5) On the one hand, then, we have decision – that is, identification as opposed to identity; and on the other, the discernible marks of contingency in the decision, that is power. The ensemble of these marks cannot therefore be objective; it must be the location of an absence. This location is precisely that of the subject. Subject equals the pure form of the structure's dislocation, of its ineradicable distance from itself. An examination of the subject's forms of presence in the structure

must therefore be an exploration of contingency's discursive forms of presence in the field of objectivity — or more precisely, the ways in which objectivity is subverted by contingency. Or in a third formulation, which amounts to the same, it must analyse the emergence of the subject as the result of the collapse of objectivity.

When we speak of politics here, we are not referring to any regional category. 'Politics' is an ontological category: there is politics because there is subversion and dislocation of the social. This means that *any* subject is, by definition, political. Apart from the subject, in this radical sense, there are only *subject positions* in the general field of objectivity. But the subject, as understood in this text, cannot be objective: it is only constituted on the structure's uneven edges. Thus, to explore the field of the subject's emergence in contemporary societies is to examine the marks that contingency has inscribed on the apparently objective structures of the societies we live in.

26.   Let us begin by identifying the basic dimensions of this antithetical relationship between subject and structure.

(a) *Any subject is a mythical subject.* By myth we mean a space of representation which bears no relation of continuity with the dominant 'structural objectivity'. Myth is thus a principle of reading of a given situation, whose terms are external to what is representable in the objective spatiality constituted by the given structure. The 'objective' condition for the emergence of myth, then, is a structural dislocation. The 'work' of myth is to suture that dislocated space through the constitution of a new space of representation. Thus, the effectiveness of myth is essentially hegemonic: it involves forming a new objectivity by means of the rearticulation of the dislocated elements. Any objectivity, then, is merely a crystallized myth. The moment of myth's realization is consequently the moment of the subject's eclipse and its reabsorption by the structure — the moment at which the subject is reduced to 'subject position'. If the condition for the mythical character of a space is its distance vis-à-vis what is representable in the space of the dominant structural objectivity (a distance which is only made possible by the latter's dislocation), the subject is only subject insofar as s/he mediates between both spaces — a mediation which is not itself representable since it has no space of its own.

(b) *The subject is constitutively metaphor.* The condition for any representation (and hence for any literality) is the presence of two spaces that can be mutually related through a one to one correlation of their constitutive elements. And the condition of possibility of this one to one correlation is that there should be something identical constituting the ultimate reality of both the represented space and the space of representation. It is in this sense that the Wittgenstein of the *Tractatus* sustained that the possibility of language referring to reality depended on both sharing the same logical form. But what happens in the case of the subject is exactly the opposite. The mythical space constituted by the subject does not have the same 'logical form' as the structure whose principle of reading the subject becomes. On the contrary, it is the critique and substitution of this 'form' which characterizes the mythical operation. The mythical space is presented as an alternative to the logical form of the dominant structural discourse. However, for reasons mentioned earlier, the mythical space cannot function as a critical alternative to another space if the latter is fully constituted, as if it were simply a question of choosing between the two. Between two fully constituted spaces lacking any common foundation, there is not the slightest criterion for a choice. It is only if one of the spaces is dislocated that the other can appear as its inverted image. But, one could ask, does not this inverted image keep (as its negative reverse) the same logical form of the structural space? The answer is clearly negative. If the mythical space was opposed to a full 'logical form' of the dominant structural space, then we would indeed be faced with an inverted image. But it is not the 'structurality' of the dominant structure to which the mythical space is opposed, but its *de*-structuring effects. The mythical space is constituted as a critique of the lack of structuration accompanying the dominant order. In this sense, however, the mythical space has a dual function and a split identity: on the one hand it is its own literal content — the proposed new order; but on the other, this order symbolizes the very principle of spatiality and structurality. The critical effects of the mythical space on the dominant structural space will therefore increase the latter's destructuration: (1) the mythical space will appear as pure positivity and spatiality, and to this end it will present that to which it is opposed as a non-space, a non-place where a set of dislocations are added together; (2) in order to conceive of itself as a space — as the point of a fully realized objectivity — it will have to present those dislocations as equivalent, but as systematic, nonetheless. But as this systematic character cannot be that of a structure, it must be referred back to a transcendent point, to an initial non-place of the dislocations that will be conceived as the *source* of the latter. The transcendent *origin* of the structural dislocations is thus opposed to the *objective* immanence of the mythical space. The metaphorical nature of mythical space thus stems from the fact that the concrete or literal content of myth represents something different from itself: the very principle of a fully achieved literality. The fascination accompanying the vision of a promised land or an ideal society stems directly from this perception or intuition of a fullness that cannot be granted by the reality of the present. Myth only springs forth as a metaphor on a ground dominated by this peculiar absence/presence dialectic. But as we have seen, this dialectic between absence (dislocation of the structure) and presence (identification with an unachieved fullness) is nothing but the space of the subject. The subject (lack within the structure) only takes on its specific form of representation as the metaphor of an absent structure.

(c) *The subject's forms of identification function as surfaces of inscription.* As we have seen, if the subject is the metaphor of an absent fullness, it means that the concrete content of its forms of identification will function as the very representation of fullness, of all possible fullness. But this means that once myth — or, what amounts to the same thing, the forms of identification giving the subject its only discursive presence possible — has achieved a certain social acceptance, it will be used as an inverted form of representation of all possible kinds of structural dislocation. Any frustration or unsatisfied demand will be compensated for or offset by the myth of an achieved fullness. This indetermination of myth — as the means of expression by which specific dislocations might be overcome — is a direct consequence of its metaphorical nature, of the possibility it opens for the expression of the form of fullness itself, beyond any concrete dislocation. This means that myth functions as a surface on which dislocations and social demands can be inscribed. The main feature of a surface of inscription is its incomplete nature: if the inscription process was complete, there would be an essential symmetry between the surface and the inscription left on it, thus eliminating any distance between the act of expression and what is expressed by it. But if the process is never complete, the symmetry is broken and our view is displaced from what is inscribed to the process of inscription itself. In this sense, social myths are essentially incomplete: their content is constantly reconstituted and displaced.

(d) *The incomplete character of the mythical surfaces of inscription is the condition of possibility for the constitution of social imaginaries.* The relation between the surface of inscription and what is inscribed on it is therefore essentially unstable. There are two extreme possibilities here. The first is the complete hegemonization of the surfaces of inscription by what is inscribed on them. As we mentioned earlier: the moment of inscription is eliminated in favour of the literality of what is inscribed. The other possibility is symmetrically opposite: the moment of representation of the very form of fullness dominates to such an extent that it becomes the unlimited horizon of inscription of *any* social demand and *any* possible dislocation. In such an event, myth is transformed into an imaginary. The imaginary is a horizon: it is not one among other objects but an absolute limit which structures a field of intelligibility and is thus the condition of possibility for the emergence of any object. In this sense, the Christian millennium, the Enlightenment and positivism's conception of progress, communist society are all imaginaries: as modes of representation of the very form of fullness, they are located beyond the precariousness and dislocations typical of the world of objects. Put another way, it is only because there are 'failed' objects, quasi-objects, that the very form of objectivity must free itself from any concrete entity and assume the character of a horizon.

With these considerations as our starting point, we can determine the collective imaginaries' pattern of constitution and dissolution. The condition for the emergence of an imaginary is the metaphorization of the literal content of a particular social demand. Let us suppose that a particular social group is suffering a range of dislocations in its customary practices and proposes a series of measures to overcome them. This body of measures constitutes a certain spatial model – an ideal model in this sense: the mythical space of a possible social order. From the beginning, the duality of this space – literal content and metaphorical representation of fullness – is present, but insofar as the mythical space is directly linked to a specific dislocation, the possibilities for the expansion and autonomization of the moment of metaphorical representation are severely limited. Yet the very fact that this mythical order is from the beginning something more than the terrain of the original dislocation entails the possibility – which may or may not be realized – of radicalizing the metaphorical moment of the representation. Thus, it only needs other dislocations and demands to be added to the fullness that the mythical space must represent for the metaphorical moment to become autonomous from the literality of the original dislocation, and for the mythical space to be transformed into an imaginary horizon. Gramsci saw this process as the transition from a *corporatist class* to a *hegemonic class*, which for him involved the 'universalization' of the demands of a particular group. What our analysis adds to the Gramscian conception is the idea that this transition is only possible because the duality of the representation has been present from the start; because all mythical space is external to the dislocation it purports to suture; and because any group, from this point of view, is exterior to its own demands. This also shows us what the logic of the dissolution of collective imaginaries is: insofar as a mythical space begins to absorb less social demands, and an increasing number of dislocations that cannot be integrated into that space of representation coexist, the space is, so to speak, re-literalized; its power of metaphorization is reduced, and its dimension of horizon is thus lost.

There is therefore a double movement governing the constitution of collective identities. On the one hand, no collective imaginary appears essentially linked to a literal content. As a collective imaginary represents the very form of 'fullness', the latter can be 'embodied' by the most diverse of contents. In this sense, the imaginary signifiers forming a community's horizon are tendentially empty and essentially ambiguous. On the other hand, however, it would be fundamentally incorrect to suppose that such ambiguity might be offset by the literality of the various social demands giving content to the imaginary in every historical juncture. This would mean assuming that the demands are self-transparent discourses, when in actual fact we know that their very constitution requires the intervention of mythical spaces and imaginary horizons. The process is considerably more complex and involves a constant interpenetration between these two dimensions. It is important to point out that there is no necessary relation between the dislocation as such (which, as we have seen, is pure *temporality*) and the discursive *space* that is to constitute its principle of reading and its form of representation. That is to say that the imaginary horizon on which a particular dislocation is inscribed — which thus transforms it into a demand and introduces a principle of intelligibility into the situation as an ensemble — is external to the dislocation as such and cannot be deduced from the latter. There is therefore no common measure between the dislocated structure and the discourse aiming to introduce a new order and a new articulation.

Consider the German economic crisis of the 1920s, for example, and its devastating effects on the middle classes. All routine expectations and practices — even the sense of self-identity — had been entirely shattered. There was thus a generalized dislocation of traditional patterns of life. That National Socialist discourse emerged as a possible response to the crisis and offered a principle of intelligibility for the new situation is not something that stemmed *necessarily* from the crisis itself. That the crisis was resolved in favour of Nazism cannot be deduced *from the terms* of the crisis themselves. What occurred was something different: it was that Nazi discourse was the only one in the circumstances that addressed the problems experienced by the middle classes as a whole and offered a principle for their interpretation. Its victory was the result of its *availability* on a terrain and in a situation where no other discourse presented itself as a real hegemonic alternative. From our previous analysis, it can be clearly gathered why mere availability is on occasion enough to ensure the victory of a particular discourse: for if the mythical space has the dual function of expressing its concrete content and representing 'fullness' as such — and since there is no common measure between the dislocation and the forms of its discursive 'spatialization' — then the mere fact that it presents itself as the embodiment of fullness is enough to ensure its acceptance. The discourse of a 'new order' is often accepted by several sectors, not because they particularly like its content but because it is the discourse of *an* order, of something that is presented as a credible alternative to a crisis and a generalized dislocation.

This does not mean, of course, that *any* discourse putting itself forward as the embodiment of fullness will be accepted. The acceptance of a discourse depends on its credibility, and this will not be granted if its proposals clash with the basic principles informing the organization of a group. But it is important to point out that the more the objective organization of that group has been dislocated, the more those 'basic principles' will have been shattered, thereby widening the areas of social life that must be reorganized by a mythical space. The collapse of liberal and rationalist convictions among widespread sectors of the population with the emergence of the totalitarianisms of the twentieth century is just one extreme example of this process. There is therefore a dual movement. On the one hand mythical space, as the incarnation of the form of fullness as such, metaphorically transfers this embodying function to its concrete content and thus manages hegemonically to impose a particular social order. It is only through this overdetermination of functions that this social order is imposed and consolidated. But this overdetermination, which is the source of its strength, is also — and this is the second movement — the source of its weakness: for if the very form of fullness has a space of representation, then the latter will be the locus to which *any* specific demand will be referred and where *any* specific dislocation will find the inverted form of its expression. The relation between the literal content of the mythical space and its function of representing the general form of fullness is a *radically* hegemonic and unstable relation; one that is exposed to an 'outside' that it is *essentially* incapable of mastering. This opens either the possibility that the moment of the general form of fullness might predominate — in which case the literal content will be deformed and transformed through the addition of an indefinite number of social demands — or that the literal content of the mythical space might predominate — in which case its ability to hegemonize the general form of fullness will be reduced; a growing coexistence will exist between unexpressed demands and a *supposed* universality that is incapable of delivering the goods; and the mythical space will lose its dimension of imaginary horizon. In practice, mythical spaces move on an unstable balance between these extremes: for longer or shorter periods they have a certain relative elasticity beyond which we witness their inexorable decline.

27.   In speaking of 'mythical spaces' and their possible transformation into imaginary horizons, it is important to point out that we are not referring to anything that is essentially 'primitive' and whose re-emergence in contemporary societies would constitute an outbreak of irrationalism. On the contrary, myth is constitutive of any possible society. As we have seen, any space formed as a principle for the reordering of a dislocated structure's elements is mythical. Its mythical character is given by its radical discontinuity with the dislocations of the dominant structural forms. The welfare state, for example, was a myth aimed at reconstructing the operation of capitalist societies following the Great Depression. A society from which myth was radically excluded would be either an entirely 'spatial' and 'objective' society — where any dislocation had been banished, like the model for the operation of a perfect machine — or one in which dislocations lacked any space for representation and transcendence. In other words, either the cemetery or the lunatic asylum.

But it is not just that myth is not absent from the functioning of contemporary societies: it is also that the latter are required by their very dynamics to become increasingly mythical. This is linked to the proliferation of dislocations peculiar to advanced capitalism — the era, as we saw, of disorganized capitalism. The combined effects of commodification, of bureaucratic rationalization, and of the increasingly complex forms of division of labour — all require constant creativity and the continuous construction of spaces of collective operation that can rest less and less on inherited objective, institutional forms. But this means that in contemporary societies the (mythical) space of the subject is widened at the expense of structural objectivity. We live today in societies that are in many ways less 'alienated' than in the past: that is to say societies in which there is a greater indeterminacy of our position within them and in which we are more free to decide our movements and identity. They are also societies in which social reproduction depends less and less on repetitive practices and requires the constant production of social myths. In one sense we can say that the duality between subject and object is being overcome: the classical problem of knowledge as the adequation between knowing and being disappears in that myth constitutes the subject and being of objects at the same time. But the transparency — if it can be called transparency — of myth is very different from that presupposed by the Hegelian abolition of the knowing/being duality found, for example, in Lukács. While for Lukács this abolition involves the consummation of a fullness that makes the alienated existence of the subject in relation to the being of the object impossible (a consummation which thus entails the radical reduction of the real to the rational), in the case of myth the opposite occurs. It is insofar as any fullness is denied to both subject and object that myth can establish the reality of both, thus transcending the division from which epistemological discourse emerges.

But this is the point at which a decisive question is posed for our discourse. Does not the *recognition* of the mythical — or contingent — character of the spatial configurations making us up as subjects already involve a certain exteriority to that mythical space and, by extension, to any space? As the ground of the subject (extended at the cost of the structure) must pay the concomitant price of its dissolution as a *locatable* ground, does not the transcendence of epistemological discourse give rise to a paradox? If any representation involves spatiality, does not the recognition of the mythical nature of any space entail forgoing any intelligibility of the *place* from which such a recognition is verified? These are crucial questions which should be answered, in our view, by drawing up close to what constitutes the specificity, in its most radical sense, of the societies in which we live. Reformulated in different, but equivalent terms, it is the question of the very possibility of a *community* in an era of generalized politics. In the following pages, we will deal with this issue from a particular angle: the way in which the discourses constituting community spaces have dealt with those realities denied the dignity of spatial representation.

28.   Politics and space are antinomic terms. Politics only exist insofar as the spatial eludes us. Or — and this amounts to the same thing — political victory is equivalent to the elimination of the specifically political nature of the victorious practices. That is why any revolution must cultivate the

myth of 'origins'; in order to establish itself as the source of all positivity, it must rub out the contingent traces of its 'ignoble' beginnings. As we know, spatiality means coexistence within a structure that establishes the positive nature of all its terms. Dislocation, on the other hand, means the impossibility of that coexistence: particular elements only manage to obtain positivity (i.e. objectivity) at the expense of the elimination of others. The representation of both as positive differential realities in the same space is therefore impossible. Only if the antagonistic elements are presented as anti-space, as anti-community, do they manage to obtain a form of discursive presence. This discourse of dislocation and antagonism, however, will not only be non-spatial but the very negation of space as such; and as we saw, the mythical space will therefore appear as the realization of the principle of pure spatiality. This offers us two starting points: an analysis of the forms of exclusion that have historically provided the conditions for the construction of a pure spatiality, and the forms of discursive presence that have been granted to the non-spatial.

Let us start by considering two historical approaches to the problem of politics which display the common characteristic of making impossible — strictly unthinkable — the political dimension of all social practice. The first is Plato's text on the possibility and limits of community. (If I do not attempt to unify the different approaches under a term like 'political philosophy' it is because this would assume the unity of an object of reflection, which is precisely what is in question.) For Plato, politics cannot be a radical construction based on the experience of dislocation, since an ideal objectivity of the community *previous to any experience* tells us what the community *is*. Any maladjustment between empirically existent communities and the form of community as such is therefore reduced to a problem of knowledge. The statesman is not an 'ideologist' — a builder of myths; nor is he even the possessor of a wisdom or 'know-how' like the Aristotelian *phronimos*: rather he is a philosopher — the possessor of a knowledge in the rigorous sense of the term. Platonic thought addresses the *problem* of politics — the issue of dislocation — but is a non-political response to that problem. If dislocation involves contingency, and contingency power, the absence of dislocation leads in the Platonic schema to a radical communitarian essentialism that eliminates the very question of power and thus the possibility of politics.

In Plato's scheme, there was no power to share; what was 'shareable' was the Form of the Good written into the structure of the community. The results of this line of argument were two-fold: the idea of citizenship was severed

from the idea of meaningful participation in the making of political decisions; and the idea of political community, that is, a community that seeks to
resolve its internal conflicts through political methods, is replaced by the
idea of the virtuous community devoid of conflict and, therefore, devoid of
'politics'. Plato did not deny that each member of the community, no matter
how humble his contribution, had a right to share the benefits of the
community; what he did deny was that this contribution could be erected
into a claim to share in political decision-making.[28]

This communitarian schema was so absolutely spatial that nothing in it
could be left to the discretion of a temporal intrusion — dislocation.
Everything, including the number of the community's inhabitants, had
to be mastered by a simultaneity in which being and knowledge entered
into strict correspondence. And yet how is it not possible to note that the
essentialism of the Platonic republic can only constitute itself starting
from its *other* — from a radical contingency which is its very condition of
possibility? For the incarnation of the philosopher in the actual ruler, to
the *empirical* search for which Plato dedicated a great part of his life, is a
fortuitous fact which escapes all intelligibility. But if the tyrant of Syra-
cuse refused, as the King of Prussia would do many centuries later, to
play the august role of incarnating the rationality prepared for him by
philosophy, then this revealed much more than an empirical circum-
stantial *fault*. It showed that rationality, if it must be embodied in a
contingent historical force, is itself mere contingency and that to be
achieved it must therefore be constituted as power. The simultaneity or
pure spatiality of the constitutive moments of the Platonic community
thus require as their condition of possibility the purely temporal, dislocated instance of an irrational incarnation. It is not necessary to go over
all the forms through which ancient thought attempted to reduce
temporal dislocation to spatiality: it is enough to recall the efforts to
write all historical change into a theory of cyclical sequence that Polybius
would dream of having overcome definitively through the perfect
balance of the Roman constitution.

Our second example of an approach which makes politics unthinkable can be found in Hobbes, where the element of dislocation, of the
impossibility of an order, represents much more than the dimension of
impurity and contingency found in all empirical reality: it is the very
definition of the state of nature. The important thing from the point of
view of our problem is that if the state of nature is conceived as dislocation pure and simple, and as absence of any order in the generalized

struggle of everyone against everyone else, then its antithetical opposite is not an order with a specific content, but order *tout court*, the very form of order independent of any content. Let us recall the point we made earlier: the more a system of norms and beliefs constituting a community has been shattered by dislocations, the less the new order's relation and continuity with that system will be; and the more its specific content will represent the order's abstract and general principle. This indifference to the specific content of the order, which grows insofar as its point of departure is an increasingly deep dislocation, finds its logical culmination in Hobbes's theory: as the initial state is defined as a state of nature which makes *any* organization of the community impossible, its antithesis (the principle of order) will be identified with the will of the ruler, *whatever* the content of that will might be. On the one hand, it could be said that we are faced here with the same elimination of politics as in Plato: both the Hobbesian monarch and the Platonic philosopher-king concentrate the whole of power in their hands, and the moment of argumentation, dissension and antagonism characterizing politics is equally eliminated. But on the other hand, we could say that the ruler of Hobbes is the antithesis of Plato's; while the legitimacy of the Platonic ruler depends on his *knowledge* of what the community *essentially is*, Hobbes's monarch must *invent* and *construct* the communitarian order, since the community, outside the order constituted by the ruler, is merely the chaos peculiar to the state of nature. The Platonic communitarian space is never mythical, since it is what it has always essentially been, and its corruption is associated with the close interpenetration between evil and ignorance, which bases the legitimacy of power on knowledge. The Hobbesian communitarian space is mythical through and through in the sense we defined earlier: it is based on an act of radical creation. There is therefore something fundamentally modern in Hobbes: while in Plato power stems from the recognition of a pre-existent objectivity, in Hobbes socio-political objectivity stems from power.

This contrast between Plato and Hobbes thus shows us how politics is impossible in both cases. But it also shows us, as its reverse side, the conditions that a community must meet to be a wholly political community. Let us dwell on this problem. As we saw, politics is impossible in Plato because community has a being prior to any decision; and in Hobbes because decision excludes all plurality and deliberation. But in that case a political community must necessarily be an essentially incomplete community in which its being must be constantly redefined and recreated. And this constitutive incompletion has two dimensions: (1) it is an incompletion of the community for which the decisions are taken — in other words, the community has no being other than that derived from those decisions: and (2) it must also be an incompletion of those taking the decisions. For if political actors were not contingent and limited, they would be omnipotent, in which case their decisions would endow the community with a complete being, thus eliminating incompletion. Thus, if the first dimension distances us from Plato, the second does the same with Hobbes. A history of the presence of the political moment in the representation of communitarian spaces in Western thought must therefore be a history of the ways in which incompletion — or dislocation, which amounts to the same thing — has been given a discursive presence. This history could be conceived as an account of the long process by which the community has come to terms with its political nature.

As we have seen, any representation of a dislocation involves its spatialization. The way to overcome the temporal, traumatic and unrepresentable nature of dislocation is to construct it as a moment in permanent structural relation with other moments, in which case the pure temporality of the 'event' is eliminated. As we said, diachrony is one of the forms of synchrony. The main form of this spatial domesticization of time in ancient thought was the theory of the cycle: the succession of different kinds of government in relation to the constitutive excesses of each is a process that always recommences. Thus, while there is no form of government that does not produce dislocatory effects — and contain the seeds of its own dissolution — the cycle does not dissolve and is therefore constituted as a pure space providing the means of representation of any possible dislocation. This circular reduction of time to space is the limit that thought on historicity and contingency reached in classical antiquity. (As we earlier pointed out, the only exception is Polybius, for whom the Roman conquest effectively breaks the cycle, but in order to constitute an even purer spatiality that eliminates not just the representation of structural dislocations, but their very *possibility*.)

29.   The dominant figure of thought on dislocation in classical antiquity was *corruption*. Corruption is essentially inherent to political forms and leads to their decline and replacement in the cyclical succession. And the boundary of essence establishing the eidetic purity of these forms only allows corruption to be conceived as non-being. In the case of ancient thought it would be totally senseless to speak of a 'fullness of time', since the incorruptible is intemporal. Any 'apocalypse' is excluded

from this perspective. It is Judaeo-Christian thought that is to introduce a radical diachrony, thus providing a new discursive surface for the insertion of dislocations. In the first place the latter are no longer conceived in terms of corruption, but *evil*. There is nothing inherent to social forms which internally generates their decline; rather it is the intervention of perverse powers.

> And I stood upon the sand of the sea and saw a beast rise up out of the sea, having ... ten horns. ... And it was given to him to make war with the saints, and to overcome them: and power was given to him over all kindreds, and tongues, and nations. And all that dwell upon the earth shall worship him, whose names are not written in the book of life.... And I beheld another beast coming up out of the earth ... And he doeth great wonders ... and deceiveth them that dwell upon the earth by means of those miracles which he had power to do.[29]

Dislocation here is merely an event, a sudden intervention originating from an absolute outside that bears no relation whatsoever to the previous situation. It is also the intervention of a new and identifiable force, rather than the result of the deterioration of a pre-existent reality. Diachrony is not therefore dominated by any regularity, be it cyclical or of any other kind. But neither is diachronic succession the recording of a series of unstructured events, as apocalyptic discourse is organized around a promise. If the radicality of thought on dislocation requires the absolute unintelligibility of evil — and, as a result, its reduction to a mere event and its personification as a malign power — the final victory of God is assured, and the advent of the pure space of a fullness guaranteed. As divine plans are inscrutable, none of the phases of apocalyptic diachrony can be explained in terms of a necessary or logical succession: in this way the nature of pure dislocated event of each of the moments of this history is maintained, but at the same time they are endowed with a surface of discursive inscription. But in the second place, the hinge of the transition to the kingdom of God on earth cannot consist of just another moment in the series of events recorded by diachrony. If all previous historical actors have been limited in their inability to prevail over the powers of evil, the actor who has the strength to objectively suppress evil and to impose divine justice must himself be divine, or at least have been transformed by God into the incarnation of his omnipotence. He must therefore be a limitless actor.

Then the heavens shall be opened in a tempest, and Christ shall descend with great power; and a fiery brightness shall go before him, and a countless host of angels; and all that multitude of godless shall be annihilated, and torrents of blood shall flow.... When peace has been brought about and every evil suppressed, that righteous and victorious King will carry out a great judgement on the earth of the living and the dead, and will hand over all heathen peoples to servitude under the righteous who are alive, and will raise the [righteous] dead to eternal life, and will himself reign with them on earth, and will found the Holy City, and this kingdom of the righteous shall last for a thousand years.[30]

In the third and final place, an apocalyptic reading of the real creates the conditions for a permanent gap between eschatological identities and the empirical actors embodying them. This means, on the one hand, that knowledge is based on an operation of recognition: it is a question of detecting behind limited empirical agents the limitless and universal actors that they embody (hence assertions such as 'the Pope is the Antichrist'). And on the other hand, the very idea that the relation between empirical agent and eschatological actor must be conceived as an incarnation assumes that a rigid separation exists between both – eschatological reality does not give rise to any contamination by empirical appearances. The price that the apocalyptic inscription of dislocations has had to pay is therefore clear: the emergence of a permanent zone of friction between the universal/necessary and the contingent.

30.   In his admirable book, *The Legitimacy of the Modern Age*,[31] Hans Blumenberg has introduced the concept of 'reoccupations'. By this he means the process by which particular notions, associated with the advent of a new vision and new problems, have the function of replacing ancient notions that had been formed on the ground of a different set of issues, with the result that the latter end up imposing their demands on the new notions and inevitably deforming them. Something like this happens with the arrival of modern ideologies of radical social transformation which 'reoccupy' a ground that had been formed, in its essential structural determinations, by the medieval millenialist apocalypse. As we saw, the latter had a dual function; on the one hand it affirmed dislocation's character as 'mere event'; but on the other it gave it a discursive presence by conceiving it as a moment in the march towards the realization of the millennium (with the inscrutability of divine plans – which only become manifest in revelation – constituting the key point that

kept the two dimensions together). But it only needed the eclipse of God from the scene, while at the same time maintaining the image of a necessary transition to the chiliastic world of a homogeneous, reconciled (and therefore non-dislocated) society for all the intrinsic tensions of apocalyptic discourse to be fully manifested.

The first requirement of a rationalist and naturalist discourse presenting itself as an attempt to radically reconstruct society, is for all transitions to be intramundane. In that case the achievement of the universality peculiar to a transparent society can only be the result of the transference of the omnipotence of the Creator to the *ens creatum*. But with inexorable logic it then follows that there can be no dislocation possible in this process. If everything that happens can be explained *internally* to this world, nothing can be a mere event (which entails a radical temporality, as we have seen) and everything acquires an absolute intelligibility within the grandiose scheme of a pure spatiality. This is the Hegelian–Marxist moment. As we have pointed out from the very start of this essay, the moment of negativity — of evil (in the apocalyptic discourse), of dislocation — becomes mere appearance in the general movement of reason. Modern rationalism thus adapted badly to the ground of medieval eschatology in its 'reoccupation' of the latter. Its maintenance of a radical representability of the real — which is what the Middle Ages attempted in opposition to the characteristic 'non-being' of the corruption of classical thought — thus depends on eliminating any thought of dislocation. But this equally opens the symmetrically opposite possibility: that of maintaining dislocation's nature as pure event or temporality, in which case its representation becomes impossible. Dislocation cannot therefore be conceived as the corruption and non-being of a pure *eidos*, but nor can it be inscribed as the manifestation of the fierce struggle with the forces of evil. What remains, then, is the mere temporality and incompletion of something that has become essentially unrepresentable. The Enlightenment, the 'great narratives' of the nineteenth century and the totalitarianisms of the twentieth were clearly oriented in the direction of the first alternative (combining it — inconsistently in many cases — with a quasi-eschatological reiteration of the image of the struggle against evil forces). By contrast, our age — the age of the democratic revolution — is beginning to explore the possibilities of historical action that the second alternative opens.

31. At the time of writing — a year that has seen Tiananmen Square, the collapse of the regimes in Eastern Europe and the beginning of a

process of political transformation with unpredictable results in the Soviet Union — it is obviously easy to indulge in facile teleologies and present the whole process from the Enlightenment to the Russian Revolution as a continuum, or rather a progression, that was to culminate in the Peking massacres or the execution of Ceausescu. But such images are superficial and absurd. The very notion of 'reoccupation' that we invoked above conspires against them: if new ideas, new discourses, new social demands adapt badly to the ground they reoccupy, it is this tension that must provide a starting point, not the supposed teleological unity of a single field embracing the whole of its contents.

But this should not allow us to forget the reality and operativeness of the reoccupied ground, as well as the way in which some basic dimensions of the medieval millennium have continued to determine fundamental structures of radical thought right up to the present. All such dimensions can be summed up in a single fact: the *universal* nature of the history of the millennium — which is the condition of the limitless representability made possible by such a history. This also requires the universality of the actors and society in which the millennium is finally realized. In secularist versions of the millennium this universality is maintained in all its force, but as it is not easy for them to establish the distinction between concrete agents and the eschatological universality they embody, there is a constant process of metaphorical — or rather metonymical — transference between both. The logics of 'incarnation' are thus fundamentally ambiguous. Let us give a couple of examples. As we showed elsewhere,[32] the very notion of socialism as *social* management of the production process was conceived in opposition to a mode of reproduction based on the search for individual profit. If the 'social' of 'social management' acquired meaning simply through opposition to the 'individual', such meaning was reduced to the abstract universality of the community. Who is the subject of *social* management then? The sociological hypothesis of communitarian universality being ultimately self-transparent — through the growing homogenization of society — has not been realized in any concrete experience, since the agents meant to *embody* 'the social' (the state or the party, for example) were always limited agents. This is the point where the metonymical transference takes place: just as gold has the dual function of having its own use value and of embodying the general form of value, the concrete particularity of an institution or social force takes on the function of representing universality itself. As we have seen, this operation is not impossible; and we can even assert that it is inherent to any process of political construction. The implicit duality of any mythical space means that *any* concrete content can also come to express the very form of fullness — that is to say universality. The ground of that duality is a priori undecidable in either direction. All depends on how the process of universalization is conceived. If communitarian universality establishes a relation of total equivalence with the social order advocated by a particular group, the incarnation will not be contingent; in fact there will be no incarnation at all, since the 'idea' and the 'body' in which it is to be incarnated have a relation of indissoluble necessity between them. An objective process has guaranteed positions from which a knowledge of the social proves possible. The dictatorship of the proletariat bases its legitimacy on the same privileged access to knowledge as the Platonic philosopher-king, with the difference that in the latter the unity between monarchical power and knowledge was fortuitous, while in the case of the dictatorship of the proletariat there is a millenialist—naturalist theory of history explaining why the latter incarnation of the universal has an objective and necessary character. In this case, (1) the social imaginary is totally reduced to mythical space in the sense that myth loses its character as a *limitless* surface of inscription; and (2) myth denies its own character as such, since on presenting itself as a necessary social order, it establishes a relation of essential continuity with the social demands that it determines as legitimate from its own inside, thus annulling any distance between the dislocations of the structure and the mythical surface on which they are to be inscribed. This obviously means that any other social demand is excluded from the pure space of the transparent society.

It is this closed nature of a space denying its mythical character that allows the indivisible unity between empirical actors and their universal 'functions' or 'tasks' to be welded together. It is perfectly clear that this fusion between empiricity and universality/rationality is at the root of the totalitarian potentialities of the 'social management' advocated by socialism. But it is important to add that this fusion is the result of the 'reoccupation' by socialist discourse of the ground of the universalist diachrony that is inherent to the Christian apocalypse. This point is crucial. For the current crisis of socialism is to a large extent that of the long-term effects of this reoccupation; and in order for the demands on which the socialist myth has been based to regain validity and acquire new historical possibilities, it only needs them to be inscribed in a discourse different from that of 'social management' — by which we mean an abstract universality that must be embodied. But this means moving in the opposite direction to the discourse of eschatological universality. We shall return to this point shortly.

The second example refers to the agent leading the historical emergence of the reconciled society. The reconciled society is the realization of the essence of humankind. It is therefore the full realization of a pure universality. How is it then possible for limited, partial and contingent agents to constitute historically something that patently transcends their powers? We have already seen how the Christian apocalypse solved this problem: by advocating the divine exteriority of the saviour from those to be saved. But this solution was not possible for a rationalist/naturalist eschatology. It thus asserted, firstly, that contingent limitations were not really limitations, but the necessary steps of reason towards self-awareness; and secondly, that the advent of the reconciled society required the emergence of a social actor whose own particularity would express the pure essence of humanity. Once again, the moment of incarnation dissolves: the proletariat, on liberating itself, liberates humanity as a whole. How this process worked in practice is well known. The supposed abolition of the subject's mythical nature crashed against a contingency unyielding to any rationalist reduction. And this meant that increasingly tortuous expedients and formulas were resorted to. Universality did not correspond to the proletariat, but to its historical interests which had to be expressed through a party, etc. What had originally been put forward as the abolition of any contingent embodiment gave way in practice to a migration of the universal through successive bodies — from class to party, from the party to the autocrat, etc. The same eschatological ambition automatically gave way to this authoritarian escalation, once the contingency of the concrete social actors rebelled against the role that 'Reason' had reserved for them. A considerable part of the tragic history of our time is contained in this game of hide and seek between 'Reason' and its various embodiments.

32.   We must now go on to question ourselves on the second alternative to the eclipse of God. This is not based on the advocacy of an intrinsic positive logic of the intramundane, which necessarily leads to the elimination of all dislocation, but on the assertion of the latter's constitutive nature, which leads to the crisis of all spatiality and the ultimate impossibility of all representation. The development of this second line of historical action is the specific ground of the democratic revolution (or rather, it is the strictly political *mode* through which democracy operates, since democracy is the very placing in question of the notion of *ground*). Let us recall the duality of mythical space, which

constitutes a concrete 'order' and represents the very form of order (or fullness) at the same time. The more this second dimension predominates, the more the mythical space will become an imaginary horizon. But this means two things. The first is that the manifestation of the very form of fullness can only take place through the growing emancipation of this form from any concrete content. In other words, this emancipation can only take place insofar as the representation of the very possibility of inscription and the representation of the materiality of the inscribed become increasingly distanced. This can only mean that the general form of fullness is exactly equivalent to the general form of possibility. That is to say that the fullness of the social does not manifest itself in any concrete social order but in the possibility of representing its radical indeterminacy, in other words its nature as a mere possibility. The second thing is that radical indeterminacy does not manifest itself through a *cancellation* of all determinations — this would consist of an operation that could only be conceivable on the basis of the fullness of the category of 'determination' and would thus leave the latter intact — but through a subversion of all determination, that is through the assertion of its presence in a context that destroys its own possibility. That is precisely what we have termed dislocation. But as we have seen, dislocation destroys all space and, as a result, the very possibility of representation.

Let us dwell for a moment on this point, however. The impossibility of representation cannot consist of the *presence* of *something* that does not have access to the space of representation. Such duality would merely be that of an exclusion, and the exclusion of the unrepresentable would precisely aid the constitution of the space of that which can be represented. Rather it is a question of an all-embracing subversion of the space of representability in general, which is the same as the subversion of spatiality itself. Let us give an example which is frequent in the constitution of political imaginaries in the Third World. Migrants from rural areas to the expanding cities bring with them a range of values, discourses and symbols, etc., from their places of origin. In the new urban environment a fresh set of antagonisms and dislocations occur in relation to their traditional way of life. A frequent reaction in such circumstances is to reaffirm traditional symbols and values of rural life as a means of creating a culture of resistance: in other words, those symbols and values operate as surfaces for the inscription of the *new* urban antagonisms and dislocations. Once the symbols' circulation has reached a certain level of generalization in the representation of a vast range of antagonisms, they become the necessary surface for the inscription of any new demand. It is for that reason that, when social groups different from those that were their original bearers – the urban middle sectors, for example – attempt to construct forms of resistance to their specific dislocations, they will increasingly invoke the symbols of resistance of internal migrants: for such symbols are the only ideological raw material expressing anti-establishment protest in that society. This constant extension of the area of the representable in the discursive surfaces formed by anti-establishment symbols has a dual effect, of course: on the one hand it consolidates that surface as the representation of the very *form* of the anti-establishment; but on the other, if it can perform this function of representing *any* demand and social protest, it is because it has been emptied of any concrete content by the very fact of its consolidation as a necessary discursive surface. The fullness of the community thus becomes an empty form and its relation with the concrete demands of the different groups is therefore essentially hegemonic and unstable.

We can see, then, the new type of link between 'particularity' and 'universality' that this kind of emptying entails. None of the problems we saw arise with the reoccupation of the space of the millenialist apocalypse disappears, but their meaning is essentially displaced; and this displacement leads us from the reoccupation of a ground to its radical deconstruction. The 'universal' does not disappear but has lost the transparency of a positive and closed world: the community 'universalizes' its values through the circulation of symbols that are stripped of any specific content to the very extent that that circulation encompasses a growing number of social demands. No universality exists other than that which is built in a pragmatic and precarious way by that process of circulation which establishes an equivalence between an increasingly wide range of demands. But this means that the problem of the tension implicit in any 'embodiment' disappears, since the essential asymmetry between the particularity of the demands and the universality of the values never gives rise to a reconciliation in which any particularity would be finally reabsorbed into a universal and transparent order. There is no *Pax Romana* for the social 'order'. But for that very reason the problem of 'embodiment' does not simply reoccupy the ground of the apocalypse in its teleological or naturalist–rationalist forms; rather, in its new form, it makes that ground impossible. It is no longer a question of a necessary universality 'searching' for the historical force that might embody it. On the contrary, since all universality is only built through the overdetermination of an indefinite and open range of concrete demands, it is a question of the force intended to embody such 'relative universalities' being indeterminate; and such a force will only be the result of a hegemonic struggle. This is exactly what politics consists of.

There are two aspects here: on the one hand, since no force is the incarnation of the universal in and by itself, a 'collective will' will only consolidate its hegemony if it manages to appear to other groups as the force capable of providing the best social arrangement possible to secure and expand a universality that transcends it. The asymmetry between 'relative universality' and the force embodying it thus paves the way for a democratic competition between groups, as the 'universal' is not commensurate with any of the forces that might momentarily embody it. On the other hand, however, the 'universal' does not have, independently of the successive forces embodying it, a fixed existence and meaning either. There is no longer a definable *eidos* outside of its corrupt forms, nor a Kingdom of God that can be apprehended through revelation. This means that the question of power, the intrinsic impurity of antagonisms and struggles, penetrate the field of the universal itself. Recognition of the historical limitation of social agents is the very condition for democracy; but for the same reason, power is paradoxically the very condition for freedom.

A reflection on a limited historical case — that of internal migrants in Third World countries — has provided the point of departure for our presentation of such theoretical developments. Yet it would be a mistake to think that the validity of the analysis is limited to this and similar cases alone. On the contrary, both the fragmentation and growing limitation of social actors, and the permanent dissociation between social imaginaries and the mythical spaces capable of embodying them, are a process that is deeply rooted in the democratic revolution of the last two centuries, as well as in the overall state of contemporary societies. In relatively stable societies there is no distancing between inscription surfaces and what is inscribed on them. 'Order' is immanent in social relations; and in all forms of counter-society, the *content* of mythical space absorbs any possible dimension of horizon. There is therefore no room for the constitution of the duality of mythical space and social imaginary. But the situation changes in societies that have gone through the experience of capitalism and the uneven and combined development inherent to it.

Let us pick up on several points of our analysis. The fragmentation and growing limitation of social actors is linked to the multiplication of the dislocations produced by 'disorganized capitalism'. It follows from this that more and more areas of social life must become the product of *political* forms of reconstruction and regulation. But the very abundance of such dislocations and their intrinsic antagonisms means that the limitation and fragmentation of the social actors they give rise to also increase. This fragmentation, however, does not mean atomization: isolated demands are overdetermined in the constitution of social imaginaries, and mythical spaces — which compete for the hegemonization of the imaginaries — articulate demands in various ways. In turn, the role of those spaces and imaginaries in transforming dislocations into demands is absolutely central. There is thus no longer any room for the base/superstructure dichotomy: any social level — if we can speak of levels to refer to something that is essentially non-spatial — can be the location of mythical re-articulations and imaginary aggregations. Society, then, is ultimately unrepresentable: any representation — and thus any space — is an attempt to constitute society, not to state what it is. But the antagonistic moment of collision between the various representations cannot be reduced to space, and is itself unrepresentable. It is therefore mere event, mere temporality. For reasons we have explained, this final incompletion of the social is the main source of our political hope in the contemporary world: only it can assure the conditions for a radical democracy.

33.   Let us draw the final conclusions. The state of social struggles in the contemporary world offers several grounds for political optimism. They at least create the preconditions for a radicalization of democracy, which is increasingly becoming the reference point for the construction of a new left. We are faced with a growing fragmentation of social actors, but this, far from being the cause for any nostalgia for the lost 'universal class', must be the source for a new militancy and a new optimism. One of the consequences of fragmentation is that the issues, which are the rallying point for the various social struggles, acquire greater autonomy and face the political system with growing demands. They thus become more difficult to manipulate and disregard. The self-evidence and homogeneity of the subject of *social* control in traditional socialist discourse has disappeared. Instead, a plurality of subjects exercise a democratic and negotiated control of the productive process on the basis of this fragmentation, thus avoiding any form of dictatorship, whether by the market, the state or direct producers. The indeterminacy of the relations between the different demands of the social actors certainly does open the possibility for their articulation by the right; but insofar as such articulations are not *necessary*, the field of possibilities for historical action is also widened, as counter-hegemonic struggles become possible in many areas traditionally associated with the sedimented forms of the status

quo. The future is indeterminate and certainly not guaranteed for us; but that is precisely why it is not lost either. The current expansion of democratic struggles in the international arena gives cause for cautious optimism.

Two final points. The first is concerned with the relation between reason and emancipation that we referred to at the beginning of this chapter. To what extent does placing in question the rationalism characterizing the project of modernity not mean undermining the foundations of the emancipatory project linked to it? From the earlier development of our argument it is clear what our reply will be. In our perspective it is a question of historically constituting the subject to be emancipated — indeed, emancipation and constitution are part of the same process. But in that case, why prefer one future over another? Why choose between different types of society? There can be no reply if the question is asking for a kind of Cartesian certainty that pre-exists any belief. But if the agent who must choose is someone who *already* has certain beliefs and values, then criteria for choice — with all the intrinsic ambiguities that a choice involves — can be formulated. Such an acceptance of the facticity of certain strata of our beliefs is nothing but the acceptance of our contingency and historicity. We could even go so far as to say that it is the acceptance of our 'humanity' as an entity to be constructed; while in the case of rationalism, we *have been given* 'humanity' and are merely left with the secondary task of realizing it historically. For the reasons we have identified, this recognition of our limitation and contingency, of the precarious and pragmatic construction of the universality of our values — a pragmatism that leaves the perverse dialectics of 'necessary embodiments' behind — is the very condition for a democratic society. To reformulate the values of the Enlightenment in the direction of a radical historicism and to renounce its rationalistic epistemological and ontological foundations, then, is to expand the democratic potentialities of that tradition, while abandoning the totalitarian tendencies arising from its reoccupation of the ground of apocalyptic universalism.

This leads us to the final question concerning the current debate over the 'end of history'. Does this formula have any purchase in providing an adequate name for our present social and political experience? If the 'end of history' is understood as the end of a conceptually graspable object encompassing the whole of the real in its diachronic spatiality, we are clearly at the end of 'history'. But from that perspective, 'history' is a quasi-transcendental category, an attempt to inscribe the totality of events and dislocations in conceptual forms transcending them. In another sense, however, we can say that we are at the *beginning* of history, at the point where historicity finally achieves full recognition. For insofar as any 'transcendentality' is itself vulnerable, any effort to spatialize time ultimately fails and space itself becomes an event. In this sense history's ultimate unrepresentability is the condition for the recognition of our radical historicity. It is in our pure condition of event, which is shown at the edges of all representation and in the traces of temporality corrupting all space, where we find our most essential being, which is our contingency and the intrinsic dignity of our transitory nature. In one of the most crucial passages of his work Ortega y Gasset recalls that a proverb can be heard in the thirsty deserts of Libya saying: 'Drink from the well and leave the place to your neighbour.'

Notes

1. Ernesto Laclau and Chantal Mouffe, *Hegemony and Socialist Strategy*, London 1985.

2. L. Wittgenstein, *Tractatus Logico-Philosophicus*, London 1981, p. 189.

3. K. Marx, *A Contribution to the Critique of Political Economy*, Moscow 1971, pp. 20–21.

4. K. Marx and F. Engels, *Communist Manifesto*, in *Selected Works*, Moscow 1969, p. 108.

5. We will be using the notion of 'constitutive outside' in the sense it has received in Derrida's theory.

6. G. A. Cohen, *Karl Marx's Theory of History. A Defence*, Oxford 1978.

7. *Ibid.*, p. 150.

8. *Ibid.*, pp. 152–3.

9. *Ibid.*, p. 153.

10. A. Levine and E. Olin Wright, 'Rationality and Class Struggle', *New Left Review*, no. 123, Sept/Oct 1980, pp. 47–68.

11. *Ibid.*, p. 61.

12. *Ibid.*, p. 61.

13. *Ibid.*, p. 62.

14. *Ibid.*, p. 63.

15. Aristotle, *Metaphysics*, V, XXX, 1. Cambridge Mass. 1980, p. 289.

16. Aristotle, V, XXX, 3–4, p. 291.

17. Quoted by R. Barthes, *Mythologies*, New York 1972, pp. 157–8.

18. I take this expression from H. Staten, *Wittgenstein and Derrida*, Oxford 1985, p. 12.

19. K. Marx, *Capital*, vol. 3, London 1974, p. 108.

20. C. Lefort, *The Political Forms of Modern Society*, Oxford 1985, p. 142.

21. *Ibid.*, p. 143.

22. K. Marx, *The Revolutions of 1848*, Harmondsworth 1973, p. 98. See the excellent

book by M. Löwy, *The Politics of Combined and Uneven Development,* London 1981, where this and other texts by Marx and Engels on the class base of the democratic revolution are exhaustively discussed.

23. K. Marx and F. Engels, *The Russian Menace to Europe,* London 1953, pp. 222–3.

24. L. Trotsky, *History of the Russian Revolution,* quoted by Löwy, pp. 87–8.

25. Löwy, p. 88.

26. Lefort, p. 159.

27. S. Lasch and J. Urry, *The End of Organized Capitalism,* Cambridge 1987; C. Offe, *Disorganized Capitalism,* Cambridge Mass. 1985.

28. S. Wolin, *Politics and Vision,* Boston 1960, p. 57.

29. *Book of Revelation,* quoted by N. Cohn, *The Pursuit of the Millennium,* London 1984, p. 24.

30. Lactantius, quoted by Cohn, p. 28.

31. H. Blumenberg, *The Legitimacy of the Modern Age,* Cambridge Mass. 1986.

32. See the Preface to this volume.

PART II

2

The Impossibility of Society

I should like to refer here to several problems which are central to the contemporary Marxist theory of ideology. In discussing these problems, it is evident that we presently live at the centre of a theoretical paradox. The terms of this paradox could be formulated as follows: in no previous period has reflection upon 'ideology' been so much at the centre of Marxist theoretical approaches; at the same time, however, in no other period have the limits and referential identity of 'the ideological' become so blurred and problematic. If the increasing interest in ideology runs parallel to a widening of the historical effectivity attributed to what was traditionally considered as the domain of the 'superstructures' – and this widening is a response to the crisis of an economistic and reductionistic conception of Marxism – then that very crisis puts into question the social totality constituted around the base–superstructure distinction. As a consequence, it is no longer possible to identify the object 'ideology' in terms of a topography of the social.

Within the Marxist tradition, we can identify two classical approaches to the problem of ideology. These approaches have often – but not always – been combined. For one of them, 'ideology' is thought to be a *level of the social totality*; for the other, it is identified with *false consciousness*. Today, both approaches appear to have been undermined as a consequence of the crisis of the assumptions on which they were grounded: the validity of the first depended on a conception of society as an intelligible totality, itself conceived as the structure upon which its partial elements and processes are founded. The validity of the second approach presupposed a conception of human agency – a subject having an ultimate essential homogeneity whose misrecognition was postulated as the source of 'ideology'. In this respect, the two approaches were grounded in an *essentialist* conception of both society and social agency. To see clearly the problems which have led the theory of ideology to its present impasse, we need to study the crisis of this essentialist conception in its two variants.

Let me turn, first, to the crisis of the concept of social totality. The ambition of all holistic approaches had been to fix the meaning of any element or social process *outside* itself, that is, in a *system of relations* with other elements. In this respect, the base–superstructure model played an ambiguous role; if it asserted the *relational* character of the identity of both base and superstructure, at the same time it endowed that relational system with a centre. And so, in a very Hegelian fashion, the superstructures ended up taking their revenge by asserting the 'essentiality' of the appearances. More importantly, the structural totality was to present itself as an object having a positivity of its own, which it was possible to describe and to define. In this sense, this totality operated as an underlying principle of intelligibility of the social order. The status of this totality was that of an essence of the social order which had to be *recognized* behind the empirical variations expressed at the surface of social life. (Note that what is at stake here is not the opposition, structuralism, vs. historicism. It does not matter if the totality is synchronic or diachronic; the important point is that in both cases it is a *founding totality* which presents itself as an intelligible object of 'knowledge' [*cognitio*] conceived as a process or re-cognition.) Against this essentialist vision we tend nowadays to accept the *infinitude of the social*, that is, the fact that any structural system is limited, that it is always surrounded by an 'excess of meaning' which it is unable to master and that, consequently, 'society' as a unitary and intelligible object which grounds its own partial processes is an impossibility. Let us examine the double movement that this recognition involves. The great advance carried out by structuralism was the recognition of the relational character of any social identity; its limit was its transformation of those relations into a system, into an identifiable and intelligible object (i.e., into an essence). But if we maintain the relational character of any identity and if, at the same time, we renounce the *fixation* of those identities in a system, then the social must be identified with the infinite play of differences, that is, with what in the strictest sense of the term we can call *discourse* — on the condition, of course, that we liberate the concept of discourse from its restrictive meaning as speech and writing.

This first movement thus implies the impossibility of fixing meaning. But this cannot be the end of the matter. A discourse in which meaning cannot possibly be fixed is nothing else but the discourse of the psychotic.

The second movement therefore consists in the attempt to effect this ultimately impossible fixation. The social is not only the infinite play of differences. It is also the attempt to limit that play, to domesticate infinitude, to embrace it within the finitude of an order. But this order — or structure — no longer takes the form of an underlying essence of the social; rather, it is an attempt — by definition unstable and precarious — to act over that 'social', to *hegemonize* it. In a way which resembles the one we are pursuing here, Saussure attempted to limit the principle of the arbitrariness of the sign with the assertion of the relative character of that arbitrariness. Thus, the problem of the social totality is posed in new terms: the 'totality' does not establish the limits of 'the social' by transforming the latter into a *determinate* object (i.e. 'society'). Rather, the social always exceeds the limits of the attempts to constitute society. At the same time, however, that 'totality' does not disappear: if the suture it attempts is ultimately impossible, it is nevertheless possible to proceed to a relative fixation of the social through the institution of nodal points. But if this is the case, questions concerning those nodal points and their relative weight cannot be determined *sub species aeternitatis*. Each social formation has its own forms of determination and relative autonomy, which are always instituted through a complex process of overdetermination and therefore cannot be established *a priori*. With this insight, the base–superstructure distinction falls and, along with it, the conception of ideology as a necessary level of every social formation.

If we now pass to the second approach to ideology — ideology as false consciousness — we find a similar situation. The notion of false consciousness only makes sense if the identity of the social agent can be fixed. It is only on the basis of recognizing its true identity that we can assert that the consciousness of the subject is 'false'. And this implies, of course, that that identity must be *positive and non-contradictory*. Within Marxism, a conception of subjectivity of this kind is at the basis of the notion of 'objective class interests'. Here I am not going to discuss in detail the forms of constitution, the implications and the limitations of such a conception of subjectivity. I shall rather just mention the two processes which led to its progressive abandonment. In the first place, the gap between 'actual consciousness' and 'imputed consciousness' grew increasingly wider. The way this gap was filled — through the presence of a Party instituted as the bearer of the objective historical interests of the class — led to the establishment of an 'enlightened' despotism of intellectuals and bureaucrats who spoke in the name of the masses, explained to them their true interests, and imposed upon them increasing totalitarian forms of control. The reaction to this situation inevitably took the form of the assertion of the actual identity of the social agents against the 'historical interests' which burdened them. In the second place, the very identity of the social agents was increasingly questioned when the flux of differences in advanced capitalist societies indicated that the identity and homogeneity of social agents was an illusion, that any social subject is essentially decentred, that his/her identity is nothing but the unstable articulation of constantly changing positionalities. The same excess of meaning, the same precarious character of any structuration that we find in the domain of the social order, is also to be found in the domain of subjectivity. But if any social agent is a decentred subject, if when attempting to determine his/her identity we find nothing else but the kaleidoscopic movement of differences, in what sense can we say that subjects misrecognize themselves? The theoretical ground that made sense of the concept of 'false consciousness' has evidently dissolved.

It would therefore look as if the two conceptual frameworks which formerly made sense of the concept of ideology have broken up, and that the concept should consequently be eliminated. However, I do not think this to be a satisfactory solution. We cannot do without the concept of misrecognition, precisely because the very assertion that the 'identity and homogeneity of social agents is an illusion' cannot be formulated without introducing the category of misrecognition. The critique of the 'naturalization of meaning' and of the 'essentialization of the social' is a critique of the misrecognition of their true character. Without this premise, any deconstruction would be meaningless. So, it looks as if we can maintain the concept of ideology and the category of misrecognition only by inverting their traditional content. The ideological would not consist of the misrecognition of a positive essence, but exactly the opposite: it would consist of the non-recognition of the precarious character of any positivity, of the impossibility of any ultimate suture. The ideological would consist of those discursive forms through which a society tries to institute itself as such on the basis of closure, of the fixation of meaning, of the non-recognition of the infinite play of differences. The ideological would be the will to 'totality' of any totalizing discourse. And insofar as the social is impossible without some fixation of meaning, without the discourse of closure, the ideological must be seen as constitutive of the social. The social only exists as the vain attempt to institute that impossible object: society. Utopia is the essence of any communication and social practice.

3

Psychoanalysis and Marxism

To think the relationships which exist between Marxism and psychoanalysis obliges one to reflect upon the intersections between two theoretical fields, each composed independently of the other and whose possible forms of mutual reference do not merge into any obvious system of translation. For example, it is impossible to affirm – though it has often been done – that psychoanalysis *adds* a theory of subjectivity to the field of historical materialism, given that the latter has been constituted, by and large, as a negation of the validity and the pertinence of any theory of subjectivity (although certainly not of the category of 'subject'). Thus, no simple model of supplement or articulation is of the slightest use. The problem is rather that of finding an *index of comparison* between two different theoretical fields, but that, in turn, implies the construction of a new field, within which the comparison would make sense.

This new field is one which may be characterized as 'post-Marxist' and is the result of a multitude of theoretico-political interventions whose cumulative effect in relation to the categories of classical Marxism is similar to what Heidegger called a 'de-struction of the history of ontology'. For Heidegger, this 'de-struction' did not signify the purely negative operation of rejecting a tradition, but exactly the opposite: it is by means of a radical questioning which is situated beyond this tradition – but which is only possible in relation to it – that the originary meaning of the categories of this tradition (which have long since become stale and trivialized) may be recovered. In this sense, effecting a 'de-struction' of the history of Marxism implies going beyond the deceptive evidence of concepts such as 'class', 'capital', and so on, and re-creating the meaning of the originary synthesis that such concepts aspired to establish, the total system of theoretical alternatives in regard to which they represented only limited options, and the ambiguities inherent in their constitution itself – the 'hymen' in the Derridean sense – which, although violently repressed, rise up here and there in diverse discursive surfaces. It is the systematic and genealogical outline of these nuclei of ambiguity which initially allows for a destruction of the history of Marxism and which constitutes post-Marxism as the field of our current political reflection. But it is precisely in these surfaces of discursive ambiguity that it is possible to detect the presence of logics of the political which allows for the establishment of a *true* dialogue, without complacent metaphorization, between Marxism and psychoanalytic theory. I would like to highlight two points, which I consider fundamental, concerning these discursive surfaces.

1. Marxism has so often been presented as a prolongation and a culmination of the Enlightenment – and therefore as one of the pinnacles of modernity – that any attempt at deconstructing its categories must begin by focusing on two decisive points where Marxism *breaks* with the tradition of the Enlightenment. These points are: (a) the affirmation of the central character of negativity – struggle and antagonism – in the structure of any collective identity; and (b) the affirmation of the opaqueness of the social – the ideological nature of collective representations – which establishes a permanent gap between the real and the manifest senses of individual and social group actions. It is easy to see how it is possible, from these two points, to establish a dialogue with psychoanalysis. The second point may be linked to the action of the unconscious and to the plurality of 'systems' established in the various Freudian topographies. The first, by establishing the non-immanent and ever-threatened character of any collective identity (resulting from the negativity inherent to antagonism), allows the consideration of class struggle as a dialectic of identifications composed around a real/impossible kernel.

However, let us not proceed too quickly. This reading of Marxism, which sees within it not the pinnacle of modernity but rather one of its first crises, is only possible if one is unaware of at least – in an optimistic calculation – half of Marx's work. (The same could be said about Hegel.) Marxism is not only a discourse of negativity and the opaqueness of the social, it is also an attempt – perfectly compatible with the Enlightenment – to limit and master them. The negativity and opaqueness of the social only exist in 'human prehistory', which will be definitely surpassed by communism conceived as homogeneous and transparent society. It is from this mastery of totality that the moment of negativity loses its constitutive and foundational character: it shone for just a brief moment in theoretical discourse, only to dissolve an instant later into the full positivity which reabsorbed it — positivity of history and society as totalizations of their partial processes, the positivity of the subject — the social classes — as agents of history. It would be absurd to deny that this dimension of mastery/transparency/rationalism is present in Marxism. Even more: this is the dimension which reaffirms itself increasingly from the *Anti-Dühring* to Stalin.

2. Consequently, if we want to trace the genealogy of post-Marxism, we cannot stop at the dichotomy of positivity/negativity, opaqueness/transparency. We must also highlight the radical inconsistency of these two dimensions. It is necessary to detect the surface where rationalist logic meets its limits — in other words, to detect those nuclei of ambiguity, the hymen where the *arbitrariness* and the *contingency* of any logic of closure is shown. Now, in the discursive field of historical Marxism, we find a privileged zone of deconstructive effects which dissolve the rationality, positivity, and transparency of Marxist categories: this is the ensemble of phenomena linked to what is known as 'unequal and combined development'.

Let us consider the problem in its simplest terms. 'Unequal and combined development' exists when a synchronic articulation occurs between stages which Marxist theory considers as successive (for example, the articulation between democratic tasks and the socialist leadership of those tasks). The key term to describe this articulation is 'hegemony'. In fact, the concept of hegemony as it was developed in the Marxist tradition, from Plekhanov and Axelrod to Gramsci, is that of a dislocation of a 'strategy' which is irreducible to a full presence that encloses, as a self-sufficient totality, the differential ensemble of its terms. Hegemony exists when that which would have been a rational succession of stages is interrupted by a *contingency* that cannot be subsumed under the logical categories of Marxist theory: in other words, it exists when the (democratic) tasks, which in a 'normal' development would have corresponded to a class (the bourgeoisie), must pass, given the weakness of the latter, to another class (in this case, the working class). A moment of reflection suffices to realize that what is explicitly thought in this relationship — the actors of the hegemonic relationship (the social classes), the class nature of the hegemonized task — is that which, strictly speaking, is absent to the extent that normal development has been dislocated; while that which is actually present — the relationship of dislocation — is *named* but not *thought.* Therefore, hegemony is in reality a hinge, given that on the one hand it sutures the relationship between two elements (the task and the agent); but, on the other hand, since this suture is produced in the field of a primary and insurmountable relationship of dislocation, we can only attribute a character of inscription to it, not one of necessary articulation. In other words, the hegemonic relationship can be thought only by assuming the category of *lack* as a point of departure. We can clearly see the pertinence of some central concepts of Lacanian theory. The hegemonic subject is the subject of the signifier, which is, in this sense, a subject without a signified; and it is only from this logic of the signifier that the hegemonic relationship as such may be conceived. But in this case, the categories of negativity and opaqueness, which we presented as characteristic of that first crisis of modernity represented by the Hegelian/Marxist moment, are not reabsorbed as a partial moment by any rationalist transparency. They are constitutive. Thus, there is no *Aufhebung*. This is precisely the point where the logic of the unconscious, as the logic of the signifier, reveals itself as an essentially political logic (insofar as politics, from Machiavelli onward, have primarily been the thought of dislocation); and where the social, ultimately irreducible to the status of full presence, also reveals itself as political. The political thus acquires the status of an ontology of the social.

Therefore, the 'de-struction' of the history of Marxism is not a speculative operation — an epistemological operation, if you will — given that it presupposes no duality of subject/object, but rather the generalization of the logic of the signifier to the ensemble of its theoretical categories. Consequently, these categories are neither *removed* nor *reabsorbed* by a higher rationality but *shown* in their contingency and historicity. For the same reason, this generalization is not a speculative/abstract process, but a practical/discursive one. It is the generalization of the phenomena of the 'unequal and combined development' of the imperialist age into any social identity which, as in the Heideggerian image of the broken hammer, transforms the *dislocation* into a horizon from which all identity may be thought and constituted (these two terms being exactly synonymous).

This indicates the direction and the way in which a possible confluence of (post-)Marxism and psychoanalysis is conceivable, neither as the addition of a supplement to the former by the latter nor as the introduction of a new causal element — the unconscious instead of economy — but as the coincidence of the two, around the logic of the signifier as a logic of unevenness and dislocation, a coincidence grounded on the fact that the latter is the logic which presides over the possibility/impossibility of the constitution of *any* identity.

4

Post-Marxism without Apologies
with Chantal Mouffe

Why should we rethink the socialist project today? In *Hegemony and Socialist Strategy* we pointed out some of the reasons. As participating actors in the history of our time, if we are actually to assume an interventionist role and not to do so blindly, we must attempt to wrest as much light as possible from the struggles in which we participate and from the changes which are taking place before our eyes. Thus, it is again necessary to temper 'the arms of critique'. The historical reality whereof the socialist project is reformulated today is very different from the one of only a few decades ago, and we will carry out our obligations as socialists and intellectuals only if we are fully conscious of the changes and persist in the effort of extracting all their consequences at the level of theory. The 'obstinate rigour' that Leonardo proposed as a rule for intellectual work should be the only guideline in this task; and it leaves no space for complacent sleights of hand that seek only to safeguard an obsolete orthodoxy.

Since we have referred in our book to the most important of these historical transformations, we need do no more here than enumerate them: structural transformations of capitalism that have led to the decline of the classical working class in the post-industrial countries; the increasingly profound penetration of capitalist relations of production in areas of social life, whose dislocatory effects – concurrent with those deriving from the forms of bureaucratization which have characterized the Welfare State – have generated new forms of social protest; the emergence of mass mobilizations in Third World countries which do not follow the classical pattern of class struggle; the crisis and discrediting of the model of society put into effect in the countries of so-called 'actually existing socialism', including the exposure of new forms of domination established in the name of the dictatorship of the proletariat.

There is no room here for disappointment. The fact that any reformulation of socialism has to start today from a more diversified, complex
and contradictory horizon of experiences than that of fifty years ago –
not to mention 1914, 1871 or 1848 – is a challenge to the imagination
and to political creativity. Hopelessness in this matter is only proper to
those who, to borrow a phrase from J.B. Priestley, have lived for years in a
fools' paradise and then abruptly move on to invent a fools' hell for
themselves. We are living, on the contrary, one of the most exhilarating
moments of the twentieth century: a moment in which new generations,
without the prejudices of the past, without theories presenting themselves as 'absolute truths' of history, are constructing new emancipatory
discourses, more human, diversified and democratic. The eschatological
and epistemological ambitions are more modest, but the liberating aspirations are wider and deeper.

In our opinion, to rethink socialism in these new conditions compels
us to undertake two steps. The first is to accept, in all their radical
novelty, the transformations of the world in which we live – that is to
say, neither to ignore them nor to distort them in order to make them
compatible with outdated schemas so that we may continue inhabiting
forms of thought which repeat the old formulae. The second is to start
from this full insertion in the present – in its struggles, its challenges, its
dangers – to interrogate the past: to search within it for the genealogy of
the present situation; to recognize within it the presence – at first
marginal and blurred – of problems that are ours; and, consequently, to
establish with that past a dialogue which is organized around continuities
and discontinuities, identifications and ruptures. It is in this way, by
making the past a transient and contingent reality rather than an absolute
origin, that a *tradition* is given form.

In our book we attempted to make a contribution to this task, which
today starts from different traditions and in different latitudes. In almost
all cases we have received an important intellectual stimulus from our
reviewers. Slavoj Žižek, for example, has enriched our theory of social
antagonisms, pointing out its relevance for various aspects of Lacanian
theory.[1] Andrew Ross has indicated the specificity of our line of argument in relation to several attempts in the United States to address
similar problems, and has located it within the general framework of the
debate about post-modernity.[2] Alistair Davidson has characterized the
new Marxist intellectual climate of which our book is part.[3] Stanley
Aronowitz has made some interesting and friendly criticisms from the
standpoint of the intellectual tradition of the American Left.[4] Philip

Derbyshire has very correctly underlined the theoretical place of our text in the dissolution of essentialism, both political and philosophical.[5] David Forgacs has posed a set of important questions about the political implications of our book, which we hope to answer in future works.[6]

However, there have also been attacks coming — as was to be expected — from the fading epigones of Marxist orthodoxy. In this article we will answer the criticisms of one member of this tradition: Norman Geras.[7] The reason for our choice is that Geras — in an extremely unusual gesture for this type of literature — has done his homework: he has gone through our text thoroughly and has presented an exhaustive argument in reply. His merits, however, end there. Geras's essay is well rooted in the literary genre to which it belongs: the pamphlet of denunciation. His opinion about our book is unambiguous: it is 'profligate', 'dissolute', 'fatuous', 'without regard for normal considerations of logic, of evidence, or of due proportion'; it is 'shame-faced idealism', an 'intellectual vacuum', 'obscurantism', 'lacking all sense of reasonable constraint', 'lacking a proper sense of either measure or modesty'; it indulges in 'elaborate theoretical sophistries', in 'manipulating concepts' and in 'tendentious quotations'. After all this, he devotes forty pages (one third of the May–June 1987 issue of *New Left Review*) to a detailed analysis of such a worthless work. Furthermore, despite the fact that Geras does not know us personally, he is absolutely definite about the psychological motivations that led us to write the book — 'the pressure ... of age and professional status'; 'the pressures of the political time ... not very congenial, in the West at least, to the sustenance of revolutionary ideas'; 'the lure of intellectual fashion'; 'so-called realism, resignation or merely candid self-interest', etc. — conceding, however, that such perverse motivations are perhaps not 'consciously calculated for advantage'. (Thank you, Geras.) It is, of course, up to the reader to decide what to think about an author who opens an intellectual discussion by using such language and such an avalanche of *ad hominem* arguments. For our part, we will only say that we are not prepared to enter into a game of invective and counter-invective; we will therefore declare from the start that we *do not know* the psychological motivations behind Geras's inspiration to write what he does and that, not being his psychiatrists, we are quite uninterested in them. However, Geras also makes a series of substantive — though not substantial — criticisms of our book, and it is to these aspects of his piece that we shall refer. We shall first consider his critique of our theoretical approach and then move on to his points concerning the history of Marxism and the political issues that our book addresses. Let us start with the central category of our analysis: the concept of discourse.

Discourse

The number of absurdities and incoherences that Geras has accumulated concerning this point is such that it is simply impossible to use his critical account as the framework for our reply. We will therefore briefly outline our conception of the social space as discursive, and then confront this statement with Geras's criticisms.

Let us suppose that I am building a wall with another bricklayer. At a certain moment I ask my workmate to pass me a brick and then I add it to the wall. The first act – asking for the brick – is linguistic; the second – adding the brick to the wall – is extralinguistic.[8] Do I exhaust the reality of both acts by drawing the distinction between them in terms of the linguistic/extralinguistic opposition? Evidently not, because, despite their differentiation in those terms, the two actions share something that allows them to be compared, namely the fact that they are both part of a total operation which is the building of the wall. So, then, how could we characterize this totality of which asking for a brick and positioning it are, both, partial moments? Obviously, if this totality includes both linguistic and non-linguistic elements, it cannot itself be either linguistic or extralinguistic; it has to be prior to this distinction. This totality which includes within itself the linguistic and the non-linguistic, is what we call discourse. In a moment we will justify this denomination; but what must be clear from the start is that by discourse we do not mean a combination of speech and writing, but rather that speech and writing are themselves but internal components of discursive totalities.

Now, turning to the term discourse itself, we use it to emphasize the fact that every social configuration is *meaningful*. If I kick a spherical object in the street or if I kick a ball in a football match, the *physical* fact is the same, but *its meaning* is different. The object is a football only to the extent that it establishes a system of relations with other objects, and these relations are not given by the mere referential materiality of the objects, but are, rather, socially constructed. This systematic set of relations is what we call discourse. The reader will no doubt see that, as we showed in our book, the discursive character of an object does not, by any means, imply putting its *existence* into question. The fact that a football is only a football as long as it is integrated within a system of socially constructed rules does not mean that it thereby ceases to be a physical object. A stone exists independently of any system of social relations, but it is, for instance, either a projectile or an object of aesthetic contemplation only within a specific discursive configuration. A diamond in the market or at the bottom of a mine is the same physical object; but, again, it is only a commodity within a determinate system of social relations. For that same reason it is the discourse which constitutes the subject position of the social agent, and not, therefore, the social agent which is the origin of discourse — the same system of rules that makes that spherical object into a football, makes me a player. The existence of objects is independent of their discursive articulation to such a point that we could make of that mere existence — that is, existence extraneous to any meaning — the point of departure of social analysis. That is precisely what behaviourism, which is the opposite of our approach, does. Anyway, it is up to the reader to decide how we can better describe the building of a wall: whether by starting from the discursive totality of which each of the partial operations is a moment invested with a meaning, or by using such descriptions as: X emitted a series of sounds; Y gave a cubic object to X; X added this cubic object to a set of similar cubic objects; etc.

This, however, leaves two problems unsolved. The first is this: is it not necessary to establish here a distinction between meaning and action? Even if we accept that the meaning of an action depends on a discursive configuration, is not the action itself something different from that meaning? Let us consider the problem from two angles. Firstly, from the angle of meaning. Here the classical distinction is between semantics — dealing with the meaning of words; syntactics — dealing with word order and its consequences for meaning; and pragmatics — dealing with the way a word is actually used in certain speech contexts. The key point is to what extent a rigid separation can be established between semantics and pragmatics — that is, between meaning and use. From Wittgenstein onwards it is precisely this separation which has grown ever more blurred. It has become increasingly accepted that the meaning of a word is entirely context-dependent. As Hanna Fenichel Pitkin points out:

> Wittgenstein argues that meaning and use are intimately, inextricably related, because use helps to determine meaning. Meaning is learned from, and shaped in, instances of use; so both its learning and its configuration depend on pragmatics.... Semantic meaning is compounded out of cases of

a word's use, including all the many and varied language games that are played with it; so meaning is very much the product of pragmatics.[9]

The use of a term is an act – in that sense it forms part of pragmatics; on the other hand, the meaning is only constituted in the contexts of actual use of the term: in that sense its semantics is entirely dependent upon its pragmatics, from which it can be separated – if at all – only analytically. That is to say, in our terminology, every identity or discursive object is constituted in the context of an action. But, if we focus on the problem from the other angle, every non-linguistic action also has a meaning and, therefore, we find within it the same entanglement of pragmatics and semantics that we find in the use of words. This leads us again to the conclusion that the distinction between linguistic and non-linguistic elements does not overlap with the distinction between 'meaningful' and 'not meaningful', since the former is a secondary distinction that takes place within meaningful totalities.

The other problem to be considered is the following: even if we assume that there is a strict equation between the social and the discursive, what can we say about the natural world, about the facts of physics, biology or astronomy that are not apparently integrated in meaningful totalities constructed by men? The answer is that natural facts are also discursive facts. And they are so for the simple reason that the idea of nature is not something that is already there, to be read from the appearances of things, but is itself the result of a slow and complex historical and social construction. To call something a natural object is a way of conceiving it that depends upon a classificatory system. Again, this does not put into question the fact that this entity which we call stone exists, in the sense of being present here and now, independently of my will; nevertheless the fact of its being a stone depends on a way of classifying objects that is historical and contingent. If there were no human beings on earth, those objects that we call stones would be there nonetheless; but they would not be 'stones', because there would be neither mineralogy nor a language capable of classifying them and distinguishing them from other objects. We need not stop for long on this point. The entire development of contemporary epistemology has established that there is no fact that allows its meaning to be read transparently. For instance Popper's critique of verificationism showed that no fact can prove a theory, since there are no guarantees that the fact cannot be explained in a better way – therefore, determined in its meaning – by a later and more comprehensive theory. (This line of thought has gone far beyond the limits of Popperism; we could mention the advance represented by Kuhn's paradigms and by Feyerabend's epistemological anarchism.) And what is said of scientific theories can also be applied to everyday languages that classify and organize objects.

Geras's Four Theses

We can now go to Geras's criticisms. They are structured around four basic theses: (1) that the distinction between the discursive and the extra-discursive coincides with the distinction between the fields of the spoken, written and thought, on the one hand, and the field of an external reality on the other; (2) that affirming the discursive character of an object means to deny the existence of the entity designated by that discursive object; (3) that denying the existence of extra-discursive points of reference is to fall in the bottomless abyss of relativism; (4) that affirming the discursive character of every object is to incur one of the most typical forms of idealism. Let us see.

We can treat the first two claims together. Geras writes:

> Every object is constituted as an object of discourse means all objects are given their being by, or are what they are by virtue of, discourse; which is to say (is it not?) that there is no pre-discursive objectivity or reality, that objects not spoken, written or thought about do not exist.[10]

To the question posed between brackets '(is it not?)', the answer is simply 'no, it is not'. The reader who has followed our text to this point will have no difficulty in understanding why. For – returning to our previous example – whether this stone is a projectile, or a hammer, or an object of aesthetic contemplation depends on its relations with me – it depends, therefore, on precise forms of discursive articulation – but the mere existence of the entity stone, the mere material and existential substratum does not. That is, Geras is making an elementary confusion between the being (*esse*) of an object, which is historical and changing, and the entity (*ens*) of that object which is not. Now, in our interchange with the world, objects are never given to us as mere existential entities; they are always given to us within discursive articulations. Wood will be raw material or part of a manufactured product, or an object for contemplation in a forest, or an obstacle that prevents us from advancing; the mountain will be protection from enemy attack, or a place for a touring trip, or the source for the extraction of minerals, etc. The mountain would not be any of these things if I were not here; but this does not mean that the mountain does not exist. It is because it exists that it can be all these things; but none of them follows necessarily from its mere existence. And as a member of a certain community, I will never encounter the object in its naked existence — such a notion is a mere abstraction; rather, that existence will always be given as articulated within discursive totalities. The second mistake Geras makes is that he reduces the discursive to a question of either speech, writing or thought, while our text explicitly affirms that, as long as every non-linguistic action is meaningful, it is also discursive. Thus, the criticism is totally absurd; it involves changing our concept of discourse midstream in the argument, and establishing an arbitrary identification between the being of an object and its existence. With these misrepresentations it is very easy, evidently, to attribute imaginary inconsistencies to our text.

The third criticism — relativism — does not fare any better. Firstly, 'relativism' is, to a great extent, an invention of the fundamentalists. As Richard Rorty has pointed out:

> 'Relativism' is the view that every belief on a certain topic, or perhaps about *any* topic, is as good as every other. No one holds this view.... The philosophers who get *called* 'relativists' are those who say that the grounds for choosing between such opinions are less algorithmic than had been thought.... So the real issue is not between people who think one view as good as another and people who do not. It is between those who think our culture, or purpose, or intuitions cannot be supported except conversationally, and people who still hope for other sorts of support.[11]

Relativism is, actually, a false problem. A 'relativist' position would be one which affirmed that it is the same to think 'A is B' or 'A is not B'; that is to say, that it is a discussion linked to the being of the objects. As we have seen, however, outside of any discursive context objects *do not have being*; they have only *existence*. The accusation of the 'anti-relativist' is, therefore, meaningless, since it presupposes that there is a *being* of things as such, which the relativist is either indifferent to or proclaims to be inaccessible. But, as we have argued, things only have being within a certain discursive configuration, or 'language game', as Wittgenstein would call it. It would be absurd, of course, to ask oneself today if 'being a projectile' is part of the true being of the stone (although the question would have some legitimacy within Platonic metaphysics); the answer, obviously, would be: it depends on the way we use stones. For the same reason it would be absurd to ask oneself if, outside all scientific theory, atomic structure is the 'true being' of matter — the answer will be that atomic theory is a way we have of classifying certain objects, but that these are open to different forms of conceptualization that may emerge in the future. In other words, the 'truth', factual or otherwise, about the being of objects is constituted within a theoretical and discursive context, and the idea of a truth outside all context is simply nonsensical.

Let us conclude this point by identifying the status of the concept of discourse. If the *being* — as distinct from existence — of any object is constituted within a discourse, it is not possible to differentiate the discursive, in terms of being, from any other area of reality. The discursive is not, therefore, an object among other objects (although, of course, concrete discourses are) but rather a theoretical *horizon*. Certain questions concerning the notion of discourse are, therefore, meaningless because they can be made only about objects within a horizon, not about the horizon itself. The following remark of Geras's must be included within this category:

> One could note again, for instance, how absolutely everything — subjects, experience, identities, struggles, movements — has discursive 'conditions of possibility', while the question as to what may be the conditions of possibility of discourse itself, does not trouble the authors so much as to pause for thought.[12]

This is absurd. If the discursive is coterminous with the being of objects — the horizon, therefore, of the constitution of the being of every object — the question about the conditions of possibility of the being of discourse is meaningless. It is equivalent to asking a materialist for the conditions of possibility of matter, or a theist for the conditions of possibility of God.

Idealism and Materialism

Geras's fourth criticism concerns the problem of idealism and we have to consider it in a more detailed way. The first condition for having a rational discussion, of course, is that the meaning of the terms one is using should be clear. Conceptual elucidation of the idealism/materialism opposition is particularly important in view not only of the widely differing contexts in which it has been used, but also of the fact that these contexts have often overlapped and so led to innumerable confusions. The idealism/materialism opposition has been used in attempts to refer to, roughly speaking, three different types of problem.

1. The problem of the existence or non-existence of a world of objects external to thought. This is a very popular mistake which Geras incurs throughout his discussion. For the distinction here is not between idealism and materialism, but between idealism and realism. A philosophy such as Aristotle's, for example, which certainly is not materialist in any possible sense of the term, is clearly realist. The same can be said of the philosophy of Plato, since for him the Ideas *exist* in a heavenly place, where the mind contemplates them as something external to itself. In this sense, the whole of ancient philosophy was realist, since it did not put into question the existence of a world external to thought – it took it for granted. We have to reach the modern age, with a philosophy such as Berkeley's, to find a total subordination of external reality to thought. However, it is important to realize that in this sense Hegel's absolute idealism, far from denying the reality of an external world, is its unequivocal affirmation. As Charles Taylor has asserted:

> This (absolute idealism) is paradoxically very different from all other forms of idealism, which tend to the denial of external reality, or material reality. In the extreme form of Berkeley's philosophy, we have a denial of matter in favour of a radical dependence on the mind – of course God's, not ours. Hegel's idealism, far from being a denial of external material reality, is the strongest affirmation of it; it not only exists but necessarily exists.[13]

If this is the question at issue our position is, therefore, unequivocally realist, but this has little to do with the question of materialism.

2. What actually distinguishes idealism from materialism is its affirmation of the ultimately conceptual character of the real; for example, in Hegel, the assertion that everything that is real is rational. Idealism, in its sense of opposition to materialism and not to realism, is the affirmation not that there do not *exist* objects external to the mind, but rather that the innermost nature of these objects is identical to that of mind – that is to say, that it is ultimately *thought*. (Not thought of individual minds, of course; not even of a transcendent God, but *objective thought*.) Now, even

if idealism in this second sense is only given in a fully coherent and developed form in Hegel, philosophers of antiquity are also predominantly idealist. Both Plato and Aristotle identified the ultimate reality of an object with its *form* — that is, with something 'universal', and hence conceptual. If I say that this object which is in front of me is rectangular, brown, a table, an object, etc., each of these determinations could also be applied to other objects — they are then 'universals', that is *form*. But what about the individual 'it' that receives all these determinations? Obviously, it is irrational and unknowable, since to know it would be to subsume it under a universal category. This last individual residue, which is irreducible to thought, is what the ancient philosophers called *matter*. And it was precisely this last residue which was eliminated by a consistent idealist philosophy such as Hegel's: it asserted the ultimate rationality of the real and thus became absolute idealism.

Thus, form is, at the same time, both the organizing principle of the mind and the ultimate reality of an object. As it has been pointed out, form

cut(s) across the categories of epistemology and ontology for the being of the particular is itself exhaustively defined according to the requirements of knowledge.... Thought, word and thing are defined in relation to thinkable form, and thinkable form is itself in a relation of reciprocal definition with the concept of entity.[14]

The true line of divide between idealism and materialism is, therefore, the affirmation or negation of the ultimate irreducibility of the real to the concept. (For example, a philosophy such as that of the early Wittgenstein, which presented a picture theory of language in which language shared the same 'logical form' as the thing, is entirely within the idealist field.) It is important to note that, from this point of view, what has been traditionally called 'materialism' is *also* to a great extent idealist. Hegel knew this so well that in his *Greater Logic* materialism is presented as one of the first and crudest forms of idealism, since it assumes identity between knowledge and being. (See *Greater Logic*, First Section, Chapter Two, final 'remark'.) Commenting on this passage, W.T. Stace points out:

Atomism alleges that this *thing*, the atom, is the ultimate reality. Let it be so. But what is this thing? It is nothing but a congeries of universals, such perhaps as 'indestructible', 'indivisible', 'small', 'round', etc. All these are universals, or thoughts. 'Atom' itself is a concept. Hence even out of this materialism proceeds idealism.[15]

Where, in all this, does Marx fit in? The answer cannot be unambiguous. In a sense, Marx clearly remains within the idealist field – that is to say, within the ultimate affirmation of the rationality of the real. The well-known inversion of dialectics cannot but reproduce the latter's structure. To affirm that the ultimate law of motion of history is given not by the change of ideas in the minds of human beings but rather by the contradiction, in each stage, between the development of productive forces and the existing relations of production, does not modify things at all. For what is idealist is not the affirmation that the law of motion of history is the one rather than the other, but the very idea that there is an ultimate law of motion that can be conceptually grasped. To affirm the transparency of the real to the concept is equivalent to affirming that the real is 'form'. For this reason the most determinist tendencies within Marxism are also the most idealist, since they have to base their analyses and predictions on inexorable laws which are not immediately legible in the surface of historical life; they must base themselves on the internal logic of a closed conceptual model and transform that model into the (conceptual) essence of the real.

3. This is not, however, the whole story. In a sense which we have to define more precisely, there is in Marx a definite movement away from idealism. But before we discuss this, we must characterize the structure and implications of any move away from idealism. As we have said, the essence of idealism is the reduction of the real to the concept (the affirmation of the rationality of the real or, in the terms of ancient philosophy, the affirmation that the reality of an object – as distinct from its existence – is *form*). This idealism can adopt the structure which we find in Plato and Aristotle – the reduction of the real to a hierarchical universe of static essences; or one can introduce movement into it, as Hegel does – on condition, of course, that it is movement *of the concept* and thus remains entirely within the realm of form. However, this clearly indicates that any move away from idealism cannot but systematically weaken the claims of form to exhaust the reality of the object (i.e. the claims of what Heidegger and Derrida have called the 'metaphysics of presence'). But, this weakening cannot merely involve an affirmation of the thing's *existence* outside thought, since this 'realism' is perfectly compatible with idealism in our second sense. As has been pointed out,

what is significant from a deconstructive viewpoint is that the sensible thing, even in a 'realist' like Aristotle, is itself unthinkable except in relation to intelligible form. Hence, the crucial boundary for Aristotle, and for philosophy generally, does not pass between thought and thing *but within each of these, between form and formlessness or indefiniteness.*[16]

The Instability of Objects

Thus, it is not possible to abandon idealism by a simple appeal to the external object, since (1) this is compatible with the affirmation that the object is form and thus remains within the field of idealism and the most traditional metaphysics; and (2) if we take refuge in the object's mere 'existence', in the 'it' beyond all predication, we cannot say anything about it. But here another possibility opens up at once. We have seen that the 'being' of objects is different from their mere existence, and that objects are never given as mere 'existences' but are always articulated within discursive totalities. But in that case it is enough to show that no discursive totality is absolutely self-contained — that there will always be an outside which distorts it and prevents it from fully constituting itself — to see that the form and essence of objects are penetrated by a basic instability and precariousness, and that this is *their most essential possibility.* This is exactly the point at which the movement away from idealism starts.

Let us consider the problem more closely. Both Wittgenstein and Saussure broke with what can be called a referential theory of meaning — i.e. the idea that language is a nomenclature which is in a one-to-one relation to objects. They showed that the word 'father', for instance, only means what it does because the words 'mother', 'son', etc., also exist. The totality of language is, therefore, a system of differences in which the identity of the elements is purely relational. Hence, every individual act of signification involves the totality of language (in Derridean terms, the presence of something always has the *traces* of something else which is absent). This purely relational or differential character is not, of course, exclusive to linguistic identities but holds for all signifying structures — that is to say, for all social structures. This does not mean that everything is language in the restricted sense of speech or writing but rather that the relational or differential structure of language is the same for all signifying structures. So, if all identity is differential, it is enough that the system of differences is not closed, that it suffers the action of external discursive structures, for any identity (i.e., the *being*, not the *existence* of things) to be unstable. This is what shows the impossibility of attributing to the being of things the character of a fixed essence, and what makes possible the weakening of *form* which constituted the cornerstone of traditional metaphysics. Human beings socially construct their world, and it is through this construction — always precarious and incomplete — that they give to a thing its being.[17] There is, then, a third meaning of the idealism/materialism opposition which is related neither to the problem of the external existence of objects, nor to a rigid counterposition of form and matter in which the latter is conceived as the 'individual existent'. In this third opposition, a world of fixed forms constituting the *ultimate* reality of the object (idealism) is challenged by the relational historical and precarious character of the world of forms (materialism). For the latter, therefore, there is no possibility of eliminating the gap between 'reality' and 'existence'. Here, strictly speaking, there are two possible conceptual strategies: either to take 'idealism' and 'materialism' as two variants of 'essentialism'; or to consider that all essentialism, by subordinating the real to the concept, *is* idealism, and to see materialism as a variety of attempts to break with this subordination. Both strategies are, of course, perfectly legitimate.

Let us return at this point to Marx. There is in his work the beginning, but only the beginning, of a movement in the direction of materialism. His 'materialism' is linked to a radical relationalism: ideas do not constitute a closed and self-generated world, but are rooted in the ensemble of material conditions of society. However, his movement towards relationalism is weak and does not actually transcend the limits of Hegelianism (an inverted Hegelianism continues to be Hegelian). Let us look at these two moments:

1. One possible way of understanding this embeddedness of ideas in the material conditions of society would be in terms of signifying totalities. The 'state' or the 'ideas' would not be self-constituted identities but rather 'differences' in the Saussurean sense, whose only identity is established relationally with other differences such as 'productive forces', 'relations of production', etc. The 'materialist' advance of Marx would be to have shown that the area of social *differences* which constitutes the signifying totalities is much wider and deeper than it had been supposed hitherto; that the material reproduction of society is part of the discursive totalities which determine the meaning of the most 'sublime' forms of political and intellectual life. This allows us to overcome the apparently insoluble problems concerning the base/superstructure relation: if state,

ideas, relations of production, etc., have purely differential identities, the presence of each would involve the presence of the others – as the presence of 'father' involves the presence of 'son', 'mother', etc. In this sense, no *causal* theory about the efficacy of one element over another is necessary. This is the intuition that lies behind the Gramscian category of 'historical bloc': historical movement is explained not by laws of motion of history but by the organic link *between* base and super-structure.

2. However, this radical relationalism of Marx is immediately trans-lated into idealistic terms. 'It is not the consciousness of men that deter-mines their existence, but their social existence that determines their consciousness.'[18] This could be read, of course, as a reintegration of consciousness with existence, but the expression could not be more unfortunate, since if social existence *determines* consciousness, then consciousness cannot be part of social existence.[19] And when we are told that the anatomy of civil society is political economy, this can only mean that there is a specific logic – the logic of the development of productive forces – which constitutes the *essence* of historical development. In other words, historical development can be rationally grasped and is therefore *form*. It is not surprising that the Preface to the *Critique of Political Economy* depicts the outcome of the historical process exclusively in terms of the contradiction between productive forces and relations of production; nor is it surprising that class struggle is *entirely* absent from this account. All this is perfectly compatible with the basic premises of Hegelianism and metaphysical thought.

Let us now sum up our argument in this section. (1) The idealism/realism opposition is different from the idealism/materialism opposition. (2) Classical idealism and materialism are variants of an essentialism grounded on the reduction of the real to *form*. Hegel is, therefore, perfectly justified in regarding materialism as an imperfect and crude form of idealism. (3) A move away from idealism cannot be founded on the *existence* of the object, because nothing follows from this existence. (4) Such a move must, rather, be founded on a systematic weakening of form, which consists in showing the historical, contingent and constructed character of the *being* of objects; and in showing that this depends on the reinsertion of that being in the ensemble of relational conditions which constitute the life of a society as a whole. (5) In this process, Marx constitutes a transitional point: on the one hand, he showed that the meaning of any human reality is derived from a world of social relations much vaster than had previously been perceived; but on the other hand, he conceived the relational logic that links the various spheres in clearly essentialist or idealistic terms.

A first sense of our post-Marxism thus becomes clear. It consists in a deepening of that relational moment which Marx, thinking within a Hegelian and, in any case, nineteenth-century matrix, could only take so far. In an age when psychoanalysis has shown that the action of the unconscious makes all signification ambiguous; when the development of structural linguistics has enabled us to understand better the functioning of purely differential identities; when the transformation of thought – from Nietzsche to Heidegger, from pragmatism to Wittgenstein – has decisively undermined philosophical essentialism, we can reformulate the materialist programme in a much more radical way than was possible for Marx.

Either/Or

At this point we should consider Geras's general methodological reproach that we have based our main theoretical conclusions on a false and rigid 'either/or' opposition; that is to say, that we have counterposed two polar and exclusive alternatives, without considering the possibility of intermediate solutions that avoid both extremes. Geras discusses this supposed theoretical mistake in relation to three points: our analysis of the concept of 'relative autonomy'; our treatment of Rosa Luxemburg's text on the mass strike; and our critique of the concept of 'objective' interest. As we will show, in all three cases Geras's criticism is based on a misrepresentation of our argument.

Firstly, 'relative autonomy'. Geras quotes a passage of our book where we sustain, according to him, that

> *either* the basic determinants explain the nature, as well as the limits, of that which is supposed to be relatively autonomous, so that it is not really autonomous at all; *or* it is, flatly, *not* determined by them and they cannot be basic determinants ... Laclau and Mouffe here deny to Marxism the option of a concept like relative autonomy. No wonder that it can only be for them the crudest sort of economism.[20]

Geras proposes, instead, the elimination of this 'inflexible alternative'. If, for example, his ankle is secured to a stout post by a chain he may not be able to attend a political meeting or play tennis, but he can still read and sing. Between total determination and partial limitation there is a whole range of intermediate possibilities. Now, it is not very difficult to realize that the example of the chain is perfectly irrelevant to what Geras intends to demonstrate, since it involves no more than a sleight of hand whereby a relation of determination is transformed into a relation of limitation. Our text does not assert that the state in capitalist society is not *relatively* autonomous, but rather, that we cannot conceptualize 'relative autonomy' by starting from a category such as 'determination in the last instance by the economy'. Geras's example is irrelevant because it is not an example of a relation of determination: the chain tied to his ankle does not *determine* that Geras reads or sings; it only limits his possible movements — and, presumably, this limitation has been imposed *against* Geras's will. Now, the base/superstructure model affirms that the base not only limits but *determines* the superstructure, in the same way that the movements of a hand determine the movements of its shadow on a wall. When the Marxist tradition affirms that a state is 'capitalist', or that an ideology is 'bourgeois', what is being asserted is not simply that they are in chains or prisoners of a type of economy or a class position, but rather that they express or represent the latter at a different level. Lenin, who, unlike Geras, *knew* what a relation of determination is, had an instrumentalist theory of the state. His vision is, no doubt, a simplistic one, but it has a considerably higher degree of realism than the chain of Geras, the latter seeming to suggest that the capitalist state is a prisoner limited by the mode of production in what otherwise would have been its spontaneous movements.

What our book asserts is not that the autonomy of the state is absolute, or that the economy does not have any limiting effect vis-à-vis the state's action, but rather that the concepts of 'determination in the last instance' and 'relative autonomy' are *logically* incompatible. And, when we are dealing with logical matters, alternatives *are* of the either/or type. This is what we have to show. In order to do so let us put ourselves in a situation most favourable to Geras: we will take as an example not a 'vulgar' Marxism but a 'distinguished' Marxism, one that avoids crude economism and introduces all imaginable sophistication in thinking the base/superstructure relation. What conceptual instruments does such a Marxism have to construct the concept of 'relative autonomy' starting from the concept of 'determination in the last instance'? We can only think of two types of attempt:

1. It might be argued that the base determines the superstructure not in a direct way but through a complex system of *mediations*. Does this

allow us to think the concept of 'relative autonomy'? By no means. 'Mediation' is a dialectical category; even more: it is the category out of which dialectics is constituted, and belongs, therefore, to the internal movement of the concept. Two entities that are related (and constituted) via mediations are not, strictly speaking, separate entities: each is an internal moment in the self-unfolding of the other. We can extend the field of mediations as much as we want: in this way we would give a less simplistic vision of social relations, but we would not advance a single step in the construction of the concept of relative autonomy. This is because autonomy — relative or not — means *self-determination*; but if the identity of the supposedly autonomous entity is constituted by its location within a totality, and this totality has an *ultimate* determination, the entity in question *cannot* be autonomous. According to Lukács, for instance, facts only acquire meaning as moments or determinations of a totality; it is within this totality — which could be as rich in mediations as we want — that the meaning of any identity is established. The exteriority that a relation of autonomy would require is therefore absent.

2. So, let us abandon this attempt to use the concept of mediation and try instead a second line of defence of the logical compatibility of the two concepts. Could we, perhaps, assert that the superstructural entity is *effectively* autonomous — that is to say, that no system of mediations links it to the base — and that determination in the last instance by the economy is reduced to the fact that the latter *always* fixes the limits of autonomy (i.e., that the possibility of Geras's hair growing as Samson's to the point that he would be able to break the chain, is excluded)? Have we made any advance with this new solution? No; we are exactly at the same point as before. The *essence* of something is the ensemble of necessary characteristics which constitute its identity. Thus, if it is an a priori truth that the limits of autonomy are always fixed by the economy, then such limitation is not external to that entity but is part of its essence. The autonomous entity is an internal moment of the same totality in which the determination in the last instance is constituted — and hence there is no autonomy. (All this reasoning is, actually, unnecessary. To affirm at the same time that the intelligibility of the social whole proceeds from an ultimate determination, and that there are internal entities to that totality which escape that determination, was inconsistent from the beginning.)

Autonomy and Determination

What happens if, instead, we abandon the concept of 'determination in the last instance by the economy'? It does not follow either that the autonomy is absolute, or that the 'economy' in a capitalist society does not impose fundamental structural limits on what can be done in other spheres. What *does* follow is (a) that the limitation and interaction between spheres cannot be thought in terms of the category of 'determination'; and (b) that there is no *last instance* on the basis of which society can be reconstructed as a rational and intelligible structure, but rather that the relative efficacy of each sphere depends on an unstable relation of antagonistic forces which entirely penetrates the social. For example, the structure of capitalist relations of production in a certain moment will impose limits on income distribution and access to consumer goods; but conversely, factors such as working-class struggles or the degree of union organization will also have a limiting effect on the rate of profit that can be obtained in a political and economic conjuncture. In our book we made reference to something that has been shown by numerous recent studies: namely, that the transition from absolute to relative surplus value, far from being the simple outcome of the internal logic of capital accumulation, is, to a large extent, the result of the efficacy of working-class struggles. That is to say, the economic space itself is structured as a political space, and the 'war of position' is not the superstructural consequence of laws of motion constituted outside it. Rather, such laws penetrate the very field of what was traditionally called the 'base' or 'infrastructure'. If *determination* was a *last* instance, it would be incompatible with autonomy, because it would be a relation of omnipotence. But, on the other hand, an *absolutely* autonomous entity would be one which did not establish an antagonistic relation with anything external to it, since for an antagonism to be possible, a partial efficacy of the two opposing forces is a prerequisite. The autonomy which both of them enjoy will therefore *always* be relative.

Our book states this clearly in the same paragraph which Geras quotes:

If ... we renounce the hypothesis of a final closure of the social, it is necessary to start from a plurality of political and social spaces which do not refer to any ultimate unitarian basis. Plurality is not the phenomenon to be explained, but the starting point of the analysis. But if, as we have seen, the identity of these spaces is always precarious, it is not possible simply to affirm the equation between autonomy and dispersion. *Neither total autonomy nor total subordination is, consequently, a plausible solution.*[21]

The suggestion that we have set up a rigid alternative between total autonomy and absolute subordination is, therefore, simply an invention by Geras. All our analyses try, on the contrary, to overcome that 'either/or' alternative — see, for instance, our critique of the symmetrical essentialisms of the totality and the elements (pp. 103–5), or our discussion of the concept of representation (pp. 119–22). In order to overcome the alternative, however, it is necessary to construct a new terrain that goes beyond its two terms, and this implies a break with metaphysical categories such as the 'last instance' of the social. Geras also tries, apparently, to overcome this alternative, but he only proceeds by the trick of affirming determination in the last instance *theoretically* whilst eliminating it in the concrete example that he gives (the one of the chain). His overcoming of the alternative is, therefore, wishful thinking, and his discourse is lodged in permanent incoherence.

Geras's other two examples of our 'either/or' reductionism can be discussed briefly, since they repeat the same argumentative strategy — and the same mistakes. Firstly, the case of Rosa Luxemburg. Geras quotes a fragment of our book where, *according to him*, we affirm that Marxism rests upon a well-known alternative:

> either capitalism leads through its necessary laws to proletarianization and crisis; or else these necessary laws do not function as expected, in which case … the fragmentation between different subject positions ceases to be an 'artificial product' of the capitalist state and becomes a permanent reality.

On which Geras comments: 'It is another stark antithesis. *Either* pure economic necessity bears the full weight of unifying the working class; or we simply have fragmentation.'[22] This time, however, Geras has omitted a 'small' detail in his quotation; and his misquotation is so flagrant that he puts us — this time for sure — before the 'either/or' alternative of having to conclude that he is intellectually either irresponsible or dishonest. The 'detail' is that our text poses this alternative, not in respect of Marxism in general, but in respect of what would be, by *reductio ad absurdum*, their extreme reductionist or essentialist versions. The quotation comes from a passage where, after having pointed out the presence of a double historical logic in the text of Rosa Luxemburg — the logic of structural determinism and the logic of spontaneism — we proceeded to what we called an 'experiment of frontiers'. That is to say, we tried to see what logical consequences would follow from an imaginary extension of the operative area of either determinism or spontaneism. Thus we pointed out that it is *only* if Marxist discourse becomes *exclusively* determinist (that is, only in the imaginary case of our experiment) that the iron alternative to which Geras refers is posed. Our book presented the history of Marxism, on the contrary, as a sustained effort to escape the 'either/or' logic of determinism. It is exactly in these terms that we refer to the increasing centrality and area of operativity of the concept of 'hegemony'. In fact, the second step of our experiment – the moving of frontiers in a direction that expands the logic of spontaneism – is conducive to the political alternatives which our text suggests, and which are very different from those possible within a determinist model.

Misquotations apart, it is interesting to see how Geras himself attempts to escape the 'either/or' alternative. As in the case of relative autonomy, his solution is a mixture of journalistic impressionism and theoretical inconsistency. (It is significant that, despite his insulting and aggressive tone, Geras is suspiciously defensive and moderate when it comes to presenting his own political and theoretical proposals.) 'Why,' he asks,

> may we not think that between this devil and that blue sea there is something else: notwithstanding the wide diversity, a common structural situation, of exploitation, and some common features, like lack of autonomy and interest at work, not to speak of sheer unpleasantness and drudgery, and some pervasive economic tendencies, proletarianizing ones among them, and such also as create widespread insecurity of employment; all this providing a solid, objective *basis* – no more, but equally no less – for a unifying socialist politics? Why may we not?[23]

Why may we not indeed? All these things happen under capitalism, in addition to some more things that Geras omits to mention: imperialist exploitation, increasing marginalization of vast sectors of the population in the Third World and in the decaying inner cities of the post-industrial metropolis, ecological struggles against pollution of the environment, struggles against different forms of racial and sexual discrimination, etc. If it is a matter of *enumerating* the unpleasant features of the societies in which we live, which are the basis for the emergence of numerous antagonisms and contesting collective identities, the enumeration has to be complete. But if it is a matter, on the contrary, of answering such fragmentation with a theory of the necessary *class* nature of anti-capitalist agents, no mere descriptive enumeration will do the trick. Geras's 'classist' alternative is constituted only by means of interrupting at a certain point his enumeration of the collective antagonisms generated by late capitalism. The vacuity of this exercise is obvious. If Geras wants to found 'classism' on something other than the determinism of 'necessary laws of history', he has to propose a theoretical alternative of which there is not the slightest sign in his article.

Finally the question of 'objective interests'. Ours is a criticism not of the notion of 'interests' but of their supposedly *objective* character: that is to say, of the idea that social agents have interests of which they are not conscious. To construct an 'interest' is a slow historical process, which takes place through complex ideological, discursive and institutional practices. Only to the extent that social agents participate in collective totalities are their identities constructed in a way that makes them capable of calculating and negotiating with other forces. 'Interests', then, are a social product, and do not exist independently of the consciousness of the agents who are their bearers. The idea of an *'objective* interest' presupposes, instead, that social agents, far from being part of a process in which interests are constructed, merely *recognize* them — that is to say, that those interests are inscribed in their nature as a gift from heaven. How it is possible to make this vision compatible with a non-essentialist conception of the social, only God and Geras know. Again, we are not dealing with an 'either/or' alternative. There *are* interests, but these are precarious historical products which are always subjected to processes of dissolution and redefinition. What there are not, however, are *objective* interests, in the sense in which they are postulated in the 'false consciousness' approach.

The History of Marxism

Let us move now to Geras's criticisms of our analysis of the history of Marxism. The centrality we give to the category of 'discourse' derives from our attempt to emphasize the purely historical and contingent character of the being of objects. This is not a fortuitous discovery which could have been made at any point in time; it is, rather, deeply rooted in the history of modern capitalism. In societies which have a low technological level of development, where the reproduction of material life is carried out by means of fundamentally repetitive practices, the 'language games' or discursive sequences which organize social life are predominantly stable. This situation gives rise to the illusion that the being of objects, which is a purely social construction, belongs to things themselves. The idea of a world organized through a stable ensemble of essential forms is the central presupposition in the philosophies of Plato and Aristotle. The basic illusion of metaphysical thought resides precisely in this unawareness of the historicity of being. It is only in the contemporary world, when technological change and the dislocating rhythm of capitalist transformation constantly alter the discursive sequences which construct the reality of objects, that the merely historical character of being becomes fully visible. In this sense, contemporary thought as a whole is, to a large extent, an attempt to cope with this increasing realization, and the consequent moving away from essentialism. In Anglo-American thought we could refer to the pragmatist turn and the anti-essentialist critique of post-analytic philosophy, starting from the work of the later Wittgenstein; in continental philosophy, to Heidegger's radicalization of phenomenology and to the critique of the theory of the sign in post-structuralism. The crisis of normative epistemologies, and the growing awareness of the non-algorithmic character of the transition from one scientific paradigm to another, point in the same direction.

What our book seeks to show is that this history of contemporary thought is *also* a history internal to Marxism; that Marxist thought has also been a persistent effort to adapt to the reality of the contemporary world and progressively to distance itself from essentialism; that, therefore, our present theoretical and political efforts have a genealogy which is internal to Marxism itself. In this sense we thought that we were contributing to the revitalization of an intellectual tradition. But the difficulties here are of a particular type which is worth discussing. The article by Geras is a good example. We learn from it, with amazement, that Bernstein and Sorel 'abandoned' Marxism — and in Geras this has the unmistakable connotation of betrayal. What can we think about this ridiculous story of 'betrayal' and 'abandonment'? What would one make of a history of philosophy which claimed that Aristotle betrayed Plato, that Kant betrayed Leibniz, that Marx betrayed Hegel? Obviously, we would think that for the writer who reconstructs history in that way, the betrayed doctrine is an object of worship. And if we are dealing with a religious object, any dissidence or attempt to transform or to contribute to the evolution of that theory would be considered as apostasy. Most supporters of Marxism affirm its 'scientific' character. Science appears as separated by an absolute abyss from what mortal men think and do — it

coincides with the distinction between the sacred and the profane. At a
time when the philosophy of science is tending to narrow the epistemological gap between scientific and everyday languages, it seems deplorable that certain sectors of Marxism remain anchored to an image of
science which is more appropriate to popular manuals from the age of
positivism.

But this line of argument does not end here. Within this perspective
the work of Marx becomes an *origin* – that is to say, something which
contains within itself the seed of all future development. Thus, any
attempt to go beyond it *must* be conceptualized as 'abandonment'. We
know the story very well: Bernstein betrayed Marx; European social
democracy betrayed the working class; the Soviet bureaucracy betrayed
the revolution; the Western European Communist parties betrayed their
revolutionary vocation; thus, the only trustees of 'revolution' and 'science' are the small sects belonging to imaginary Internationals which, as
they suffer from what Freud called the 'narcissism of small differences',
are permanently splitting. The bearers of Truth thus become fewer and
fewer.

The history of Marxism that our book outlines is very different and is
based on the following points. (1) Classical Marxism – that of the Second
International – grounded its political strategy on the increasing
centrality of the working class, this being the result of the simplification
of social structure under capitalism. (2) From the beginning this prediction was shown to be false, and within the bosom of the Second International three attempts were made to respond to that situation: the
Orthodox Marxists affirmed that the tendencies of capitalism which
were at odds with the originary Marxist predictions were transitory, and
that the postulated general line of capitalist development would eventually assert itself; the Revisionists argued that, on the contrary, those tendencies were permanent and that Social Democrats should therefore cease
to organize as a revolutionary party and become a party of social reforms;
finally revolutionary syndicalism, though sharing the reformist interpretation of the evolution of capitalism, attempted to reaffirm the radical
perspective on the basis of a revolutionary reconstruction of class around
the myth of the general strike. (3) The dislocations proper to uneven and
combined development obliged the agents of socialist change – fundamentally the working class – to assume democratic tasks which had not
been foreseen in the classical strategy, and it was precisely this taking up
of new tasks which was denominated 'hegemony'. (4) From the Leninist
concept of class alliances to the Gramscian concept of 'intellectual and

moral' leadership, there is an increasing extension of hegemonic tasks, to the extent that for Gramsci social agents are not classes but 'collective wills'. (5) There is, then, an internal movement of Marxist thought from extreme essentialist forms – those of Plekhanov, for example – to Gramsci's conception of social practices as hegemonic and articulatory, which virtually places us in the field, explored in contemporary thought, of 'language games' and the 'logic of the signifier'.

The axis of our argument is that, at the same time that essentialism disintegrated within the field of classical Marxism, new political logics and arguments started to replace it. If this process could not go further, it was largely due to the political conditions in which it took place: under the empire of Communist parties which regarded themselves as rigid champions of orthodoxy and repressed all intellectual creativity. If today we have to carry out the transition to post-Marxism by having recourse to a series of intellectual currents which are outside the Marxist tradition, it is to a large extent as a result of this process.

An Atemporal Critique

We will reply point by point to Geras's main criticisms of our analysis of the history of Marxism. First, he suggests that we have designed a very simple game, choosing at random a group of Marxist thinkers and separating the categories they inherited from classical Marxism from those other aspects of their work in which, confronted with a complex social reality, they were forced to move away from economic determinism. We are then alleged to have given medals to those who went furthest in this direction. This is, obviously, a caricature. In the first place, our main focus was not on economic determinism but on essentialism (it is possible to be absolutely 'superstructuralist' and nevertheless essentialist). In the second place, we did not consider 'any Marxist' at random but narrated an intellectual history: one of progressive disintegration within Marxism of the originary essentialism. Geras says nothing of this history. However, the image he describes fits his own vision well: for him there is no internal history of Marxism; Marxist categories have a validity which is atemporal and it is only a question of complementing them here and there with a bit of empiricism and good sense.

Secondly, we are supposed to have contradicted ourselves by saying that Marxism is monist and dualist at the same time. But there is no contradiction here: what we asserted was that Marxism becomes dualist as a result of the failure of monism. A theory that starts by being pluralist would run no risk of becoming dualist.

Thirdly, Geras alleges that we have presented ourselves as the latest step in the long history of Marxism, and so fallen into the error, criticized by Althusser, of seeing in the past only a pre-announcement of oneself. Here, at least, Geras has posed a relevant intellectual question. Our answer is this: any history that deserves its name and is not a mere chronicle must proceed in the way we have proceeded – in Foucault's terms, history is always history of the present. If today I have the category 'income distribution', for instance, I can inquire about the distribution of income in ancient times or in the Middle Ages, even if that category did not exist then. It is by questioning the past from the perspective of the present that history is constructed. Historical reconstruction is impossible without *interrogating* the past. This means that there is not an *in-itself* of history, but rather a multiple refraction of it, depending on the traditions from which it is interrogated. It also means that our interpretations themselves are transitory, since future questions will result in very different images of the past. For this very reason, Althusser's critique of teleological conceptions of the past is not applicable in our case; we do not assert that we are the *culmination* of a process that was pre-announced, as in the transition from the 'in itself' to the 'for itself'. Although the present organizes the past, it can have no claim to have disclosed its 'essence'.

Finally, at several points Geras questions our treatment of texts by Trotsky and Rosa Luxemburg. In the case of Trotsky, we are said to have made use of 'tendentious quotations'. What we actually said was that: (1) Pokrovsky posed a *theoretical* question to Trotsky: namely, whether it is compatible with Marxism to attribute to the state such a degree of autonomy from classes as Trotsky does in the case of Russia; and (2) Trotsky, instead of answering theoretically, gave an account of Russian development and attempted to deal with the specific *theoretical* aspect of Pokrovsky's question only in terms of the contrast between the greenness of life and the greyness of theory ('Comrade Pokrovsky's thought is gripped in a vice of rigid social categories which he puts in place of live historical forces', etc.).[24] Thus the type of question that Pokrovsky's intervention implied – one referring to the degree of autonomy of the superstructure and its compatibility with Marxism – is not tackled by Trotsky at any point. The reader can check all the passages of Trotsky to which Geras refers and in none of them will s/he find a *theoretical* discussion concerning the relationship between base and superstructure. As for the idea that we demanded from Trotsky a theory of relative autonomy when we have affirmed its impossibility in another part of our book, we have already seen that this last point is a pure invention by Geras.

In the case of Rosa Luxemburg it is a question not of misquotations but of simplifications — that is, we are supposed to have reduced everything to the 'symbol'. Geras starts by enumerating five points, with which it would be difficult to disagree because they are simply a summary of Rosa Luxemburg's work on the mass strike. Our level of analysis is different, however, and does not contradict any of the five points in Geras's summary. The fifth point, for instance, reads: 'economic and political dimensions of the overall conflict interact, intersect, run together.'[25] A further nine-point enumeration then explains what this interaction is, and we would not disagree with it either since it merely gives examples of such interaction. What our text asserts — and what Geras apparently denies without presenting the slightest argument — is that through all these examples a specific social logic manifests itself, which is the logic of the symbol. A meaning is symbolic when it is a second meaning, added to the primary one ('rose', for example, can symbolize 'love'). In the Russian Revolution, 'peace', 'bread' and 'land' symbolized a variety of other social demands. For example, a strike for wage demands by any group of workers will, in an extremely repressive political context, also symbolize opposition to the system as a whole and encourage protest movements by very different groups; in this way an increasing relation of overdetermination and equivalence is created among multiple isolated demands. Our argument was that: (1) this is the mechanism described by Rosa Luxemburg in *The Mass Strike*; (2) it is, for her, the central element in the constitution of the unity between economic struggle and political class struggle; (3) her text is conceived as an intervention in the dispute between syndicalist and party theoreticians about the relative weight of economic and political struggle. Since Geras does not present any argument against these three theses, it makes little sense to prolong this discussion.[26]

Radical Democracy

As is usual in sectarian literature, when it comes to talking about politics Geras has remarkably little to say. But we do need to deal with his assertion that it is an axiom that socialism should be democratic.[27] The fact is that for any person who does not live on Mars, the relation between socialism and democracy is axiomatic only in Geras's mind. Has Geras ever heard of Stalinism, of the one-party system, of press censorship, of the Chinese Cultural Revolution, of the Polish coup d'état, of the entry of Soviet tanks into Prague and Budapest? And if the answer is that nothing of the kind is *true* socialism, we have to be clear what game we are playing. There are three possibilities. The first is that Geras is constructing an ideal model of society in the way that the utopian socialists did. Nothing, of course, prevents him from doing so and from declaring that in Gerasland collective ownership of the means of production and democracy go together; but in that case we should not claim to be speaking about the real world. The second possibility is to affirm that the authoritarian states of the Soviet bloc represent a transitory and necessary phase in the passage towards communism. This is the miserable excuse that 'progressive' intellectuals gave to support the worst excesses of Stalinism, from the Moscow trials onwards. The third possibility is to assert that these states are 'degenerate forms' of socialism. However, the very fact that such 'degeneration' is possible clearly indicates that the relation between socialism and democracy is far from being axiomatic.

For us the articulation between socialism and democracy, far from being an axiom, is a political project; that is, it is the result of a long and complex hegemonic construction, which is permanently under threat and thus needs to be continuously redefined. The first problem to be discussed, therefore, is the 'foundations' of a progressive politics. For Geras this presents the following difficulty: has not our critique of essentialism eliminated any possible basis for preferring one type of politics to another? Everything depends on what we understand by 'foundation'. If it is a question of a foundation that enables us to decide with apodictic certainty that one type of society is better than another, the answer is no, there cannot be such a foundation. However, it does not follow that there is no possibility of reasoning politically and of preferring, for a variety of reasons, certain political positions to others. (It is comical that a stern critic of 'either/or' solutions such as Geras confronts us with exactly this type of alternative.) Even if we cannot decide algorithmically about many things, this does not mean that we are confined to total nihilism, since we can reason about the *verisimilitude* of the available alternatives. In that sense, Aristotle distinguishes between *phronesis* (prudence) and *theory* (purely speculative knowledge). An argument founded on the apodicticity of the conclusion is an argument which admits neither discussion nor any plurality of viewpoints; on the other hand, an argument which tries to found itself on the verisimilitude of its conclusions, is essentially pluralist, because it needs to make reference to other arguments and, since the process is essentially open, these can always be contested and refuted. The logic of verisimilitude is, in this sense, essentially public and democratic. Thus, the first condition of a radically democratic society is to accept the contingent and radically open character of all its values – and in that sense, to abandon the aspiration to a single foundation.

At this point we can refute a myth, the one which has it that our position is incompatible with humanism. What we have rejected is the idea that humanist values have the metaphysical status of an essence and that they are, therefore, prior to any concrete history and society. However, this is not to deny their validity; it only means that their validity is constructed by means of particular discursive and argumentative practices. The history of the production of 'Man' (in the sense of human beings who are bearers of rights in their exclusive human capacity) is a recent history – of the last three hundred years. Before then, all men were equal only in the face of God. This history of the production of 'Man' can be followed step by step and it has been one of the great achievements of our culture; to outline this history would be to reconstruct the various discursive surfaces where it has taken place – the juridical, educational, economic and other institutions, in which differences based on status, social class or wealth were progressively eliminated. The 'human being', without qualification, is the overdetermined effect of this process of multiple construction. It is within this discursive plurality that 'humanist values' are constructed and expanded. And we know well that they are always threatened: racism, sexism, class discrimination, always limit the emergence and full validity of humanism. To deny to the 'human' the status of an essence is to draw attention to the historical conditions that have led to its emergence and to make possible, therefore, a wider degree of realism in the fight for the full realization of those values.

The Transformation of Political Consciousness

Now, the 'humanization' of increasingly wider areas of social relations is linked to the fundamental process of transformation of political consciousness in Western societies during the last two hundred years, which is what, following Tocqueville, we have called the 'democratic revolution'. Our central argument is that socialism is an integral part of the 'democratic revolution' and has no meaning outside of it (which, as we will see, is very different from saying that socialism is axiomatically democratic). In order to explain our argument we will start from an analysis of the capitalist/worker relation. According to the classical Marxist thesis, the basic antagonism of capitalist society is constituted around the extraction of surplus value by the capitalist from the worker. But it is important to see where the antagonism resides. A first possibility would be to affirm that the antagonism is inherent in the very form of the wage-labor/capital relation, to the extent that this form is based on the appropriation by capital of the worker's surplus labour. However, this solution is clearly incorrect: the capitalist/worker relation considered as form — that is to say, insofar as the worker is considered not as flesh and blood but only as the economic category of 'seller of labour power' — is not an antagonistic one. Only if the worker *resists* the extraction of his or her surplus-value by the capitalist does the relation become antagonistic, but such resistance cannot be logically deduced from the category 'seller of labour power'. It is only if we add a further assumption, such as the 'homo oeconomicus' of classical political economy, that the relation becomes antagonistic, since it then becomes a zero-sum game between worker and capitalist. However, this idea that the worker is a profit-maximizer in the same way as the capitalist has been correctly rejected by all Marxist theorists.

Thus, there is only one solution left: that the antagonism is not intrinsic to the capitalist relation of production as such, but rather, that it is established *between* the relation of production and something external to it — for instance, the fact that below a certain level of wages the worker cannot live in a decent way, send his/her children to school, have access to certain forms of recreation, etc. The pattern and the intensity of the antagonism depend, therefore, to a large extent, on the way in which the social agent is constituted *outside the relations of production.* Now, the further we are from a mere subsistence level, the more the worker's expectations are bound up with a certain perception of his or her place in the world. This perception depends on the participation of workers in a variety of spheres and on a certain awareness of their rights; and the more democratic-egalitarian discourses have penetrated society, the less will workers accept as natural a limitation of their access to a set of social and cultural goods. Thus, the possibility of deepening the anti-capitalist struggle itself depends on the extension of the democratic revolution. Even more: anti-capitalism is an internal moment of the democratic revolution.[28]

However, if this is right, if antagonism is not intrinsic to the relation of production as such but is established between the relation of production and something external to it, then two consequences follow. The first is that there are no a priori privileged places in the anti-capitalist struggle. We should remember that for the Second International – for Kautsky, particularly – the idea of the centrality of the working class was linked to: (a) a vision of the collapse of capitalism as determined by the contradiction between forces and relations of production which would lead to increasing social misery – that is say, to the contradiction between the capitalist system as a whole and the vast masses of the population; and (b) to the idea that capitalism would lead to proletarianization of the middle classes and the peasantry, as a result of which, when the crisis of the system came about, everything would be reduced to a simple showdown between capitalists and workers. However, as the second process has not taken place, there is no reason to assume that the working class has a privileged role in the anti-capitalist struggle. There are many points of antagonism between capitalism and various sections of the population (environmental pollution, property development in certain areas, the arms race, the flow of capital from one region to another, etc.), and this means that we will have a variety of anti-capitalist struggles. The second consequence is that the potential emergence of a radical anti-capitalist politics through the deepening of the democratic revolution, will result from global political decisions taken by vast sectors of the population and will not be linked to a particular position in the social structure. In this sense there are no *intrinsically* anti-capitalist struggles, although a set of struggles, within certain contexts, could *become* anti-capitalist.

Democratic Revolution

If everything then depends on the extension and deepening of the democratic revolution, we should ask what the latter itself depends on and what it ultimately consists of. Marx correctly observed that capitalism only expands through permanent transformation of the means of production and the dislocation and progressive dissolution of traditional social relations. Such dislocation effects are manifest, on the one hand, in commodification, and on the other hand, in the set of phenomena linked to uneven and combined development. In these conditions, the radical instability and threat to social identities posed by capitalist expansion necessarily leads to new forms of collective imaginary which reconstruct those threatened identities in a fundamentally new way. Our thesis is that egalitarian discourses and discourses on rights play a fundamental role in the reconstruction of collective identities. At the beginning of this process in the French Revolution, the public space of citizenship was the exclusive domain of equality, while in the private sphere no questioning took place of existing social inequalities. However, as Tocqueville clearly understood, once human beings accept the legitimacy of the principle of equality in one sphere they will attempt to extend it to every other sphere of life. Thus, once the dislocations generated by capitalist expansion became more general, more and more sectors constructed the legitimacy of their claims around the principles of equality and liberty. The development of workers' and anti-capitalist struggles during the nineteenth century was a crucial moment in this process, but it was not the only or the last one: the struggles of the so-called 'new social movements' of the last few decades are a further phase in the deepening of the democratic revolution. Towards the end of the nineteenth century Bernstein clearly understood that future advances in the democratization of the state and of society would depend on autonomous initiatives starting from different points within the social fabric, since rising labour productivity and successful workers' struggles were having the combined effect that workers ceased to be 'proletarian' and became 'citizens', that is to say, they came to participate in an increasing variety of aspects of the life of their country. This was the start of the process that we have called the 'dispersion of subject positions'. Bernstein's view was, without any doubt, excessively simplistic and optimistic, but his predictions were fundamentally correct. However, it is important to see that from this plurality and dislocation there does not follow an increasing integration and adaptation to the system. The dislocatory effects that were mentioned above continue to influence all these dispersed subject positions, which is to say that the latter become the points which make possible a new radicalization, and with this, the process of the radical democratization of society acquires a new depth and a new impulse. The result of the process of dispersion and fragmentation whose first phases Bernstein described, was not increasingly conformist and integrated societies: it was the great mobilizations of 1968.

There are two more points which require discussion. The first refers to liberalism. If the radical democratization of society emerges from a variety of autonomous struggles which are themselves overdetermined by forms of hegemonic articulation; if, in addition, everything depends on a proliferation of public spaces of argumentation and decision whereby social agents are increasingly capable of self-management; then it is clear that this process does not pass through a direct attack upon the state apparatuses but involves the consolidation and democratic reform of the liberal state. The ensemble of its constitutive principles — division of powers, universal suffrage, multi-party systems, civil rights, etc. — must be defended and consolidated. It is within the framework of these basic principles of the political community that it is possible to advance the full range of present-day democratic demands (from the rights of national, racial and sexual minorities to the anti-capitalist struggle itself). The second point refers to totalitarianism. Here Geras introduces one of his usual confusions. In trying to present our critique of totalitarianism, he treats this critique as if it presupposed a fundamental identity between communism and fascism. Obviously this is not the case. Fascism and communism, as types of society, are totally different. The only possible comparison concerns the presence in both of a certain type of political logic by which they are societies with a State Truth. Hence, while the radical democratic imaginary presupposes openness and pluralism and processes of argumentation which never lead to an ultimate foundation, totalitarian societies are constituted through their claim to master the foundation. Evidently there is a strong danger of totalitarianism in the twentieth century, and the reasons are clear: insofar as dislocatory effects dominate and the old structures in which power was immanent dissolve, there is an increasing tendency to concentrate power in one point from which the attempt is made 'rationally' to reconstruct the ensemble of the social fabric. Radical democracy and totalitarianism are, therefore, entirely opposite in their attempts to deal with the problems deriving from dislocation and uneven development.

To conclude, we would like to indicate the three fundamental points on which we consider it necessary today to go beyond the theoretical and political horizon of Marxism. The first is a philosophical point which relates to the partial character of Marx's 'materialism', to its manifold dependence on crucial aspects of the categories of traditional metaphysics. In this respect, as we have tried to show, discourse theory is not just a simple theoretical or epistemological approach; it implies, by asserting the radical historicity of being and therefore the purely human nature of truth, the commitment to show the world for what it is: an entirely social construction of human beings which is not grounded on any metaphysical 'necessity' external to it — neither God, nor 'essential forms', nor the 'necessary laws of history'.

The second aspect refers to the social analyses of Marx. The greatest merit of Marxist theory has been to illuminate fundamental tendencies in the self-development of capitalism and the antagonisms that it generates. However, here again the analysis is incomplete and, in a certain sense, parochial — limited, to a great extent, to the European experience of the nineteenth century. Today we know that the dislocation effects which capitalism generates at the international level are much deeper than the ones foreseen by Marx. This obliges us to radicalize and to transform in a variety of directions Marx's conception of the social agent and of social antagonisms.

The third and final aspect is political. By locating socialism in the wider field of the democratic revolution, we have indicated that the political transformations which will eventually enable us to transcend capitalist society are founded on the plurality of social agents and of their struggles. Thus the field of social conflict is extended, rather than being concentrated in a 'privileged agent' of socialist change. This also means that the extension and radicalization of democratic struggles does not have a final point of arrival in the achievement of a fully liberated society. There will always be antagonisms, struggles, and partial opaqueness of the social; there will always be history. The myth of the transparent and homogeneous society — which implies the end of politics — must be resolutely abandoned.

We believe that, by clearly locating ourselves in a post-Marxist terrain, we not only help to clarify the meaning of contemporary social struggles but also give to Marxism its theoretical dignity, which can only proceed from recognition of its limitations and of its historicality. Only through such recognition will Marx's work remain present in our tradition and our political culture.

Notes

1. Slavoj Žižek, 'La société n'existe pas', L'Age, Paris, October–December 1985.
2. Andrew Ross, m/f 11/12, 1986.
3. Alastair Davidson, Thesis Eleven, no. 16, Melbourne 1987.
4. Stanley Aronowitz, 'Theory and Socialist Strategy', Social Text, Winter 1986/87.
5. Philip Derbyshire, City Limits, 26 April 1985.
6. David Forgacs, 'Dethroning the Working Class?', Marxism Today, May 1985.
7. Norman Geras, 'Post-Marxism?', New Left Review 163, May–June 1987.
8. This example, as the reader will realize, is partly inspired by Wittgenstein.
9. Hanna Fenichel Pitkin, Wittgenstein and Justice, Berkeley 1972. See also Stanley Cavell, Must We Mean What We Say? New York 1969, p. 9.

10. Geras, p. 66.

11. R. Rorty, *Consequences of Pragmatism*, Minneapolis 1982, pp. 166–7.

12. Geras, p. 69.

13. Ch. Taylor, *Hegel*, Cambridge 1975, p. 109.

14. H. Staten, *Wittgenstein and Derrida*, Oxford 1985, p. 6.

15. W.T. Stace, *The Philosophy of Hegel*, New York 1955, pp. 73–4.

16. Staten, p. 7.

17. In the same manner as reactionary theoreticians, Geras considers that he can fix the being of things once and for all. Thus, he says that to call an earthquake an expression of the wrath of God is a 'superstition', whilst calling it a 'natural phenomenon' is to state 'what it is'. The problem is not, of course, that it does not make perfect sense in our culture to call certain beliefs 'superstitions'. But, to counterpose 'superstitions' to 'what things *are*' implies: (1) that world views can no longer change (that is to say, that our forms of thought concerning the idea of 'the natural' cannot be shown in the future to be contradictory, insufficient, and therefore 'superstitious'); (2) that, in contrast to men and women in the past, we have today a direct and transparent access to things, which is not mediated by any theory. With such reassurances, it is not surprising that Geras regards himself as a functionary of truth. It is said that at some point Mallarmé believed himself to be the individual mind which embodied the Absolute Spirit, and that he felt overwhelmed. Geras makes the same assumption about himself far more naturally. It is perhaps worthwhile remarking that Geras's naive 'verificationism' will today hardly find defenders among philosophers of any intellectual orientation. W.V. Quine, for instance, who is well anchored in the mainstream tradition of Anglo-American analytic philosophy, writes: 'I do ... believe in physical objects and not in Homer's gods, and I consider it a scientific error to believe otherwise. But in point of epistemological footing the physical objects and the gods differ only in degree and not in kind. Both sorts of entities enter our conception only as cultural posits.... Moreover, the abstract entities which are the substance of mathematics — ultimately classes and classes of classes and so on up — are another posit in the same spirit. Epistemologically these are myths on the same footing with physical objects and gods, neither better nor worse except for differences in the degree to which they expedite our dealings with sense experiences.' 'Two Dogmas of Empiricism', in *From a Logical Point of View*, New York 1963, pp. 44–5.

18. K. Marx, *A Contribution to the Critique of Political Economy*, London 1971, p. 21.

19. Geras reasons in a similar way. Referring to a passage in our text where we write that 'the main consequence of a break with the discursive/extra-discursive dichotomy, is the abandonment of the thought/reality opposition', Geras believes that he is making a very smart materialist move by commenting: 'A world well and truly *external* to thought obviously has no meaning outside the thought/reality opposition' (p. 67). What he does not realize is that in saying so he is asserting that thought is not part of reality and thus giving credence to a purely idealist conception of mind. In addition, he considers that to deny the thought/reality dichotomy is to assert that everything is thought, while what our text denies is the *dichotomy* as such, with precisely the intention of reintegrating thought to reality. (A deconstruction of the traditional concept of 'mind' can be found in Richard Rorty, *Philosophy and the Mirror of Nature*, Princeton 1979.)

20. Geras, p. 49.

21. E. Laclau, C. Mouffe, *Hegemony and Socialist Strategy*, London 1985, p. 140.

22. Geras, p. 50.

23. Ibid., p. 50.

24. L. Trotsky, *1905*, London 1971, p. 333.

25. Geras, p. 60.

26. One further point concerning Rosa Luxemburg. Geras sustains (p. 62) that we deny that Rosa Luxemburg had a theory of the mechanical collapse of the capitalist system. This is not so. The point that we make is rather that nobody has pushed the metaphor of the mechanical collapse so far as to take it literally; and that, therefore, all Marxist writers of the period of the Second International combined, in different degrees, objective laws and conscious intervention of the class in their theorizations of the end of capitalism. A second point that we make in the passage in question — and here yes, our interpretation clearly differs from Geras's — is that it is because the logic of spontaneism was not enough to ground the class nature of the social agents, that Luxemburg had to find a different grounding and was forced to appeal to a hardening of the objective laws of capitalist development. Fully to discuss this issue would obviously require far more space than we have here.

27. Geras, p. 79.

28. We would like to stress that, in our view, the various anti-capitalist struggles are an integral part of the democratic revolution, but this does not imply that socialism is *necessarily* democratic. The latter, as a form of economic organization based upon exclusion of private ownership of the means of production, can be the result, for example, of a bureaucratic imposition, as in the countries of Eastern Europe. In this sense, socialism *can be* entirely external to the democratic revolution. The compatibility of socialism with democracy, far from being an axiom, is therefore the result of a hegemonic struggle for the articulation of both.

PART III
On South Africa

This part of the book is an exchange of letters, dating from 1987, with my South African Ph.D. student, Aletta J. Norval. Given the rapid changes that have taken place in the South African scene, she has added a postscript, written in March 1990, to her original letter.

5

Letter to Ernesto

Aletta J. Norval

Pretoria

13 August 1987

Dear Ernesto

This morning, I witnessed once again the violence of apartheid encroaching upon 'ordinary' life: the arrest of young black boys in the streets of Arcadia, their only crime being their presence on the sidewalks of a white suburb. (I tried to intervene, but to no avail.) Even what appear to be the most insignificant areas of everyday life are infected by violence. Derrida has characterized apartheid as 'the violent arrest of the mark, the glaring harshness of abstract essence(heid) [that] seems to speculate in another regime of abstraction, that of confined separation'.[1] This lived violence that plays itself out in a situation of forced silence compels one to speak, although, as has been said, speaking frightens me because one always runs the risk of saying both too little and too much. But speak one must.

During the last few months, I have been writing to you about various aspects concerning the South African political landscape. Today, I want to put together the pieces of the theoretical approach that we have been discussing in our seminar in Essex, and apply them to the situation here. My aim is to construct a preliminary sketch moving beyond the essentialism that has marred so much of the otherwise thought-provoking work on South Africa (SA). Some of the categories that we have discussed, such as organic crisis, constitutive outside, antagonism, logic of equivalence and political frontier, acquire new and dramatic meanings as they

---

[1] J. Derrida, 'Racism's Last Word', *Critical Inquiry*, no. 12, 1985, p. 292.

become tools for a political analysis which is increasingly dominated by a sense of urgency.

The signs of the crisis facing the regime have been inscribed throughout society for some time now: the spiralling resistance in black communities, the development of increasingly militant trade unionism, the growth of rightwing opposition and internal dissension in the National Party (NP) ranks. One could go on enumerating these signs *ad infinitum*. It is an organic crisis, in the Gramscian sense, which precludes any discursive fixing of the identities of the social agents in an ensemble of non-antagonistic relations by the NP. The proliferation of antagonisms and schisms which cannot be accommodated by the NP leads to an increasing destabilization of the constructed frontiers: it is becoming more and more difficult for the dominant sectors to establish and to maintain clear and uninterrupted chains of equivalence which divide the social into two camps. This generalized crisis of social identities, which does not emerge from one single point, but is the result of an overdetermination of circumstances, cannot be seen as pertaining exclusively to the NP discourse, wholly separate from the other discourses operating in the social. The crisis of NP discourse must be placed against the whole social and political background which forms its discursive exterior.

The discursive exterior, the social groups that lie 'beyond' the unstable frontier (extra-parliamentary movements, militant trade unions, etc.) are asserting a presence which can no longer be ignored. This ensemble of forces forms a constitutive outside, in the Derridean sense, and it is the most important site from which the inside/dominant bloc is challenged and threatened. This process leads to a weakening of the fixity of social identities, and it has become impossible to think of these identities as being preconstituted and given in any sense. We are constantly confronted with the fact that all identities are subject to change. They are precarious, unstable and open to articulation and re-articulation in a context of constant struggle where there is a weakening of dividing lines between discourses and a proliferation of floating signifiers. The discursive nature of all social and political identities, and the political relevance of the categories which we discussed in our seminar, are fully shown in situations of organic crisis such as the present one. These categories constitute an intellectual horizon which allows us to grasp the full meaning of the social and political changes which are taking place in SA at the moment, and, even more, they are also useful tools for developing new strategies of resistance.

Let me stress those features of the category of 'constitutive outside' which are particularly important for my analysis. Reflecting on the South African situation, I have again been struck by the relevance to political analysis of Derrida's critique of the metaphysics of presence and the logic of identity. What Derrida argues about conceptual thought, namely that there is a 'non- or anti-essence that violates the boundaries of positivity by which a concept has formerly been thought to be preserved in its as-such',[2] and that the non-essence in violating positivity becomes the condition of possibility of the assertion of that positive boundary, applies not only to conceptual/philosophical thought. The non-closure he describes is the non-closure of any discursive form and can therefore also be extended to political analysis.

In our analysis of discursive formations such as the NP's apartheid discourse, this has obvious relevance. If any identity is necessarily contaminated by otherness and, as Lacan clearly shows, becomes what it is only by reference to this otherness, it means that any discursive formation, in order to signify itself as such, has to refer to something which is exteriorized in its formation. This can be seen, for example, in the construction of an 'Afrikaner identity' in the NP discourse and in the different systems of exclusion by which this construction has operated over time. Moreover, that which is exteriorized creates the possibility of constituting any identity at all; it is constitutive. Since the exterior at the same time threatens the identity of the inside by preventing it from achieving positivity, the constitutive outside can also be shown to be subversive.

As you have shown in your work, the discursive construction of identities which pierces the entire material density of the multifarious institutions, rituals and practices of the social can occur in terms of either the logic of difference or the logic of equivalence. Let me explain the way in which I see the operation of these logics in SA. According to your analysis, wherever identities are constructed in terms of the logic of difference, there is an attempt to fix the relations among social agents as a set of differential positions. Therefore, social identities are sets of stable positive differences. Here one can think for example of the attempts to create non-antagonistic 'group identities' in the NP discourse. Each group is portrayed as being merely different from the other and as occupying a specified place in the systems of relations that constitute society. However, the logic of difference never manages to constitute a fully

---

[2] H. Staten, *Wittgenstein and Derrida*, Oxford 1985, p. 18.

sutured space, since systems of difference only partially define relational identities. The contingency of systems of difference is revealed in the unfixity which equivalence introduces.

Your conclusion could equally well be applied to my earlier example; 'group identities' are not merely a question of difference: there is always the possibility of constructing equivalences, and of portraying the other as a threat. This occurred, for example, in the discourse of Malan who in the 1949 election introduced the notion of the *swart gevaar* (black danger). Here it is clear that through an expansion of a set of equivalences, positive identities are subverted. In the later Verwoerdian discourse, the subversion of the positive identities of the 'ten black nations' were once again to be found in the construction of a 'black threat' which put these 'positive' identities into question and left only a certain 'black mass' that had become anti-white. In this way, a political frontier was created which constructed what was beyond it as a negative identity. It is here that antagonistic relations can be shown to exist. Antagonism then becomes the witness of the final impossibility of constituting purely differential identities; and antagonism as impossibility can only be revealed or shown, in the Wittgensteinian sense, in the discursive practices through which positivity is put into question. That is, this impossibility is shown through the functioning of the logic of equivalence and the creation of political frontiers. I would argue that the 'dialectic' between reform and repression, between co-option and coercion is related to this unresolved tension between difference and equivalence in NP discourse.

I discussed this unstable balance in the apartheid discourse in some depth with you last year. In contrast to both the liberal and the revisionist analyses, I am inclined to argue that apartheid society cannot be understood in terms of either race-reductionism or class-reductionism. The liberal school, which explicitly rejects economic reductionism, holds that white domination must be understood as a result of an irrational racial logic. This irrational logic would then finally break down as a consequence of the needs of a rational capitalist development: whites will choose to be 'rich and mixed rather than poor and separate'. Paradoxically, the race reductionist theory can then ultimately be shown to be highly economistic since it argues that capitalism's rational logic will lead to the breakdown of apartheid. Revisionist theorists have on their part also fallen into the trap of economic reductionism by portraying apartheid as merely a superstructural phenomenon which has been devised to facilitate capital accumulation. Classes are thus made the *a priori* fundamental category of analysis. In breaking with all forms of reductionism, we have argued that what needs to be investigated is the specific discursive construction of identities in apartheid discourse. Any links that can be shown to exist between apartheid and capitalism will then be of a contingent rather than of a necessary character. I would argue that any attempt to understand what is happening in SA today will have to take account of this process of construction of identities, whether one wants to look at the politics of the dominant bloc or at that of the various radical opposition groupings.

In terms of the irresolvable tensions in the apartheid discourse, I have found that the kernel signifiers 'apartheid', 'volk' and 'race' in the Verwoerdian discourse are particularly remarkable. Each of these signifiers worked as a hymen, in the Derridian sense, in the text of the apartheid discourse. The irreducible ambiguity in these terms creates the possibility for them to assume contrasting meanings in different places. The notion 'volk' in Verwoerd's discourse, which appears in two distinct senses, is a case in point. First, the term can be used to establish differences between the various volkere, such as the Afrikaner-volk, for example. Second, 'volk' can be used to refer to the white population including both Afrikaners and the English. These two usages exemplify a crucial distinction in official discourse at the time. In the case of the former, 'volk' is utilized to ground those positive differential identities by which the separateness of the 'Afrikaner group' could be constructed through the unification of a number of heterogeneous elements. In the latter, it forms the basis for the creation of a number of equivalences on the grounds of which political frontiers could be established, such as the opposition between whites versus a 'black threat'.

The unresolved tensions found in all these signifiers are also present in the construction of identities and political frontiers. I am thinking here specifically of the 1958–66 period. The key point of the ambiguity in this era is found in the way in which the colour barrier was thought either in terms of difference or in terms of negativity. I have tried to pinpoint how the black/white frontier was established, and to reveal its essentially unstable nature by showing the presence of other chains of equivalence that made the construction of one enemy increasingly difficult. It was by means of tracing out these hymens, both in the key signifiers and in the construction of identities, that it became possible to see how apartheid discourse attempted to conceal the traces of its own discursivity by presenting itself as a transparent medium through which 'reality' could speak without mediation: that is, by presenting the (dis)ordering of society, which was a result of social and cultural construction, as natural.

The Vorster era witnessed the beginning of the decline of apartheid as a hegemonic ideology. (I am using the term ideology to denote a discourse which attempts to constitute the social as closed, to construct meanings, and to mute the effects of the infinite play of differences. I see apartheid ideology then as a specific will to totality, rather than as a belief system of a particular class, or as a false consciousness.) The discourse of 'separate development' in the years 1966–78 constructed identities mainly in terms of difference. Paradoxically, this discourse of so-called difference marked the beginning of a long period of erupting antagonisms in SA. It is these more recent developments that I now want to discuss with you.

Historical Background

Throughout the nineteenth and the first half of the twentieth centuries, Afrikaner identity was defined in opposition to that of the English-speaking sectors of society, who represented English capital and the despised liberalism. Around the time of the Anglo–Boer war this was particularly apparent. During the 1910–48 period two conceptions of Afrikanerhood were to vie with each other periodically. First, there was the conception of a 'pure' Afrikanerhood, which included only Afrikaans-speaking people, and second, there was the conception of Afrikanerhood which comprised all white South Africans, unifying English- and Afrikaans-speaking people. The first conception, however, prevailed and, until 1948, the Afrikaans/English opposition could be regarded as the main line of division in the social. The shift to a construction of the identity of the Afrikaner in terms of a black/white opposition started gradually between 1910 and 1948 and only fully matured in the 1950s. However, with the rise in the significance of the black/white opposition during the turbulent 1950s, when notorious legislation such as the Immorality Act, the Population Registration Act and the Suppression of Communism Act was introduced, it became particularly apparent. This construction of identities had strategic effects which permeated the whole of the social. For example, while up to the 1950s some space existed for legal extra-parliamentary mass political opposition, this situation changed drastically with the suppression of popular resistance culminating in the banning of the African National Congress (ANC).

In the Verwoerd era (1958–66), apartheid ideology acquired a new centrality and comprehensiveness in relation to the preceding ten years. (Although my periodization roughly follows the succession of regimes, I

do not mean to imply that each of these regimes' discourses is a homogeneous bloc. Rather, these discursive formations must be regarded as
ensembles of articulations marked by contradictions since the unity of
the discursive formation is not given through a logical coherence of its
elements, but through articulatory practices which combine the
elements in a certain way around a number of nodal points.) The most
important changes in the construction of identities during this time were
those related to the attempts to create a new positive identity by uniting
Afrikaners and the English into a 'white *volk*', one white people. But this
'unity' was immediately drawn into the relation of a white/black frontier, and thereby lost its 'positive' nature. This frontier was developed by
reference to the decolonization of Africa and the rejection of a multi-
racial state as a suitable model for SA. A chain of equivalences was
consistently created between the idea of a multi-racial state as exemplified in black Africa, black domination, heathenism and dictatorships,
which was then shown to be a threat to Western values, Christianity,
equality, and 'real' freedom. The ultimate result of this construction of
equivalences was the portrayal of the notion of a multi-racial state as
'white suicide'. This perception was then transferred to the construction
of the black subject inside SA, so that these chains of equivalences created
the black subject as constituting such a threat. A political frontier was
established which divided the world rigidly into two camps: black and
white.

  This situation was, however, further complicated by the perception of
another threat, that of communism, which was systematically linked to
the first chain of equivalences. By linking this construction to the already
present notions of a multi-racial state and black domination, it became
possible to portray all opposition to apartheid, including the English
opposition and the press, the Black Sash, the Indian National Congress
and the ANC, as communist-inspired and anti-white. This expansion of
the white/black frontier introduced into it a fundamental instability.
Since all opposition to apartheid, from both blacks and whites was
portrayed as 'communist', the simple colour-based frontier was interrupted by the introduction of the communist element. This meant that
one social actor, such as, for example, the English, could be taken up in
contradictory chains of equivalence, and once this process established
itself, it became more and more difficult to construct a single enemy.
The construction of equivalences was, however, accompanied by the
construction of identities in terms of difference. Here the notions of
'ethnic groups', different '*volkere*' and the discourse of 'grand apartheid'

which made provision for the creation of 'homelands' for each group was introduced.

Significant changes occurred in the construction of political frontiers during the regime of Vorster (1966–78), whose discourse was organized around the signifier 'separate development', which, as I have mentioned earlier, laid much more emphasis on the construction of identities in terms of difference. The construction of Afrikaner and English identities as different groups, but as both having a white identity that began in the Verwoerd era, came to full maturity under Vorster and finally led to the first split to the right from the NP since it came to power in 1948. In this discourse of difference, where racist language became unacceptable, but the other had to remain marked by otherness, the question of 'colour' also had to be redefined. The other was now constructed as simply different. But as different 'races' they still had to be kept separate. Vorster now portrayed SA as a multi-*national* state with 'homelands' that could achieve 'independence'. The process of broadening white identity, or the 'inside', started at this time.

What is important to note at this point is the survival terms in which the unification of a white identity was constructed. The communist threat already present in the discourse in the 1960s now became dominant in the process of constructing political frontiers. This increasingly led to a new division in the construction of the black subject. The homeland leaders were taken up in the system, while radical, mostly urban blacks, especially after the popular uprisings of 1976, were presented as being inspired by communist influences. (The uprisings of 1976 are significant in that the lack of overt resistance from the 1960s to the 1970s is only brought decisively to an end at that time.) All these developments led to an increasing blurring of the black/white frontier. 'Blacks' were both communist and non-communist: the inside was no longer only white but included moderate blacks and the possibility of including 'coloureds' and Indians in the inside through the tri-cameral system was being explored by a commission of inquiry.

I would therefore argue that it is possible to trace out the most significant changes in SA society, from the stages of resistance to changes in the form of the state, by carefully following the various discourses in their interaction, and the associated construction of identities over the years. Although I have here focused on the creation of social and political identities in the NP discourse, this must, as I have argued earlier, be placed in the context of the discursive construction of identities in the society as a whole. To recapitulate, it is clear that over the last decade there has been an increasing weakening of the original black/white frontier which makes the construction of a singular enemy more and more difficult. The increasing complexity and fluidity of frontiers at the same time have led to a proliferation of possible points of antagonism. It is the situation itself and not any kind of a priori classificatory system which forces me to pursue a double discussion of the present organic crisis. On the one hand there is the crisis within the dominant bloc, and on the other, there is the constitutive outside which lies at the 'source' of this crisis. Paradoxically, in order to grasp the first dimension, one must already know the second; the nature of the crisis will therefore only become clear if one could, so to speak, place the two dimensions on top of each other and thereby show the resultant instability of social identities and political frontiers, and the increasing disintegration of the attempts in the NP discourse to create stable systems of purely differential identities.

The Crisis in the Dominant Bloc

The events of the 1970s placed the government of Vorster under increasing pressure to acknowledge the various failures of orthodox ideology, and ultimately constituted the 'roots' of the present organic crisis within the dominant bloc. The possibility of moving away from certain central tenets of Verwoerdian ideology was the result of the irreducible duality in the construction of identities, in terms of the logic of difference or in terms of the logic of equivalence, in the discourse of apartheid. Vorster stressed the dimension of the Verwoerdian discourse which emphasized difference. Vorster's discourse therefore introduced an entire change in the tone of politics; racist language was no longer heard and there was a move away from 'volk' symbols to a discourse which constructed white unity. Until the early 1970s, the illusion could be maintained that the social and political order was marked by difference, without discrimination. The growing labour unrest in the early 1970s, and the Soweto uprising of 1976, however, decisively shattered this illusion.

The Botha regime, faced with a crisis which had economic, social and political dimensions, introduced a transformist strategy in the Gramscian sense. This strategy can be seen as part of an operation to construct social identities in terms of a logic of difference, and, in this case, it centred primarily on political and economic attempts to co-opt different 'communities' into the apartheid system in order to expand the threatened white hegemony. I would argue that the transformist strategy of the NP, although portrayed primarily in terms of a logic of difference, necessarily also included the construction of frontiers and, therefore, an element of force and exclusion. Let me take, as an example, the tri-cameral parliamentary system and the various reforms pertaining to the black urban community to illustrate my reading of this strategy of transformism.

The position of urban blacks was one of the main issues on the government's agenda during the late 1970s. A variety of reforms, following from the Wiehahn and Rieckert Commissions of Inquiry, were introduced. These included *inter alia* the legalization of black trade unions and the recognition, for the first time, of blacks as permanent residents in 'white' SA. The reforms, which focused primarily on the socio-economic conditions of the urban black population, and investigated the requirements of a stable workforce, had the effect of splitting the black labour force into two groups: the privileged urban insiders and the rural outsiders. Although it is impossible for me to go into the various intricacies of these reforms, there can be no doubt that they played a crucial role in the transformist strategy of the NP: they aimed at an economic form of co-option of the urban blacks, and drove a wedge between the different sectors of the black labour force. Although there were limited attempts to address the question of the political position of blacks at a local level, another attempt at co-option which miserably failed, the reforms generally amounted to an outright denial of the national political aspirations of blacks. I would thus argue that this strategy attempted to separate the realm of the 'economic' from the 'political'.

The second element of this strategy of transformism is the introduction of the 'new dispensation' for the 'coloured' and Indian communities, which took the form of a tri-cameral parliament. This reform provided these communities, for the first time, with political representation at the national level. The 'deracialization' of the political order was portrayed in the NP discourse as the logical solution to the problem of political accommodation of these 'groups' within the apartheid system. The opening up of the dominant bloc to other racial groups consisted of a fundamental reconstitution of the nation which had previously allowed only whites into the privileged inside. The proposed tri-cameral system was not, however, simply an innocent attempt to find an answer to the political accommodation of the coloureds and Indians in a system of purely differential relations. Far more than that, it was an attempt to disengage the coloured and Indian communities from black society in order to broaden the support basis of the dominant bloc in the face of a revolutionary threat. The same could be said about the reforms concerning the black urban population.

An investigation of the discursive construction of the 'revolutionary threat', and therefore of the political frontiers operating at that time, leads us back to the question of a 'total onslaught' and the Total Strategy. The Total Strategy, conceived of by the military as a comprehensive effort to utilize all the means available to the state to achieve their aim of countering this total onslaught, can be seen as an expansion of the earlier anti-communist chain of equivalences. The notion of a total onslaught, which originally emerged in the context of the decolonization of the Portugese colonies in Southern Africa when SA was perceived as 'being without its buffer states' and unprotected against the communist onslaught, played a crucial role in the construction of political frontiers. Not only was an external frontier constructed by establishing equivalences between the threat posed by the ANC, communism and Soviet expansionism, but this frontier was expanded to include the situation inside SA, and it laid the ground for a division of political space between legitimate political activities (i.e. within the limits posed by the dominant bloc) and illegitimate political resistance. While the 'external' frontier was used to legitimate the escalation of violent strikes across the border into neighbouring countries, the displacement of this frontier to the inside of the country provided the possibility for the regime's unspeakable acts of violence and repression, in 1976 and later, towards those who were placed on the other side of this frontier. Although the language of the total onslaught could no longer be used after the Nkomati accord with Mozambique was signed, the systems of equivalences continued to function, as could clearly be seen by the *ad nauseam* expansion and application to the United Democractic Front (UDF) of all the supposed terrors that the ANC represented in this discourse. As unrest escalated in the early 1980s around the Koornhof Bills and the new constitution, this system of equivalences became increasingly expanded until almost all extra-parliamentary opposition was constructed as a threat in these terms.

However, the Total Strategy, with its emphasis on survival, did not only consist of elements of repression: it also laid considerable stress on other conditions for stability. The notions of 'free enterprise' and 'economic growth', for example, became more and more prominent in the NP's discourse. The conception of white identity had become less important than the notion of a system, a way of life, which linked SA to the 'free West' and counterposed it to the 'tyranny of Marxist regimes'. It could be argued that, in this respect, an important new facet emerged in the NP discourse, a technocraticism attempting to de-politicize areas of potential conflict by constructing differential, non-antagonistic identities. This can further be shown in the changes in the form of the state that were introduced with the new constitution. Power was concentrated in the executive branch, and the roles of the cabinet, parliament and the caucus were diminished. These shifts had extensive consequences in terms of the form of politics that was to prevail in the 1980s. The establishment of four permanent cabinet committees which drew members not only from parliament but also from the ranks of business leaders and the military, signified a new approach to policymaking and a steady decrease in the authority of the electoral parties. These changes then created the conditions of possibility for the formalization of different currents present in NP discourse. The most notable of these was the direct representation of monopoly capital at the highest level of decision-making, and the establishment of a military shadow government.

The considerable depth of the present organic crisis is shown dramatically in the extent to which the regime failed to broaden the consensual basis of the dominant bloc by expanding the systems of difference, through their attempts to co-opt the coloured and Indian communities as well as the urban blacks, and, as a result, the extent to which it failed to create and maintain stable frontiers. The modest labour reforms and the inclusion of 'other racial groups' within the dominant bloc, with the retention of one of the cornerstones of apartheid ideology, the Population Registration Act, by the cautious NP nonetheless sparked off a series of antagonisms, both to the right and to the left within the dominant bloc, as well as in those social sectors which formed the constitutive outside of the NP's discursive universe. The emergence of these antagonisms radically changed the face of SA politics. It led to the erosion of at least a part of the NP's traditional basis with the breakaway far right and the formation of the Conservative Party (CP).

I will refer to the reaction of the black community to these transformist initiatives later; it is sufficient at this point simply to note that the opposition was so fierce and widespread that it effectively subverted the NP's attempts to create any stable systems of difference. The spiralling resistance led to the introduction of the first state of emergency, whose repressive nature is well known. It is generally acknowledged that the first and later states of emergency amounted to an admission by the government that it could no longer control the events in the townships in its ordinary capacity; that the forces of opposition had succeeded in creating the 'state of ungovernability' that the ANC had called for at the beginning of 1985.

Despite attempts to organize consent for their increasingly repressive response to the deepening crisis by continuously stressing the need for extraordinary measures to contain radicalism, cracks began to appear in the dominant bloc, signifying a crisis of frontiers. It is enough to mention the most relevant developments: the breakaway of the Independents (New Nats) just before the general election of 1987; the resignation of the leader of the opposition in the white's chamber of parliament in 1986; the formation of the Institute for a Democratic Alternative for South Africa (IDASA) and its Dakar talks with the ANC; and the outcome of the general election in which there was a dramatic swing to the right and the Progressive Federal Party (PFP) was replaced by the far right-wing CP as the official opposition. All these developments increasingly put into question the conventional wisdom of NP discourse.

White extra-parliamentary organizations, which play a crucial role in the challenging of frontiers, expanded in number at an unprecedented rate over the last year. Let me just mention two: the End Conscription Campaign (ECC), which has actively opposed the role of the South African Defence Force in enforcing apartheid policies and has challenged the regime's conscription of youths into a civil war, and the Five Freedoms Forum (FFF), which brought together an extremely broad alliance of extra-parliamentary movements. Organizations of this kind could ultimately represent a watershed in 'white politics' insofar as it aims to address the role of whites in SA today in a fundamentally new manner, questioning the very grounds upon which the government has constructed the divisions in the social.

The key question at this juncture is the extent to which the realignments constitute a threat to the NP and the entire apartheid structure. (I do not imply here that the demise of the NP would necessarily also mean a decline of apartheid. A scenario could easily be imagined where apartheid could survive such a demise in a new or altered form.) It is in this respect that an analysis of the role of the constitutive outside becomes significant. Within the dominant bloc divisions are multiplying. The fractions of the far right have challenged the reconstitution of the nation, and the centre left has questioned both the increasing use of violence to contain black resistance, and the validity of the inside/outside distinction (legitimate versus illegitimate resistance) as such. With the increasing splitting of the dominant bloc and the persistent attempts to disarticulate the NP discourse, it has become more and more difficult for the NP to discursively fix the political and social identities of the various social agents in a non-antagonistic manner. From the moment of the introduction of the strategy of transformism, schisms and antagonisms have erupted throughout the social. The NP's dramatically inadequate response remains one of repression and domination.

The Subversive Outside

As was the case in my earlier discussion of the NP, a consideration of the terrain from which a radical questioning of the dominant bloc took place requires that we refer back to the development of the 1970s which shattered the passivity in oppositional struggles of the previous era: the growth of the black trade union movements, the popular uprisings of 1976, and the explosion onto the scene of youth, community and student organizations in black, coloured and Indian communities, organizing protests around basic issues such as education, rents, services and housing.

The growth of the black trade union movement was the site of a major failure on the part of the state in an attempt to co-opt black resistance. Several black trade unions, after their legalization in 1979, decided to participate in state-created agencies. Instead of neutralizing their opposition, the state, however, only succeeded in opening up a legal space for these unions from which they could wage their struggles against the dominant bloc. Simultaneously, the Black Consciousness Movement (BCM), which aimed at liberating blacks from oppression by struggle founded on the construction of a positive black identity gained prominence. This movement succeeded in re-articulating the conception of 'blackness' and in unifying the African, 'coloured' and Indian communities in opposition to the apartheid regime. Using our terminology, this was achieved by constructing a new political imaginary which transformed relations of subordination into relations of oppression, and which, by giving a new content to the category of 'the oppressed', created a re-division of the social around which new antagonisms developed. Because of the effectiveness of the frontier constructed by this discourse, the NP attempted to co-opt the moderate elements of the coloured and Indian communities into the dominant bloc, and it is only against this background that the importance of the revival of Congress politics, and the role the UDF played in it, can be assessed.

The UDF was formed in February 1983 in the context of an extreme proliferation of antagonistic points. Its immediate aim was to organize resistance to the new constitution and the Koornhof Bills. The tri-cameral system, by excluding Africans, thus actually opened up the space for the organization and unification of oppositional groups. In later forming a broad anti-apartheid alliance, the UDF succeeded in establishing an overdetermination between an unprecedented amount of local struggles, by taking them up in a radical discourse of national liberation. It is in this process of articulation of a plurality of 'loose' struggles and wild antagonisms that the significance and democratic subversiveness of the UDF lies.

The specificity of UDF's discourse in the terrain of mass-based politics is largely linked to its acceptance of the Freedom Charter as a guiding document in the struggle. Political debates in the extra-parliamentary sphere have for some time now been dominated by attempts to fix the meaning of the Charter. Each movement is obliged to define its views on the transformation of SA with reference to this framework, and their identities are forged within this definition. This has led to differing and conflicting divisions of political space in oppositional discourses. The Charter has become the crucible of these discourses, and its acceptance by the UDF has signified the contiguity of the ANC and the UDF in a highly visible manner.

The construction of political identities by the black extra-parliamentary movements has been a terrain of fierce contestation, and I would argue that as long as the category of class is treated as an a priori privileged one, these constructions cannot simply be thought in class terms. Rather, in the case of UDF, it could be argued that a popular-democratic imaginary, as you have defined it in your work, has been developed. Their construction of a political identity is not based on a limited class-centred approach; the UDF has insisted that it is not a class organization, that it does not 'represent' the 'interests' of any one class, and that if the working class is to assume a central role, that role must be established through struggle. Because of this, the UDF has frequently been accused of being 'degenerately populist', and of 'endangering the class struggle'. These accusations rest on a number of illegitimate assumptions. One of them is to see populism as an 'appeal to the people above class divisions'. Such a characterization neglects the fact that populist discourses can refer to both 'the people' and to classes, which is the case with the UDF. Moreover, the attempt to negate the importance of this discourse by presenting it 'as selling out the class struggle', is based on a narrow, politically unfruitful and theoretically unjustified classism. The unity constituted around 'the people' is viewed, not as an expression of some underlying essence, but rather as a unity which is politically constructed in a process of struggle. The people, in this discursive formation, includes not only the members of the oppressed black, coloured and Indian communities, but whites as well. The division between 'the people' and the oppressive regime is therefore not made with reference to a simple black/white frontier, as was the case with the BCM. The UDF's construction of a frontier on non-racial grounds is a more radical challenge to the NP's attempts to create systems of difference in terms of race and ethnicity. I would argue that the strength of the UDF lies both in the refusal of narrowly-defined 'class politics' and in the ability to cut across racial lines, since it is this openness and strategic mobility which allows for the development of a genuinely hegemonic politics.

'The struggle', has been presented by the UDF as a non-racial, anti-capitalist, national struggle for democracy. The anti-capitalist element is an integral part of the UDF's interpretation of the Freedom Charter. However, although socialists within the UDF emphasize this dimension, the UDF generally does not present its project as socialist in character. The ensemble of equivalences developed around the notion of democracy plays an important role in establishing the UDF's stance in opposition to the regime. The latter's banal discourse on democracy is well known; in contrast, the UDF insists on a unitary state and a complete rejection of all partial or group-based solutions. (The notion of the necessity of the 'protection of minority rights' in a democratic society has also, perhaps naively, been excluded.) The UDF not only rejects the conception of group-based democracy, but also insists on the development of grassroots democracy, a people's democracy, in which the people would have control over all spheres of their lives, including control over the distribution of the national wealth. They therefore developed a notion of democracy which fundamentally challenges the present system. In terms of the extra-parliamentary/parliamentary division, this presentation of the struggle as anti-apartheid, anti-capitalist, democratic and non-racial, expels the other (the NP and the dominant bloc) by constituting its identity as fundamentally undemocratic, racist and exploitative. The resultant frontier between the regime and 'the people' is, for example, shown in the UDF's strategy to boycott those state reform initiatives which are regarded as merely an expansion of the structures of racial domination. However, as in the case of the initiatives of the NP, the construction of these frontiers must not be seen as static and unchangeable. The division between those taking part in state-created institutions and those pursuing a boycott strategy is not a hard line of division; rather, it can be crossed in pursuit of real political gains in a highly fluid strategic struggle.

The UDF's unique position on democracy and socialism also sets this movement apart from other radical discursive formations. I think it could be argued that the UDF has avoided both the pitfall of separating 'stages' of struggle (anti-apartheid and anti-capitalist) and the simple conflation of the two which leads to the danger of assuming that the overthrow of the apartheid state would necessarily lead to a breakdown of capitalism. This process of articulation is shown most clearly in the working relations between the Congress of South African Trade Unions (COSATU) and the UDF. In the case of other, more workerist unions, economistic strategies prevent the articulation of the workers' struggles to the ensemble of other struggles emerging in the community.

Against this background, the differences between the UDF and other black opposition groups, such as Inkatha and the Black Consciousness movement/National Forum (NF) can be clarified. Although the political frontiers proposed by each of these movements overlap to a certain extent, there are several points of antagonism among the various conceptions. The NF was formed in the same year as the UDF, with opposition to the same initiatives of the NP as its initial focal point. However, the NF took the Manifesto of the Azanian People as its guiding document, and identified racial capitalism as the most important source of oppression in the society. In this discourse, the main antagonism between the oppressed and the regime was located in terms of a capitalism/anti-capitalism division, and the political space was primarily divided around a racially-determined conception of class divisions; the oppressed black working class (Africans, coloureds and Indians) versus whites-as-capitalists. Oppression was seen as a simple opposition between pre-constituted social agents rather than as a complex system of relations in which subjects are constructed. Within this framework, the NF criticized the UDF as a populist movement, as having a petty-bourgeois leadership, and even as compromising the struggle by colluding with representatives of capitalism (i.e. the Kennedy visit).

The UDF/Inkatha antagonism, which has been much more prominent and has led to the deaths of at least 100 people in the past few months, can also be analysed in terms of the different construction of frontiers in the two discourses. Inkatha, a Natal-based, mainly Zulu movement under the leadership of Buthelezi, has been at least partially absorbed into the differential system developed by the NP. It represents 'ethnic' (Zulu) interests, works for partial solutions (the Kwa-Natal Indaba), and claims to be anti-apartheid, pro-free enterprise and anti-sanctions. The historically uneasy relation between the ANC and Inkatha, the formation of an Inkatha union to counter the activities of COSATU, and the state support for Inkatha's right-wing vigilantes has further fuelled the struggle between Inkatha and the UDF.

Let me conclude by referring to one last point where the UDF's construction of identities and frontiers directly challenges other radical discourses as well as that of the regime: the UDF's view of the ANC. In the UDF's discourse, the 'ANC' can be regarded as a nodal point in the Lacanian sense, in that it operates as a privileged signifier that fixes the meaning of other signifiers in that chain of signification. The construction of identities, the drawing of frontiers and the analysis of the nature of the struggle all come together at this crucial point. No solution for the crisis is imaginable without the participation of this organization which is the most important political force in the SA resistance movement.

Now, if each of the discussed discourses, in the dominant bloc and its constitutive outside respectively, was 'hegemonic' in its 'own' context, where does this leaves us? If this were the case in SA today, the struggle would indeed be futile. If, however, social identities are not viewed as being fixed and pre-constituted by some structural position, and if political interests are not seen as being given with these positions but as constructed, the analysis, the strategizing and, indeed, the struggle changes. Resistance becomes a war on all fronts to change the dividing lines and to gain as much terrain as possible. These aims can only be achieved through the development of discourses which aim at disarticulating the dominant construction of identities and political frontiers.

At this point, it is necessary to return to my discussion of the organic crisis, and to draw all the threads of this letter together. As a result of the challenges to the transformist strategy of the NP, both from within and from without the dominant bloc, splits in the dominant bloc to the left and the right have occurred. As a result, the NP's ability to dominate the construction of social and political identities has been severely limited. In addition, there has been a blurring of the political frontiers and a continuous proliferation of antagonisms. The growth of the extra-parliamentary movements which cut across traditional dividing lines has furthermore created a space from which it became possible to disarticulate elements of the discourse of the dominant bloc. In the case of the 'white' extra-parliamentary organizations, we can no longer speak of these discourses as belonging to the discursive realm of the dominant bloc. The articulation of the various progressive discursive elements provides the possibility of making inroads against the previously 'hegemonic' NP discourse, perhaps even of the construction of a new historical bloc.

It is here that the significance of the form of politics developed by the extra-parliamentary movements, and particularly by the UDF, lies. We are witnessing today the truly subversive power of a democratic discourse, which, as you argue in your book with Chantal Mouffe, facilitates the expansion of demands for equality and liberty into increasingly wider domains. Further, it is only this form of politics which creates the conditions of possibility for the disarticulation of the dominant discourse, and which can act as a 'fermenting agent' for the dissemination of democratic demands into all areas of the social.

It is clear to me that once one has accepted the radical contingency which permeates the social, a new terrain of struggle is opened up, a space in which there can be no acceptance of a given situation; rather there is an obligation to engage in the open terrain of struggle.

I would like, finally, to ask you a set of questions linked to the theoretical implications of some current political debates in South Africa. I anticipate in most cases what the general trend of your answers will be, but as these questions touch on crucial aspects of resistance struggles here, I would like you to elaborate your answers in some detail.

1. In your deconstructive reading of the Marxist tradition, you have rejected totalizing categories such as classes. Does this mean that there are no instances where it is still possible to speak of classes? Would it not be, for instance, possible to reintroduce 'classes' in our analysis as long as we accept that they are not a priori categories but contingent social constructions which only acquire meaning in particular conjunctural and relational contexts? And, if this is the case, what would the preconditions be for the development of a class-based struggle?

2. How exactly do you envisage the relation between socialism and radical democracy? If the struggle for socialism is just one dimension of the project of radical democracy, what implications would this have for the debate in SA on the 'national question', the whole problem of representation and democratization, which some sectors see as necessarily historically prior to the move towards a socialist society?

3. You refer to power as something which is constitutive of social relations; power is not something which can be seized. At the same time, you stress the fact that revolutionary transformations must be thought in terms of a process. Would you not agree that in this process there must necessarily be a moment of seizure of power, that is, that the process of 'becoming state' in Gramsci's sense must include a seizure of power in the traditional sense?

4. In your work, you have insisted that ambiguity and incompletion are the conditions of a democratic society. Democracy implies the recognition that no transparent society, as envisaged in Hegelian dialectics or in the Marxian dream of a classless society, can ever exist. A society is democratic only if full democracy is never achieved. I would like to ask you two related questions concerning democracy and Third World struggles.

(a) In your book with Chantal Mouffe, you have drawn a distinction between forms of struggle in advanced capitalist societies and those characteristic of the Third World by saying that in the latter, forms of oppression are more centralized and popular struggles are endowed with a centre, with a single and clearly defined enemy, while in the former, there is a proliferation of antagonisms which make the construction of unified chains of equivalence and the division of the social into two camps very difficult. Does this not create serious obstacles for the democratization of post-revolutionary or post-colonial societies? In other words, what are the conditions of possibility of developing a radical democratic politics in a country such as a liberated South Africa?

(b) Paradoxically, if these obstacles are to be overcome, is it not necessary to incorporate into the current, ongoing struggle for democracy some elements of the democratic imaginary and some consciousness of the impossibility of ever reaching a fully democratic society?

5. A central theme running throughout this letter concerns the duality of the discourse of the dominant bloc, which revolves around the construction of identities either in terms of difference or in terms of equivalence. I have argued that this duality coincides to a large degree with the tension in the NP discourse between reform and repression, between co-option and coercion. I have tried to set this out in terms of the Derridean notion of the constitutive outside. That is, in the same way that the stabilization of, or the construction of, positive identities is limited by chains of equivalence which introduce negativity into the

social, the construction of an inside/dominant bloc is likewise limited by what is externalized in this process. The outside is, then, simultaneously that which makes the emergence of an inside possible and that which threatens it. In more general terms, I would like to ask whether we need not here address the question of the relation between consent and coercion in our conception of the political. If we accept that coercion is always already present in consent, in the sense that consent already implies the ruling out of certain possibilities (this can probably be compared to Foucault's notion of a 'regime of truth'), what do we then make of a situation of co-option? That this is a form of violence is clear to me; could we here talk of non-violent violence or something comparable to the Derridean idea of violence by inscription? Could we not go further and talk about an 'original violence' contained in any discourse? That would mean that we would find in both difference and equivalence always already some form of coercion. In that case, we would have to ask at what point discourses become antagonistic. For example, would there be a moment of antagonism in a discourse of co-option, such as the one accompanying the institution of the tri-cameral parliament, even though it is a discourse which operates by means of difference? Since we accept that the logics of difference and equivalence operate in the same space, is there a threshold which has to be determined for the emergence of antagonism, or is there always antagonism to a greater or lesser extent?

At this point it is necessary for me to end my rather long letter. I hope everything is going well in Essex, and I am looking forward to your reply.

Sincerely yours,

Aletta

Postscript – Post-Apartheid?

March 1990

Since the letter was written in 1987, South Africa has been thrown into a process of transformation similar to the one we have witnessed in Eastern Europe. With the legalization of the ANC, SACP and other proscribed organizations, and with the release of Nelson Mandela, an era has come to an end. Yet we should be careful not to accept the notion of the ending of an era in any simplistic manner, for this would imply the

beginning of something radically new, bearing no relation at all to what
has preceded it. In both theoretical and strategic terms, this would not be
advisable. The transition from apartheid to post-apartheid society would
have to be thought within a horizon of possibilities different from the
revolutionary tradition in which radical breaks have been conceptualized
previously. The imaginary of the left which has oriented resistance
struggles in South Africa for more than four decades has itself been put
into question, forcing resistance movements to rethink their aims and
strategies. This rethinking is occurring within an interregnum in the true
sense of the word, in a fluid and unstable situation where much will
depend on the capacity of these movements to retain the initiative in the
process of moving towards a post-apartheid society.

It is in the context of thinking the nature of this future society that
much of the relevance of my earlier argument concerning non-dogmatic
forms of struggle still lies. The success of the ANC, the UDF and its
successor, the Mass Democratic Movement's actions serve as examples of
the fermenting power of democratic demands when displaced to ever
wider areas of social life. In spite of the sense of euphoria and accom-
plishment produced by these possibilities, we need to reaffirm the
necessity of continued and multifarious resistances against any efforts to
stunt the momentum of these developments. In addition, we need to
occupy these new spaces without fear of a dilution of the 'purity' of the
struggle. In creating an alternative South Africa, it is important to take
seriously the implications of the logic of hegemony and the possibilities
opened up by the current situation for the winning over of additional
allies. The creation of a new historical bloc involves a questioning and a
re-articulation of the political identity of all the forces involved, such
that no single identity can be kept pure and intact. At this point it is
necessary to affirm once again our position on the constitution of political and social identities in relation to the demands for radical democracy. The question looming on the horizon is this: what are the
implications of recognizing that the identity of the other is constitutive
of the self, in a situation where apartheid itself will have become something of the past? That is, how do we think social and political identities
as *post*-apartheid identities? The struggle for the filling up of the signifier
'post-', the act in which it will become linked to a specific signified, is a
site of struggle opened up long ago — but one whose urgency is
increasing with the possibility of that post-society on the horizon.
Whether we will be able to affirm from this site the opening up of the
self to the other, of the identity to alterity, is to be determined in the

context in which the 'post' is thought.

The filling out of the 'post-' should not be allowed to be sutured in the name of a post-colonial necessity for a closing of ranks, in the name of the construction of a unitary identity against that which has always sought to divide and thereby to dominate — apartheid. Here we enter the difficult terrain which requires the assertion of a specific South African identity, yet one which would retain a pluralism and autonomy such that it does not simply become the reverse of the construction of apartheid-identities. Such is the terrain of radical democracy, which calls forth the other in its otherness. Once again, how is this to be accomplished without constructing identities of the type found in the division of the social in apartheid discourse?

If the discourse reconstructing a unitary South African identity is one where difference is only allowable in so far as it is internal to the 'original' resistance discourse, then we are walking a similar path. If the other is merely rejected, externalized *in toto* in the movement in which post-apartheid receives its signified, we would only have effected a reversal of the order, remaining in effect in the terrain in which apartheid has organized and ruled. The systems of domination and signification which have constructed the field of apartheid will then continue to be operative — even while we wish to be 'beyond' it. However, I would argue that the nature of the 'post-' leaves open other possibilities. Through a remembrance of apartheid as other, post-apartheid could become the site from which the final closure and suturing of identities is to be prevented. Paradoxically, a post-apartheid society will then only be radically beyond apartheid in so far as apartheid itself is present in it as its other. Instead of being effaced once and for all, 'apartheid' itself would have to play the role of the element keeping open the relation to the other, of serving as watchword against any discourse claiming to be able to create a final unity. It is only then that this sickness, which has served as the signifier of all oppression, will be eradicated; it is only then that the day will come that apartheid is 'only for the memory of man'.

6

Letter to Aletta

London
10 September 1987

Dear Aletta

Thank you very much for your long, insightful and thought-provoking letter. I have learned a lot from you about South Africa, and I hope to increase that knowledge further when you come back to Essex in a couple of months. The South African people's struggle against one of the most ignominious forms of oppression which exist in the world today commands, of course, all our support and solidarity. But the importance of that struggle transcends the borders of South Africa: by laying bare the exclusionary logic of racism, it also reveals the presence – in more hidden forms – of that same logic in our societies, and thus points out to us the depth, tenacity and strategic subtlety which the struggle for radical democracy requires. There is, in this sense, a recurrent phenomenon: it is always the 'anomalous' or 'peripheral' case which reveals that which does not appear immediately visible in apparently more 'normal' cases. It was the Spanish civil war which showed the weakness and ambiguity of democratic values in the countries of Western Europe; today it is the American aggression against the Sandinista regime which lays bare the *ultima ratio* which is always a latent possibility in liberal regimes; it is, finally, the struggle against racism in South Africa which highlights the limits of egalitarian logics and the presence of discriminatory mechanisms which, in these years of neo-conservative offensive, threaten the achievements of the democratic revolution of the last two centuries. Madrid, Managua, Soweto: more than precise geographical locations in a neutral space, they are the names of political trenches indefinitely

159

expandable to all latitudes; they are, in short, the names of the frontiers through which our own political identities are constituted.

As you are aware, the concept of *political frontier* is central to my whole approach to the question of hegemony. I would even say that it is through the consolidation or dissolution of frontiers that a historical bloc is constructed or fragmented. As you have demonstrated clearly in your work, the history of apartheid has been the history of the political frontiers through which Afrikaner identity was established; and, as you point out in your letter, the organic crisis of the present regime in Pretoria is intimately bound up with the impossibility of maintaining coherent lines of exclusion and discrimination. But it is important to clarify the theoretical background against which the relevance and centrality of the category of frontier may be understood. I would say, in the first place, that the presence of frontiers is inherent to the political as such — that consequently, there is only politics where there are frontiers; and, secondly, that the political is not an internal moment of the social but, on the contrary, that which shows the impossibility of establishing the social as an objective order. I am not able in this letter to enter into the detail of this question — about which, in any case, we have had frequent discussions — but I want, nevertheless, to underline two points which are highly relevant to the questions you raise in your letter. Firstly, any advance in the understanding of present-day social struggles depends on inverting the relations of priority which the last century and a half's social thought had established between the social and the political. This tendency had been characterized, in general terms, by what we may term the systematic absorption of the political by the social. The political became either a superstructure, or a regional sector of the social, dominated and explained according to the objective laws of the latter. Nowadays, we have started to move in the opposite direction: towards a growing understanding of the eminently political character of any social identity. To use Husserlian terminology: if the social is established through the *sedimentation* of the political, through the 'forgetting of origins', the *reactivation* of the original meaning of the social consists in showing its political essence.

My second observation is that there is in the Western intellectual tradition a very precise discursive surface in which the relation between the social and the political has been thought, and that is the whole debate concerning the relationship between state and civil society. If I may limit myself to the Marxist tradition, the moment of the greatest 'forgetting of origins', of the greatest subordination of the political to the social, can be found in the work of Marx himself: the political is a superstructure. The relationship between the state and civil society is characterized by the omnipotence of the latter (or rather of its anatomy, which is the political economy). The political is merely a *supplement* of the social and, as a good reader of Derrida, you are well aware of all the ambiguities which are inherent in the 'logic of the supplement'. Well then, the subsequent history of Marxism could only be characterized as the 'revenge of the supplement'. From Rosa Luxemburg to the integral state in Gramsci, there is an escalation characterized by the increasing privileging of the political moment. In Gramsci, this is perfectly clear: the 'becoming state' of the working class is not a 'superstructural' process but the very terrain of the constitution of social relations.

The reason why I am emphasizing these two aspects is because they are fundamental for understanding the meaning of the replies I shall give to your questions. It is on this point, precisely, that the whole significance of the transition from Marxism to post-Marxism resides and which, as a theoretical approach, you share with me. Marxism, just as the greater part of the sociological tradition, is grounded on the affirmation of the objective character of the social. In this sense, Marxism is perfectly rooted in the intellectual tradition of the 'metaphysics of presence'. The central point of our 'post-Marxism' consists, by contrast, in opposing the 'objectivity' of any kind of ultimate suturing or closure, due to the negativity inherent in the 'constitutive outside' to which you refer in your letter. Accordingly there is a displacement in the very type of valid interrogation. Let us suppose, for example, a question such as: 'what is the class structure in a country X during a period Z?' What this question presupposes – as an unquestioned a priori, as a transcendental horizon, thus, for the constitution of any historicity – is that social agents are structured in terms of 'classes'. The post-Marxist question, by contrast, would be: 'what are the *historical conditions* for the constitution of social agents as classes?' Whereas the category of 'class' is, in the first approach, an objective datum, necessary and a priori for any society in which antagonistic relations exist, it comes, in the second approach, to have *conditions of possibility* which are themselves historical and contingent. Whereas classical Marxism fixed an objective meaning on history which subsequently operated as an unquestioned transcendental horizon in the analysis of concrete social processes, what we try to do is to historicize the horizon itself, that is to say, to show it in its radical contingency, which is only possible insofar as the radicalization of the interrogation opens the possibility of different contingencies. What is required, therefore, is taking one step back and inscribing Marxist theory within a horizon of broader interrogations which — without necessarily denying the former in its totality — relativizes and historicizes its categories and, above all, enables us also to think about a set of historical possibilities different from those which are thinkable within Marxism. It is not, of course, a question of advocating a system of categories valid for all possible worlds but, rather, at least for more worlds than those to which Marxist categories give us access.

This will clarify, I hope, the manner in which I shall attempt to tackle your questions. Instead of answering them directly, I will attempt to displace them and, in this sense, deconstruct them. A *direct* answer implies that the person answering fully accepts the universe of presuppositions giving meaning to the question. But, if it is at the very level of those presuppositions that the disagreement arises, then it is a case of dissolving the meaning of the question, not of answering it. (In this sense you make my task easier since, in your formulations, you proceed halfway in the deconstruction of your own questions.) Well then, to dissolve or displace a question implies a series of discursive operations which imply what has been termed a change of paradigm. And the transition from one paradigm to another is, as you know, never algorithmic. This supposes that the substitution of one form of interrogation of the social for another is, in the strict sense of the term, a hegemonic operation. It is because a discourse has exhausted the possibilities of mastering those problems that people experience as relevant with its system of questions, that new discourses, based on radically new forms of interrogation of the social, come to the forefront. This implies the appearance of a new problematic. 'Problematic' means precisely that: a *coherent* system of questions constituting the ground upon which the debate between radically different perspectives may take place. In intellectual history, the important epistemological breaks have not occurred when new solutions have been given to old problems, but when a radical change in the ground of the debate strips the old problems of their sense. This is what seems central to me today if one wishes to push forward the political debate of the left: it is necessary to construct a new language — and a new language means, as you know, new objects, new problems, new values, and the possibility of discursively constructing new antagonisms and forms of struggle. Living in England this necessity is particularly urgent — I hardly need to tell you the sensation of *déjà vu* which one experiences, of having reached a blind alley, when one hears an Arthur Scargill or a Tony Benn speaking on TV.

I shall now proceed to deal with your five points.

1. With regard to the first point, I entirely agree with you. The rejection of the category of 'class' as the preconstituted unity of the subject does not mean the rejection *tout court* of the latter but its historicization. But for this very reason I believe that the question which you ask at the end concerning the specificity of class struggle, loses its meaning (and I'm well aware that, coming from you, it's not so much a question with which you identify but rather an invitation to me to state clearly my thoughts on this matter). Because if class struggle is conceived as a *specific* struggle along with the others, this would presuppose an analytic terrain constituted around the recognition of the fragmentation and dispersal of subject positions. But the category of *class* in Marxism was not thought from within that analytic terrain; it was thought, on the contrary, in order to define the *coherent* totality of those positions starting from a precise location in the social totality: the relations of production. So much so that the 'formation' of the class was conceived of as the transition from the 'class in itself' to the 'class for itself'. It is only at the heart of this essential unity of all the positions of the social agent that the dislocation between reality and the ideal could be conceived of as 'false consciousness'. The Marxist theory of class and class struggle is a theory concerning the essential unity of the social agents around 'interests'.

Therefore, if one asserts that there are, for example, workers' struggles, but these struggles form only *one* of the subject positions of social agents, since the workers themselves participate in many others which do not have any *necessary* relation with the struggles that are waged at the level of the factory floor, one is asserting something very true, but something which is incompatible with the Marxist theory of classes. And it is not that these objects — 'classes' — should be thought differently, rather the very category of 'class' loses analytic value in the new theoretical terrain. On the one hand — returning to the example — the analytic unification of a set of struggles under the label 'workers' struggles' — struggles for wage levels, for control of working conditions, for control over the introduction of new technology — must define the theoretical status of that unification. Is it simply the unity of the struggles which take place in the same physical space? Or on the part of those very social agents conceived of as mere referents? In that case, the category of 'class' would lack any theoretical value. But if it is a category which seeks to establish the boundaries which define the identities of the agents, in that case it must lay the foundations in something for the unification of a group of positions. So, if as is increasingly evident, whatever unity existing between those struggles is precarious and derives from hegemonic articulations — and cannot be read off on the basis of any sociological descriptivism — in such a case, the fact that the workers' struggles may or may not lead to their unity in a 'class', is the result of concrete historical processes and not of an a priori theorization. On the other hand, if there are subject positions external to the relations of production which contribute to shaping the identity of the agent and there are no boundaries which establish a priori the class unity of the agent, there is no reason to suppose that the collective totalities, which will constitute the — relative — unity of the social agent through overdetermination with other subjectivities, have necessarily to be 'class' totalities. That is to say, we are in the Gramscian field of 'collective wills'. You know as well as I do the complexity of the process of the formation of social and political identities in Third World countries, and all the 'poverty' of 'classism' when it is applied to this kind of context. If we add to this the increasing dispersion of subject positions in advanced capitalist countries, you will agree with me that the very concept of '*class* struggle' becomes a particularly inadequate category to describe the social antagonisms in the world in which we live.

If this is the case, what is the meaning of my assertion that the categories of 'class' and 'class struggle' should not be abandoned but historicized? It comes from the fact that these categories are not simple *errors* of Marx, since they correspond well enough to what was occurring in the field of his historical and political experience. In the first place, in societies prior to capitalism the 'boundaries' of social and political identities *tended* to coincide with the unity of the group as a coherent and integrated set of subject positions. The aristocracy, the urban bourgeoisie and the peasantry, held few positions in common and tended, consequently, to live existences segregated from each other (not, of course, in the sense that there was no interaction between them, but in the sense that they had few overlapping identities). In the second place, when the working class was constituted, it was *still* in the same situation: living in certain well-defined neighbourhoods, having a low level of consumption, enjoying limited forms of access to education and health assistance, and, above all, having to spend many hours subjected to the discipline of the factory which was the centre around which the life of the workers was organized. In these circumstances, the problem of the dispersion and overlapping of subject positions could not really arise for Marx nor for his contemporaries. The group as a set of integrated positions (the *class*)

presented itself as the agent of struggle. *Ergo*, 'class struggle'. So much so
that, for Marx, 'non-antagonistic society' and 'classless society' were
synonomous. Marx's vision of 'class struggle' was, therefore, relatively
correct and it accorded fairly well with social reality because the society
of his time *was* to a large extent a class society. But the society in which
we are living a century later is an increasingly less classist society, because
the unity of group positions on which the Marxist notion of 'class' is
based no longer obtains. We have exploitation, antagonisms, struggles,
but the latter — workers' struggles included — are increasingly less *class*
struggles.

Three observations must be made at this point. The first is that there
is no relation between the entry into an increasingly less classist society
and a decline in its antagonistic potential. In Western Europe, for
example, the working class as a unified group has done nothing but
decline. Think, for example, of the red belts in France, still a centre of
proletarian life and culture at the end of the Second World War but
which entered into a rapid process of disintegration in the following
decades. This, however, does not mean that we are entering into increasingly integrated societies, since the era of 'disorganized capitalism'
implies that the fragmentation of subject positions which it generates is
accompanied by the proliferation of new antagonisms and points of
rupture. These form the basis for the development of new types of
struggles — workers' struggle, among others — which also pose new
problems. Consequently, the left must today face up to questions such as
the following: how to unify, so as to generate certain political effects, a
set of struggles based on a dispersion of subject positions? How to constitute new political forms which are not the *product* of a unification already
given at the level of a mythic 'structure' but are themselves the source of
whatever unification may exist? How to reconcile unifying effects at a
certain level with the autonomy of fragments at another? All these questions take us beyond the theoretical and political horizon of Marxism.

If it is accepted that the horizon of analysis of social identities is
constituted by categories such as *dispersion* and *articulation*, my second
observation is that 'social classes', such as Marxism would understand
them, are merely *one* historically determined form, of establishing a
certain unity between the different subject positions of social agents. To
what extent do social classes exist nowadays? It would certainly be false
to say that they have entirely disappeared. If one thinks of the workers in
a mining enclave, for example, it is evident that the category of class may
to a large extent be useful in characterizing them, since one finds a

fundamental continuity and stability between all their subject positions. And the same could be said for a variety of other sectors. But if one thinks of the generalization of the phenomena of combined and uneven development in contemporary society, of the rapid rate of technological transformation and of the increasing commodification which takes place in late capitalism, it is clear that the prevailing tendencies lead to the decline of 'classes' as a form of constituting collective identities. This could also be reformulated in the following terms: there is a decline of the *social* – as a set of sedimented objectivities – and an expansion of the field of the *political.* (Once again, as you know, when I speak of the decline of classes I am not implying that there is a general decline in social inequalities, but that the existing inequalities – which in many cases tend to increase – can be characterized less and less as class inequalities.)

Finally, my third observation is connected with the manner in which this problem of classes sheds light on the general type of relation which exists, for us, between 'Marxism' and 'post-Marxism'. The transition from one to the other could be characterized as a widening of horizons. In the same way that non-Euclidean geometries *do not negate* the geometry of Euclid, but rather present it as a special case within a universe of wider alternatives, the basic categories of Marxism must be presented as specific historical forms within a wider universe of possible articulations. If we start from the axiomatic statement that in any society social antagonisms are class antagonisms, the fact that in certain societies they adopt this latter form is not something which has to be explained historically, since it is an a priori principle in the reading of *any* social situation. But if, by contrast, 'classes' are historical and contingent forms of articulation, in that case, the question arises concerning the *conditions of possibility* of constituting social agents as classes. With this, the level of historicity of analysis is radically deepened.

2.   My reply to your second point is symmetrical to the one I gave to the first. To pose the question of priority between democratic struggle and socialist struggle, implies two presuppositions: (a) that the two must be conceived of separately; (b) that the relation between the two must be conceived of in terms of a *periodization* (that is to say, that it is a question of stages). On this point, the South African debate is simply the reformulation, for the nth time, of the terms of the classical debate in Russian social-democracy, which opposed Plekhanov, Lenin and Trotsky, and which dominated the discussion of the Third International with regard

to the course of revolutions in colonial and semi-colonial countries. Today, however, it is necessary at all costs to go beyond this horizon.

In the first place, as you know, I do not conceive the set of demands characteristic of socialism in their classical sense as something *separate* from democratic demands, but as an internal moment of the democratic revolution. Just as people have demands for political participation, for racial equality, for access to education, they also have demands for economic equality, for control of working conditions, and so forth. Different demands traditionally considered as socialist and others usually considered as democratic will combine diversely in different circumstances creating an identity or popular bloc opposed to power. The important strategic discussion is not, consequently, the debate concerning the seizure of power in which all the participants accept the differentiation between democratic and socialist demands and merely disagree on the priority of some demands over others or their combination; but, rather, how to constitute a historical bloc which will maximize the possibilities of advancing the democratic revolution on the basis of articulating a set of demands which do not have amongst them any essence which may determine a priori their separation or their unity. In the second place, if the problem is posed as a contingent articulation of diverse demands in the specific unity of a historical bloc, it is also clear that each of these demands is united with the others as the consequence of a struggle. The outcomes of which are always reversible and cannot be fixed by any aprioristic theory concerning periods and stages. The history of Marxism, from this point of view, is the history of the progressive disintegration of that originating 'stagism'. (If, in the theory of 'combined and unequal development', we already discovered a certain almost surreal dislocation of the rigid stagism of Kautsky and Plekhanov, the accentuation of these dislocations in late capitalism obliges us to theoretically go beyond the articulatory and recomposite forms which were conceivable in the Marxist theoretical horizon.)

3. Here, once again, it is a matter of raising doubts about the very meaning of the question. One has to see what the classical notion of 'seizure of power' implied. At the very least, without doubt, it involved the following suppositions: (a) that a fundamental social antagonism was *transferred* from the economic to the political sphere; (b) that a new social force proceeded, through this transfer, to the revolutionary reconstruction of society; (c) that this political moment was the decisive foundational act in the transition from one type of society to another. Now

then, as you indicated, what the Gramscian perspective leads to is the radical deconstruction of the very concept of 'seizure of power' as it is conceived of in this sense. Think of a category such as 'war of position'. This supposes that social forces engaged in struggle do not simply *occupy* an increasingly wider political terrain, but they transform themselves and also the terrain in the course of this process of occupation; in this sense they do not *seize* state power but *become* state. This implies, in the first place, that there is a pluralization of the ambits of struggle which lead to a politicization of the social; but also, in the second place, that there is not *one* point which represents *the* moment in which society is turned upside down. As you can see, this does not mean that in many cases the violent overthrow of a regime is not necessary, but that, even in such cases, this overthrow is not an origin but an internal moment of a multifaceted and much larger hegemonic process. In this sense the 'war of movement', far from being the opposite pole of the 'war of position', is a constituent part of the latter. Thus, the 'war of position' is wholly incompatible with the traditional notion of 'seizure of power' to which you refer. This supposes the Jacobin notion of a pure *foundational* moment; it is, if you like, the reverse and at the same time the complement of a *sedimented* vision of the social: to the extent that the latter is characterized by the 'forgetting of origins', it can only endow itself with the vision of its origin under the mythic form of an *absolute* foundation — that is to say, of a radical elimination of *difference*.

4.   Let me respond separately to your two questions about democracy and Third World struggles and then establish the common root of both. I will begin with the second. My reply to your suggestion that it is necessary from the outset to incorporate the basic components of a democratic imaginary in any liberation struggle is, unhesitatingly, *yes*. Here it is necessary to distinguish a series of problems. At the base of any struggle lies, as I believe you agree with me, the experience of dislocation and antagonism. But antagonism is the disruption of a system of differences, of a symbolic universe, by an 'outside' which negates it — the Real, in the Lacanian sense — which impedes it from fully constituting itself. So, the response to the dislocation is the *imaginary* reconstitution of the negated identity. This requires discursive surfaces which offer a new principle of reading to the situation, forms which reconstruct an identity no longer given by its immanent participation in the objectivity of a symbolic system. But precisely because the antagonism is *constitutive* and may not be reduced to any positivity which may re-absorb it, those discursive

surfaces on which the experience of the dislocation will have to be inscribed are something which cannot be read on the basis of the negated identities. I say this in order to affirm that the reason why elements of a democratic imaginary have not occupied a more central place in the liberation movements of the Third World, has much to do with the theoretical, political and strategic discourses which were available in these countries. It is not true to say that the absence may be explained merely by external circumstances such as political isolation, imperialist aggression, internal counter-revolution and so on. Obviously there are situations in which it is necessary to adopt emergency measures which imply the curtailment of a set of civil rights. But nobody will ever convince me that the repression of homosexuality or abstract art is necessary for the security of the state. But if there is no rational and necessary link between the negated identities and the discursive surfaces which reconstruct those identities on the level of the imaginary, then alternative surfaces, in which the democratic element is present from the beginning, *are* possible. Nobody can demonstrate that discourses such as Leninism, Maoism and other similar ones constitute the only forms of political understanding and calculation which are compatible with the struggle of the masses. But the new democratic imaginary has to be created, and its creation implies a radical change in the conception of the political. In this sense, the first thing to bear in mind is the nature of the obstacles which oppose this change, and thus I go on to answer your first question.

The central obstacle preventing the democratization of emancipatory discourses is the fact that, as you point out, while ambiguity and indeterminacy are central features of democracy, emancipatory discourses tend to manifest themselves as total ideologies which seek to define and master the foundations of the social. And this responds to a deep psychological need: as the immanence of a symbolic system is threatened, as identities have been shattered by a plurality of dislocatory processes, identification with a new ideology tends to make the latter the surface of inscription for an ever increasing plurality of antagonisms thereby transforming it into a *total* horizon. And the more this horizon comes to be hegemonic, the more the imaginary mastery of the foundation will present itself as the elimination of any ambiguity and indeterminacy. This process is inevitable in the construction of any collective will and of hegemony.

How then to make this compatible with a radical democracy? I think that here the decisive step consists in making the very democratic indeterminacy the totalizing horizon of the social, in making the radical absence of foundation the basis for a critique of any form of oppression. Let me explain myself. Think of the ambiguity of Jacobinism during the French Revolution. On the one hand, it constitutes, without doubt, the starting point of modern totalitarianism: the dissolution of the plurality of the social by terror, the affirmation that society must be radically reconstituted from a single political point, the postulation of a rationality and complete transparency in social relations. But, on the other hand, all this is done in terms of an empty and indeterminable universality: the rights of man and of the citizen, and this is incompatible with the concentration of legitimacy in one point of the social fabric — on the contrary, the egalitarian logics tend to disperse and to diversify it. The very indeterminacy of the terms in which the subjects of rights are defined implies that these may be indefinitely expanded, in all directions, without any positive content binding them necessarily to a specific type of society.

Once the legitimacy of equality has been established, there is a systematic weakening of the 'absolutism' of any identity. For this very reason, the tendency to propose an exclusive choice between 'universalism' — conceived as the privileging of the 'ethnia of the west' — and the diverse forms of particularism (national, cultural and so forth), which characterize the identities of the peoples of the Third World, has always seemed absurd to me. Today, it is precisely because any identity is constituted within a horizon opened up by the democratic revolution, and because the latter makes of its indeterminacy and lack of essence a new universality, that no form of social organization, neither that of the West nor any other, can take on the paradigmatic value of a model. If, on the one hand, any historical experience affirms the legitimacy of its individuality, on the other, this individuality is only constituted as such on the basis of the universalism of the indeterminacy constituted by egalitarian logics. Whereas totalitarian 'universalisms' tend to postulate *models* of social organization, which through repetition in an infinite number of cases transforms them into the essence of the social, in the case of democratic universalism we have a radical relativization of any model. This leads to the weakening of the totalitarian pretension which may lurk behind emancipatory discourses. In our age (the age of post-isms), with the decline of political totalitarian myths — the Fatherland of socialism, *the* Party, *the* Class — the possibility is increasingly opened to link emancipatory discourses to that affirmation and practice of democracy to which you refer.

5. The problems which your question raises are important and complex. Like you, I believe that the opposition between consent and coercion must not be conceived of as an exclusive polarity. Consent and coercion are, rather, ideal limitative situations. What would be, in effect, a type of consent which excluded any coercion? An identity so perfectly achieved and sutured that it would leave no space for any *identification* in the Freudian sense of the term. But this is exactly the possibility which our entire critique of the objectivist conception of social relations excludes. As you say, the mere choosing of possible courses of action and the exclusion of others implies, in itself, a form of violence. It is important to state precisely why. If the choosing of a course of action were algorithmic, in that case there would be no coercion, because the different courses of action, although materially possible, could only have been undertaken as a consequence of a subjective error of judgment. If I make a mistake in a mathematical calculation, the erroneous solution is not a possibility which belongs to the field of mathematics itself. But if the decision *is not* algorithmic, in that case to decide implies something very different: it implies *creating* something which was not predetermined and, at the same time, cancelling out of existence possibilities which will not now be realized. Since the outcome of the situation is indeterminate in terms of the data which this latter affords us, to choose a course of action implies an act of coercion with respect to other possible courses of action.

The act of coercion is frequently seen as though it were a matter of violence which one subject exerts upon another in which the unity and homogeneity of both is assumed. But if, when I decide, I am taking a course of action which was not predetermined, in that case the decision does not follow automatically from what I *already* was, but rather through it I am also constituting myself and, at the same time, repressing other possibilities open to me. Acts of interaction with things, acts of constituting my identity and acts of coercion, are one and the same process. And, if we move on to collective decisions which imply a large number of people, it is highly probable that those other possibilities which I am discarding may be chosen by other groups. At this point, the 'repression' or the 'coercion' which divides the very individuality of the social agents, merely manages to constitute their identities through acts of identification. And it is this moment of coercion implicit in any decision which gives the concept of negativity its foundational character. Let us consider the case to which you refer: that of co-option via transformism. It is usually considered to be a form of neutralization of the potential antagonism of the group. (In our terminology: the construction of a system of differences through the breaking of chains of equivalence.) If the decision between accepting the co-option and continuing the confrontation were algorithmic, and if the correct decision were the latter, the first solution could only be a phenomenon of false consciousness. That is to say, the identity of the agent would not be affected by the decision-making process. But if the decision is not algorithmic, it constitutes a radically new identity. In this case, the identity of the co-opted agents changes and (given the contingent character of the decision) this can only occur on the basis of *repressing*, of exerting *coercion*, on other possibilities. I believe that any problem of the consent/coercion relation can be seen, in this sense, in terms of the category of 'constitutive outside' which is so central to your work.

Allow me to pose the problem from yet another angle. Gödel pointed out the presence of 'undecidable' propositions in formalized structures. Now then, from the point of view of those structures, if something is undecidable, it is just so, and there is nothing which you, I or Gödel can do about it. It is simply the end of the matter. But in practical life we are constantly faced with decisions to take which are algorithmically undecidable but which, nevertheless, have to be taken. So, I would say that systems of social organization can be seen as attempts to reduce the margin of undecidability, to make way for actions and decisions that are as coherent as possible. But by the simple fact of the presence of negativity and given the primary and constitutive character of any antagonism, the hiding of the *ultimate* undecidability of any decision will never be complete and social coherence will only be achieved at the cost of repressing something which negates it. It is in this sense that any consensus, that any objective and differential system of rules implies, as its most essential possibility, a dimension of coercion. And it is for this reason that there are no systems of social relations which are not, to some extent, relations of power.

All this seems essential to me in order to pose the question of democracy. A society in which coercion has been totally eliminated would be an absolutely transparent society, absolutely identical to itself (without a constitutive outside). In it, consequently, any decision would be algorithmic. But, for this very reason, that society would in no way be a free society — or, at most, it would merely enjoy the Spinozan freedom of being conscious of necessity. One does not have freedom of choice within a mathematical structure. This is why the absolute realization of democracy and its complete disappearance are synonymous. Democracy can only exist *in the movement* toward the elimination of oppression, not in the radical elimination of the latter; in the never resolved tension between social 'decidables' and 'undecidables', which indefinitely postpones the possibility of any *Aufhebung*. But is this not the same as affirming, as we have so often done, that 'society' does not exist? Does it not mean, therefore, affirming the practice of democracy as a *revelatory* function inasmuch as it shows us, behind the sedimented forms of the social, the political moment of its originating institution?

It is time to conclude this letter and I would like to do so with an observation which brings us back to something I raised at the beginning. In the light of my preceding analysis, my affirmation of the political character of the social acquires its full meaning. If the 'political' were part of the 'social', the systems of differences constituting the objectivity of the latter, would dominate unchallenged, and then the political would not be the moment of an originating institution, but rather the phenomenal form of a supergame which would reveal a deeper objectivity. But, if the outside *is* constitutive, in that case the political moment is irreducible: any consensus is constituted through an original act of coercion and a society reveals itself to be political through and through. It is in this politicization of social relations that the metaphysics of presence finally dissolves itself: the 'undecidability' of the acts of originary institution, by revealing the constitutive outside which accompanies the emergence of all objectivity, lays bare the historicity of being. Far from being the empirical terrain in which an abstract transcendental rationality is realized, history is the background of indeterminacy and contingency which shows the intrinsic and constitutive limitation of any 'transcendentalism' and any 'rationality'. But, for the reasons which I have indicated, this itself opens the possibility of broadening the horizon of freedom, which gives all its meaning to the project of a radical democracy. It is only to the extent that something is radically called into question that our attention is directed to its historical conditions of possibility, which before we took for granted. Our time is more conscious than any other of the precariousness and contingency of those values and forms of social organization which the naive optimism of earlier ages considered guaranteed by some immanent need of history. But it is the experience of this constitutive contingency itself which leads, paradoxically, to a higher consciousness of freedom and human dignity — that is to say, to the recognition that we ourselves are the exclusive creators of our world, and the ones who have a radical and untransferable responsibility towards it.

We shall continue our discussion of these topics in Essex in a few weeks.

Yours ever,

Ernesto

PART IV
Interviews

========================= 7 =========================

Building a New Left

Strategies: *Before we ask you about your notion of post-Marxism, we would like to inquire about the genealogy of these ideas. It is clear in your early essays published in* Politics and Ideology in Marxist Theory *that you are approaching the various issues — feudalism and capitalism in Latin America, the specificity of the political, the origins of fascism, and the notion of populism — from the viewpoint that most theorists have approached these topics with theoretical terrorism, if we may use that term. That is, you seem to argue that, in the name of paradigmatic clarity and logical consistency, there has been a tendency to overlook the historical specificity of the phenomena under question. This strategy seems to point toward your more general critique of essentialist discourses you now hold. In your introduction to* Politics *you even raise the whole problem of 'class reductionism' in Marxist theory, an issue that takes on central importance in your recent work with Chantal Mouffe. At the same time, your early studies are still within the parameters of the Marxist tradition — your homage to the theoretical and practical riches of Althusser and Della Volpe are indicative of this tentative stance. What was the intellectual history behind your current theoretical position? What brought you from these first hesitant steps toward your later conception of post-Marxism?*

EL: Let me tell you, in the first place, that I do not think there is such a radical discontinuity in my intellectual evolution. In some way or another I think that evolution has been but a process of deepening some intuitions that were already there. The idea of politics as hegemony and articulation, for example, is something that has always accompanied my political trajectory. I remember that in 1984, after many years, I travelled

First published in the US journal *Strategies*, this interview with Ernesto Laclau was conducted between its editorial collective and Ernesto Laclau over several months, starting in March 1988.

to Buenos Aires with Chantal Mouffe and we were able to consult early works of mine. Chantal was surprised to read my leading articles in *Lucha Obrera* (of which I had been the editor) of twenty years earlier, in which socialist struggle was already spoken about as the struggle of the working class for the hegemonization of democratic tasks.

In that sense, I have never been a 'total' Marxist, someone who sought in Marxism a 'homeland', a complete and harmonic vision of the world, to use Plekhanov's terms. The 'language games' I played with Marxism were always more complicated, and they always tried to articulate Marxism to something else. In my first works published in England — the critiques of Poulantzas and Gunder Frank, for example — people were inclined to see a more rigorous reformulation of Marxist orthodoxy, but I do not think this has been a correct interpretation. The critique of Frank, for example, was an attempt to define capitalism as a *mode of production* to prevent the concept from losing all analytical validity; on the other hand, it is also stated that the modes of production are not a substratum or foundation, but are articulated into larger totalities, that is, *economic systems* — and at that time many already observed that the category of 'economic system' is not a Marxist category. And I do not think you can find in my writings at any time the reduction of non-classist components to the role of superstructures of classes. My critique of Poulantzas' conception of fascism was based precisely on stating the irreducibility of the 'national-popular' to classes.

As for the influence I received from thinkers like Della Volpe and Althusser, the answer is similar: it is only insofar as they allowed me to start a gradual rupture from the totalizing character of Marxist discourse — Althusser's overdetermined contradiction, Della Volpe's anti-dialectical trend — that I felt attracted by their works. In the case of Della Volpe, I think my enthusiasm for his work was, at a given point, considerably exaggerated. His reduction of historicism to teleology, his insistence on the validity of Marxism's abstract categories vis-à-vis their articulation to concrete traditions, his lack of comprehension of Gramsci's thought, go exactly in the opposite direction to what I have intended to do in the last few years. But in the case of Althusser I think a good deal of my later works can be seen as a radicalization of many themes already hinted at in *For Marx* (much more than in *Reading Capital*). I think that the sudden disappearance of the Althusserian school can be explained, to a great degree, by two factors: in the first place because it had little time to mature intellectually in a post-Marxist direction — the '68 wave created a new historical climate that turned obsolete all that analytical-interpretative elucubration around Marx's holy texts; but in the second place — and this is linked with what I said before — it is also necessary to remember that the Althusserian project was conceived as an attempt at an internal theoretical renewal of the French Communist Party — a project that gradually lost significance in the seventies.

At any rate, as far as I am concerned, the deconstruction of Marxist tradition, not its mere abandonment, is what proves important. The loss of collective memory is not something to be overjoyed about. It is always an impoverishment and a traumatic fact. One only thinks *from* a tradition. Of course, the relation with tradition should not be one of submission and repetition, but of transformation and critique. One must construct one's discourse as *difference* in relation to that tradition and this implies at the same time continuities and discontinuities. If a tradition ceases to be the cultural terrain where creativity and the inscription of new problems take place, and becomes instead a hindrance to that creativity and that inscription, it will gradually and silently be abandoned. Because any tradition may die. In that sense Marxism's destiny as an intellectual tradition is clear: it will either be inscribed as a historical, partial and limited moment within a wider historical line, that of the radical tradition of the West, or it will be taken over by the boy scouts of the small Trotskyist sects who will continue to repeat a totally obsolete language — and thus nobody will remember Marxism in twenty years' time.

Strategies: *If we may follow up on this line of inquiry for a moment — it seems clear that your theoretical position in some way reflects the concrete and practical developments in 'radical' politics in the post-1968 climate of Western democracies. Not only does one perceive an awareness in your work of the importance of those struggles associated with women's rights, gay rights, nuclear disarmament, and the ecology, but one also senses the 'presence' in your text of those 'anti-capitalist' movements (e.g., the Autonomy movement in Italy) that were inspired by Marx, but were antagonistic to conventional Marxist discourses and practices. How have these and other political developments affected your present theoretical position?*

EL: In the sense that they created the historical and political terrain that allowed me to deepen certain intuitions which up to then I had only been able to base on my Argentinian experience. The 1960s in Argentina had been a period of fast disintegration of the social fabric. After the 1966 coup d'état there was a proliferation of new antagonisms and a rapid politicization of social relations. All I tried to think theoretically later – the dispersal of subject positions, the hegemonic recomposition of fragmented identities, the reconstitution of social identifies through the political imaginary – all that is something I learnt in those years in the course of practical activism. It was evident to all of us that a narrowly classist approach was insufficient. The roots of my post-Marxism date back to that time. Well, in these circumstances the 1968 mobilizations in France, Germany and the USA seemed to confirm those intuitions and made it possible to place them in a wider political and historical terrain. Later on, already in Europe, the study of the new social movements you are referring to enabled me to advance theoretically in the direction you know through *Hegemony and Socialist Strategy*. In that sense an important role was played by my collaboration with Chantal Mouffe, who made very important contributions to the problematic we were trying to elaborate together. (The formulation of politics in terms of radical democracy, which appears in the last part of the book, is basically her contribution.)

Strategies: *In the first two chapters of* Hegemony and Socialist Strategy, *you and Chantal Mouffe construct a genealogy of the concept of hegemony as it developed out of the Marxist tradition since the Second International. In this narrative, the most striking feature is your argument that, even for Gramsci, the 'new political logic' of hegemony could not be theorized because of the dominance of essentialist categories. What are the inherent discursive limitations of the Marxist tradition?*

EL: More than about an inherent discursive limitation of the Marxist tradition I would speak about limitations that Marxism shares with the ensemble of the nineteenth-century sociological tradition. The main limitation in this respect is the 'objectivism' in the comprehension of social relations, which is ultimately reduced to the 'metaphysics of presence' which is implicit in sociological categories – that is, the assumption that society may be understood as an objective and coherent ensemble from foundations or laws of movement that are conceptually graspable. Against this, the perspective we hold affirms the *constitutive* and *primordial* character of negativity. All social order, as a consequence, can only affirm itself insofar as it represses a 'constitutive outside' which negates it – which amounts to saying that social order never succeeds in entirely constituting itself as an objective order. It is in that sense that we have sustained the *revelatory* character of antagonism: what is shown in antagonism is the *ultimate* impossibility of social objectivity. Now Marxism constituted itself as an essentially objectivist conception, as an assertion of the rationality of the real, in the best Hegelian tradition. The radically *coherent* history constituted by the development of productive forces and their combination with various types of production relations is a history without 'outside'.

Of course, from the beginning this history had to postulate a supplement not easy to integrate into its categories: this supplement is class struggle — that is, the element of negativity and antagonism. If history is an objective process, negativity cannot occupy any place in it; on the other hand, without negativity there is neither theory nor revolutionary action. Class struggle thus plays in Marxist theory the role of what Derrida has called a hymen: the theory both requires it and makes it impossible. But we do not have to regret this inconsistency: it is thanks to it that there has been a *history* of Marxism. And this history has consisted in the progressive erosion of the main body of the theory on the part of that supplement which cannot be integrated. What is positive and retrievable in Marxism is the set of categories — hegemony, in the first place — that it elaborated in the course of its distancing from its originary objectivism. As regards the latter, it is necessary to relegate it where it belongs: the museum of antiquities.

Strategies: *While you argue quite convincingly for the problem of the 'double void' in Marxism from the Second International onwards, you never sufficiently deal with Marx's theory itself. Given this omission, the inevitable comment from Marxist quarters would be that although you have shown the necessity of going beyond Marxism, you have not shown the necessity of going beyond Marx. We need only look to the historical and political texts of Marx* — The Civil War in France, The 18th Brumaire of Louis Bonaparte, *even* The Critique of the Gotha Programme — *to see a theoretical opening for a 'logic of the contingent', discussions of the materiality of ideology, etc. Thus, it would seem that your argument might lead one not to become post-Marxist, but rather to study Marx more thoroughly, to become more Marxist. How would you respond to this type of comment?*

EL: By saying that the conclusion is highly optimistic. It is true that in our book we have dealt with Marx's work only marginally, the reason being that the trajectory of Marxism we put forward there, as from the Second International, is conceived not as a 'general' history but as a genealogy of the concept of hegemony. But it would doubtless be wrong to assume that Plekhanov or Kautsky, who devoted a considerable part of their lives to the study of Marx's work — and who were certainly not hacks — have simply misread Marx. Finally, the one who said that the most advanced countries show those which are less so the mirror of their own future, or the one who wrote the Preface to the *Contribution to the Critique of Political Economy* is not an economistic commentator of the Second International, but Marx himself. That such a duality between the 'rational and objective' history — grounded on the contradiction between productive forces and relations of production — and a history dominated by negativity and contingency — grounded, consequently, on the constitutive character of class struggle — can be traced back to the work of Marx himself is something of which I am well aware. And it is evident that it is in the political and historical writings that the second moment naturally tends to become more visible. I have never said that Marx's work should be abandoned *en bloc* but deconstructed, which is very different. But precisely because that duality dominates the ensemble of Marx's work, and because what we are trying to do today is to eliminate it by asserting the primary and constitutive character of antagonism, this involves adopting a post-Marxist position and not becoming 'more Marxist' as you say. It is necessary to put an end to the tendency to transvest our ideas, presenting them as if they belonged to Marx, and proclaiming *urbi et orbi* every ten years that one has discovered the 'true' Marx. Somewhere in his writings Paul M. Sweezy says, and very sensibly at that, that instead of attempting to discover what Marx meant to say, he will make the simplifying assumption that he meant to say what he actually said.

Strategies: *In chapter three of* Hegemony, *you attempt to fill in the theoretical space left open by your deconstruction of Marxism. Central to this theoretical reconstruction is the introduction of the notion of the 'impossibility of the social', and the concepts of 'articulation' and 'antagonism'. What exactly is meant by each of these terms or concepts, and how do they provide a basis for theorizing the new political logic of hegemony?*

EL: The three concepts are interrelated. By 'impossibility of the social' I understand what I referred to before: the assertion of the ultimate impossibility of all 'objectivity'. Something is objective insofar as its 'being' is present and fully constituted. From this perspective things 'are' something determinate, social relations 'are' — and in that sense they are endowed with objectivity. Now in our practical life we never experience 'objectivity' in that way: the sense of many things escapes us, the 'war of interpretations' introduces ambiguities and doubts about the being of objects, and society presents itself, to a great degree, not as an objective, harmonic order, but as an ensemble of divergent forces which do not seem to obey any unified or unifying logic. How can this experience of the failure of objectivity be made compatible with the affirmation of an ultimate objectivity of the real? Metaphysical thought — and sociological thought, which is but its extension — respond by opting for the reaffirmation of the objectivity of the real and for the reduction of their failures to a problem of incorrect or insufficient apprehension — that is, to a problem of *knowledge*. There is a 'being' of objects — and of history and society among them — that constitutes its ultimate reality and that remains there, waiting to be discovered. In the 'war of interpretations', what is at stake is not the construction of the object, but its correct apprehension; society's irrationality is mere appearance for, behind its phenomenal forms, a deeper rationality is always at work. In that sense, the progress of knowledge is the discovery of a gradually deeper stratum of objectivity, but objectivity as such is not a point at issue.

This is the point where our approach differs (and not only ours: it is but the continuation of a multiple intellectual tradition which becomes manifest, for example, in a philosophy such as Nietzsche's). The moment of failure of objectivity is, for us, the 'constitutive outside' of the latter. The movement towards deeper strata does not reveal higher forms of objectivity but a gradually more radical contingency. The being of objects is, therefore, radically historical, and 'objectivity' is a social construction. It is in this sense that society does not 'exist' insofar as objectivity, as a system of differences that establishes the being of entities, always shows the traces of its ultimate arbitrariness and only exists in the pragmatic — and as a consequence always incomplete — movement of its affirmation.

The radical contingency of the social shows itself, as we have stated, in the experience of antagonism. If the force that antagonizes me negates my identity, the maintenance of that identity depends on the result of a struggle; and if the outcome of that struggle is not warranted by any a priori law of history, in that case *all* identity has a contingent character. Now, if, as we have shown, antagonism is the 'constitutive outside' that accompanies the affirmation of all identity, in that case all social practice will be, in one of its dimensions, *articulatory*. By articulation we understand the creation of something new out of a dispersion of elements. If society had an ultimate objectivity, then social practices, even the most innovative ones, would be essentially repetitive: they would only be the explicitation or reiteration of something that was there from the beginning. And this applies, of course, to all teleology: if the 'for itself' was not *already* contained in the 'in itself', the transition from one to the other would not be teleological. But if contingency penetrates all identity and consequently limits all objectivity, in that case there is no objectivity that may constitute an 'origin': the moment of creation is radical — *creatio ex nihilo* — and no social practice, not even the most humble acts of our everyday life, are entirely repetitive. 'Articulation', in that sense, is the primary ontological level of the constitution of the real.

And this shows why the category of 'hegemony' is something like the starting point of a 'post-Marxist' discourse within Marxism. Because Marxism was well rooted in the traditional metaphysics of the West, it was a philosophy of history. The dénouement of history was the result of '*objective* laws' which could be rationally grasped and which were independent of the will and consciousness of the agents. The Stalinist conception of the 'objective sense' of actions is but the coarse expression and the *reductio ad absurdum* of something that was implicit in Marx's theoretical project. But 'hegemony' means something very different: it means the contingent articulation of elements around certain social configurations — historical blocs — that cannot be predetermined by any philosophy of history and that is essentially linked to the concrete struggles of social agents. By *concrete* I mean *specific*, in all their humble individuality and materiality, not insofar as they incarnate the dream of intellectuals about a 'universal class'. Post-Marxism is, in this sense, a radicalization of those subversive effects of the essentialist discourse that were implicit from the beginning in the logic of hegemony.

Strategies: *If we were to look again at your early studies, it is clear that you were influenced by Althusser. In your essays on fascism and populism, for instance, you argue for the importance of Althusser's conception of ideology, especially the notion of 'ideological interpellation', for understanding the specificity of these social phenomena. What is interesting is the way in which these formulations bear a close resemblance to your notion of 'discourse' in* Hegemony and Socialist Strategy. *What are the defining characteristics of your notion of discourse, and in what way does it differ from Althusser's concept of ideology? More generally, how does your notion avoid the status of an essentialist category?*

EL: The concept of discourse in *Hegemony and Socialist Strategy* is in no way connected with the category of 'ideology' as it was formulated by

Althusser. To be more precise: while the concept of ideology was the terrain where Althusser started to *recognize* some of the problems that have become central in our approach, he could not radicalize them beyond a certain point, as his analytical terrain was limited by the straitjacket of the base/superstructure distinction. This already establishes a clear line of demarcation between the two perspectives. For Althusser, ideology, despite all the recognition of its 'materiality', is a superstructure, a regional category of the social whole — an essentially topographical concept, therefore. For us, 'discourse' is not a topographical concept, but the horizon of the constitution of any object. Economic activity is, consequently, as discursive as political or aesthetic ideas. To produce an object, for instance, is to establish a system of relations between raw materials, tools, etc., which is not simply given by the mere existential materiality of the intervening elements. The primary and constitutive character of the discursive is, therefore, the condition of any practice. And it is at this point where the fundamental watershed takes place. Confronted with the discursive character of all social practices, we can follow two courses (a) conceive those practical-discursive forms as manifestations of a deeper objectivity that constitutes its ultimate reality (the cunning of Reason in Hegel, the development and neutrality of productive forces in Marx); or (b) consider that those practical-discursive structures do not conceal any deeper objectivity that transcends them, and, at the same time, explains them, but that they are forms *without mystery*, pragmatic attempts to subsume the 'real' into the frame of a symbolic objectivity that will always be overflown in the end. The first solution only has a sense within the frame of traditional metaphysics, which, insofar as it asserted the radical capacity of the concept of grasping the real, was essentially idealistic. The second solution, on the contrary, implies stating that between the real and the concept there is an insurmountable asymmetry and that the real, therefore, will only show itself in the distortion of conceptual. This path, which is, in my view, the path of a correctly understood materialism, involves asserting the discursive character of all objectivity; if the real were transparent to the concept, then there would be no possible distinction between the objectivity of the conceptual and the objectivity of the real, and the discursive would be the neutral medium of presentation of that objectivity to consciousness. But if objectivity is discursive, if an object *qua object* constitutes itself as an object of discourse, in that case there will always be an 'outside', an ungraspable margin that limits and distorts the 'objective', and which is, precisely, the real.

This, I hope, clears up why a category like that of 'ideology', in its traditional sense, has no room in our theoretical perspective. All topography supposes a space within which the distinction between regions and levels takes place; this implies, therefore, a closure of the social whole, which is what allows it to be grasped as an intelligible structure and which assigns precise identities to its regions and levels. But if all objectivity is systematically overflown by a constitutive outside, any form of unity, articulation and hierarchization that may exist between the various regions and levels will be the result of a contingent and pragmatic *construction*, and not an essential connection that can be recognized. In that sense, it is impossible to determine a priori that something is the 'superstructure' of anything else. The concept of ideology can, nevertheless, be maintained, even in the sense of 'false consciousness', if by the latter we understand that illusion of 'closure' which is the imaginary horizon that accompanies the constitution of all objectivity. This also shows why our concept of 'discourse' does not have the status of an essentialist category: because it is precisely the concept which, by asserting the presence of the 'constitutive outside' which accompanies the institution of all identity, points to the limitation and contingency of all essence. Finally, let me point out that the concept of 'interpellation' is the phenomenon of 'identification' which Freud described at various points of his work, especially in *Group Psychology*. In its Lacanian reformulation, it presupposes the centrality of the category of 'lack'. In my own analyses, the important issue is also the reconstitution of shattered political identities through new forms of identification. The limits of the symbolic are, therefore, the limitations that the social finds to constitute itself fully as such. But in the Althusserian formulation – with all its implicit Spinozanism – the central point is the production of the 'subject effect' as an internal moment of the process of reproduction of the social whole. Instead of seeing in 'identification' an ambiguous process that shows the limits of objectivity, the former becomes precisely the opposite: an internal requirement of objectivity in the process of its self-constitution (in Spinozan terms, the subject is substance).

Strategies: *In your final chapter, you argue that what underlies political struggles for radical democracy is the 'democratic imaginary'. There are a number of questions that arise from the use of this concept: first, does not this symbolic discourse become an essentialist category in your narrative of the history of radical democracy? Secondly, it seems as if your characterization of the origin of the democratic imaginary in the French Revolution might be open to the charge of Western-centrism. Do*

*you see this democratic discourse as universal? If so, why? And, if not, what imagin-
ary functions for non-Westerm societies?*

EL: No, the democratic imaginary is the opposite of any form of essentialism. To affirm the essence of something consists in affirming its *positive identity*. And the *positive identity* of something, insofar as all identity is
relational, consists in showing its *differences* from other identities. It is
only insofar as the lord *is different* from the bondsman that his identity as
lord is constituted. But in the case of the democratic imaginary what
happens is different: what is affirmed are not *positive* and *differential*
identities but, on the contrary, the *equivalence* between them. The democratic imaginary does not constitute itself on the level of the (differential)
positivity of the social, but as a transgression and subversion of it. Consequently, there is no essentialist assertion involved. A society is democratic, not insofar as it postulates the validity of a certain type of social
organization and of certain values vis-à-vis others, but insofar as it
refuses to give its own organization and its own values the status of a
fundamentum inconcussum. There is democracy as long as there exists the
possibility of an unlimited questioning; but this amounts to saying that
democracy is not a *system* of values and a *system* of social organization, but
a certain inflection, a certain 'weakening' of the type of validity attribut-
able to any organization and any value. You must notice that there is no
scepticism here; 'weakening' the foundation of values and forms of organization also means widening the area of the strategic games that it is
possible to play, and therefore, widening the field of freedom.
    This leads me to your second question. The universality of values of
the French Revolution lies not in having proposed a certain type of *social
order* grounded on the rights of man and citizen, but in the fact that these
rights are conceived as those of an abstract universality that can expand
in the most varied directions. To affirm the rights of the people to their
self-determination presupposes the legitimacy of the discourses of
equality in the international sphere, and these are not 'natural' discourses,
but they have conditions of possibility and a specific genesis. That is why
I think it is illegitimate to oppose the 'universality' of Western values to
the specificity inherent in the various cultures and national traditions, for
asserting the legitimacy of the latter in terms different from those of an
unrestricted xenophobia involves accepting the validity of discourses –
for example, the rights of nations to self-determination – which can
only be put forward in 'universalist' terms.
    The problem of 'ethnocentrism' thus presents itself as considerably

more complex than in the past. On the one hand, there is a 'universaliza-tion' of history and political experience that is irreversible. Economic, technological, and cultural interdependence between nations means that all identity, even the most nationalistic or regionalistic, has to be constructed as specificity or alternative in a terrain that is international and that is penetrated, to a great extent, by 'universalist' values and trends. The assertion of a national, regional or cultural identity in terms of simple withdrawal or segregated existence is nowadays simply absurd. But on the other hand, that same pluridimensionality of the world we live in implies that, for instance, the link between capitalist productive techniques and the socio-cultural complexes where they were originally developed is not necessary, that there may be absolutely original forms of articulation that construct new collective identities on the basis of hegemonizing various technological, juridical, and scientific elements on the part of very different national-cultural complexes. That there has been throughout the last centuries a 'Westernization' of the world through a technological, economic and cultural revolution that started in Europe is an obvious enough fact; that those transformations are intrinsi-cally Western and that other peoples can only oppose a purely external and defensive resistance by way of defence of their national and cultural identity, seems to me essentially false and reactionary. The true ethno-centrism does not lie in asserting that the 'universalization' of values, techniques, scientific control of the environment, etc., is an irreversible process, but in sustaining that this process is linked by an essential bond, immanent to the 'ethnia of the West'.

Strategies: *One of the more salient topics in recent critical literature is that of post-modernism. Do you consider the topic an important one? And if so, how would you define this constellation of discourses and practices? Also, in what way do you feel your own theory is linked to the logic of postmodernity?*

EL: The debate around postmodernity has embraced an ensemble of loosely integrated themes, and not all of them are relevant to our theor-etico-political project. There is, however, a central aspect common to the various so-called postmodern approaches to which our theoretical perspective is certainly related, and that is what we may call a critique of the fundamentalism of the emancipatory projects of modernity. From my point of view this does not involve an abandonment of the human or political values of the project of the Enlightenment, but a different modulation of its themes. Those that for modernity were absolute essences have now become contingent and pragmatic constructions. The beginning of postmodernity can, in that sense, be conceived as the achievement of a multiple awareness: epistemological awareness, insofar as scientific progress appears as a succession of paradigms whose transformation and replacement is not grounded on any algorithmic certainty; ethical awareness, insofar as the defence and assertion of values is grounded on argumentative movements (conversational movements, according to Rorty), which do not lead back to any absolute foundation; political awareness, insofar as historical achievements appear as the product of hegemonic and contingent — and as such, always reversible — articulations and not as the result of immanent laws of history. The possibilities of practical construction from the present are enriched as a direct consequence of the dwindling of epistemological ambitions. We are going into a world that is more aware than at any other time in the past of its dangers and the vulnerability of its values but which, for that same reason, does not feel limited in its possibilities by any fatality of history. We no longer regard ourselves as the successive incarnations of the absolute spirit — Science, Class, Party — but as the poor men and women who think and act in a present which is always transient and limited; but that same limitation is the condition of our strength: we can be ourselves and regard ourselves as the constructors of the world only insofar as the gods have died. There is no longer a Logos, external to us, whose message we have to decipher inside the interstices of an opaque world.

Strategies: *Since you have described hegemony as a field of articulatory practices and antagonisms grouped around various nodal points, it would seem that cultural struggles would become an extremely important area in your theory. Yet you seem to concentrate in your examples of democratic struggles on explicitly 'political' struggles. What place do you see for the struggle within, for example, the arts? In particular, what about the role of mass cultural forms?*

EL: Yes, you are right. The field of cultural struggles has a fundamental role in the construction of political identities. Hegemony is not a type of articulation limited to the field of politics in its narrow sense, but it involves the construction of a new culture — and that affects all the levels where human beings shape their identity and their relations with the world (sexuality, the construction of the private, forms of entertainment, aesthetic pleasure, etc.). Conceived in this way, hegemony is not, of course, hegemony of a party or of a subject, but of a vast ensemble of different operations and interventions that crystallize, however, in a certain configuration — in what Foucault calls a *dispositif*. And in an era when mass media play a capital role in the shaping of cultural identities, all hegemonic offensives must include, as one of its central elements a strategy concerning them.

Let me go back at this point, apropos of cultural strategies, to certain aspects related to the question of postmodernity. The aesthetic dimension — the dimension of desire that is fulfilled in the aesthetic experience — is fundamental in the configuration of a world. Plato had already understood this: beauty is for him the splendour of truth. And his 'aesthetic' project consisted in showing, behind the imperfections of the world of sensible experience, the forms or paradigms that made up their essence. There is a very clear mechanism of identification here: Platonic aesthetic experience lies in this passage from limitation, from imperfection, to that which is conceived as pure or essential form. But this essential form is also the universal, and if in aesthetic experience the individual *identifies her- or himself* with the universal, identity is achieved through repetition — of what is in me identical with other individuals.

I think this is important for the subject we are speaking about, given that the culture of the left has been constructed in a similar way. It has been, to a large extent, a culture of the elimination of specificities, of the search of that which, behind the latter, was regarded as the universal. Behind the various concrete working classes was *the* working class, whose historical destiny was established outside all specificity; the 1917 revolution was not a *Russian* revolution, but a general paradigm of revolutionary action; the activist had to reproduce in his or her behaviour all the imitative automatisms of a 'cadre'. As in many other things, Gramsci represents, in this respect, an exception and a new beginning that had few followers. Well I think that the main task of a new culture — of a postmodern culture, if you like — is to transform the forms of identification and construction of subjectivity that exist in our civilization. It is necessary to pass from cultural forms constructed as a search for the universal in the contingent, to others that go in a diametrically opposite direction: that is, that attempt to show the essential contingency of all universality, that construct the beauty of the specific, of the unrepeatable, of what transgresses the norm. We must reduce the world to its 'human scale'. From Freud we know that this is not an impossible task, that the *desire* from which this venture, or rather this constellation of cultural ventures, can be started is present there, distorting the essentialist tidiness of our world. It is necessary to pass from a culture centred on the absolute — that therefore denies the dignity of the specific — to a culture of systematic irreverence. 'Genealogy', 'deconstruction', and other similar strategies are ways of questioning the dignity of the 'presence', of the 'origins', of the form.

Strategies: *We would like to ask you a question on both the role of poststructuralism in your own work and about the politics of poststructuralism in general. It is clear in your recent book that there are close affinities between some of your ideas and those of poststructuralists (in particular, Foucault and Derrida). However, poststructuralists have long been accused of promoting views of language, history, and so forth, that are implicitly nihilistic and apolitical; or if political, they have been interpreted as either anarchistic or even authoritarian. While it is hard to believe that all of these charges are true, it does raise questions about the politics of poststructuralism. Given your own commitment to radical democracy, what do you see as the political possibilities and limits of poststructuralism (especially deconstruction) as a way of furthering this project?*

EL: In the first place, let us clear up a point: there is nothing that can be called a 'politics of poststructuralism'. The idea that theoretical approaches constitute philosophical 'systems' with an unbroken continuity that goes from metaphysics to politics is an idea of the past, that corresponds to a rationalistic and ultimately idealistic conception of knowledge. At the highest point of Western metaphysics it was asserted, as you know, that 'the truth is the system'. Today we know, on the contrary, that there are no 'systems'; that those that appear as such can only do so at the cost of hiding their discontinuities, of smuggling into their structures all types of pragmatic articulations and non-explicit presuppositions. It is this game of ambiguous connections, not the discovery of underlying systematicities, that constitutes the true terrain of an intellectual history. What the currents that have been called poststructuralist have created is a certain intellectual climate, a certain horizon that makes possible an ensemble of theoretico-discursive operations arising from the intrinsic instability of the signifier/signified relation. The correct question, therefore, is not so much which is *the* politics of poststructuralism, but rather what are the *possibilities* a poststructuralist theoretical perspective opens for the deepening of those political practices that go in the direction of a 'radical democracy'. (And here we should not actually limit ourselves to poststructuralism *sensu stricto*: post-analytical philosophy as from the work of the latter Wittgenstein, the radicalization of the phenomenological project in Heidegger's work, go in an essentially similar direction.)

If we then concentrate not on a so-called — and mythical — essential connection between poststructuralism and radical democracy, but on the possible articulation, on the *possibilities* that poststructuralism opens up to think and deepen the project of a radical democracy, I think we should basically mention four aspects.

Firstly, the possibility of thinking, in all its radicality, the *indeterminate* character of democracy, which has been pointed out in numerous recent discussions, especially in Claude Lefort's works. If in a hierarchical society the differential character of the positions of the agents tends to establish a strict fixation between social signifiers and signifieds, in a democratic society the place of power becomes an empty place. The democratic logic of equality, therefore, in not adhering to any concrete content, tends to become a pure logic of the circulation of signifiers. This logic of the signifier — to use the Lacanian expression — is closely related to the growing politicization of the social, which is the most remarkable feature of democratic societies. But thinking of this democratic indetermination and contingency as constitutive involves questioning the metaphysics of presence, and with that, transforming the poststructuralist critique of the sign into a critique of the supposed closed character of any objectivity.

Secondly, going more strictly into the problem of deconstruction you refer to, the possibility of deconstructing all identity is the condition of asserting its historicity. Deconstructing an identity means showing the 'constitutive outside' that inhabits it — that is, an 'outside' that constitutes that identity, and, at the same time, questions it. But this is nothing other than asserting its contingency — that is, its radical historicity. Now, if something is essentially historical and contingent, this means that it can always be radically questioned. And it also means that, in such a case, there is no source of the social different from people's decisions in the process of the social construction of their own identities and their own existence. If history were the theatre of a process that has been triggered off outside people's contingent decisions — God's will, a fixed world of essential forms, necessary historical laws — this would mean that democracy cannot be radical, as the social would not be constructed politically, but would be the result of an immanent logic of the social, superimposed on, or expressed through all political will. But if the case is the opposite one, then this deconstruction, in showing the contingent character of all identity also shows its political character, and that radical democracy, insofar as it is based on the reactivation of the ultimate character of the social (that is, its political character), beyond its sedimented forms becomes the first historical form of what we might call *post-society*. And please note that with this I am not contraposing the essentialism of an immanent law to the essentialism of a sovereign chooser. The same contingency that is constitutive of all social identity is also constitutive of the subjectivity of the agent. These will *always* be confronted by a partially opaque and hostile society and by a *lack* that will be constitutive of their subjectivity. What I am stating is that these decisions, taken while partially ignoring the circumstances, the consequences and one's own motivation, are the *only* source of the social, and it is through them that the social is constituted. If in the traditional conceptions of a radical democracy the transparency of the social was a condition for full liberation, what I am stating now is the opposite; that it is only insofar as the social is radically contingent — and does not therefore obey any immanent *law* — that the social is on the same scale of agents which are historical, contingent and fallible themselves. True liberation does not therefore consist in projecting oneself towards a moment that would represent the fullness of time, but, on the contrary, in showing the temporal — and consequently transient — character of all fullness.

Thirdly, the systematic weakening of all essentialism paves the way for a retrieval of the radical tradition, including Marxism. Anti-essentialism, as a theoretical perspective, has a genealogy that also passes through the various radical political traditions. In the first chapters of *Hegemony and Socialist Strategy*, we have tried to show how the disaggregation of essentialist paradigms is not simply a critique *of* Marxism but a movement *within* Marxism. The Sorelian conception of myth, for example, is based on a radical anti-essentialism: there is no 'objectivity' *in itself* of the social outside the mythical reconstitution of identities and of the relations that take place through the violent confrontations of groups. And 'hegemony' in Gramsci goes in the same direction: the notion of historical bloc, which replaces in his vision the base/superstructure duality, is entirely grounded on pragmatic and contingent hegemonic articulations. We should therefore start off from the new awareness that allows us practices such as deconstruction or 'language games' to trace a political genealogy of the present. And this genealogy is the construction of a *tradition*, in the strictest sense of the term. The danger that haunts us now is not so much the continuity of the essentialist discourses of classical Marxism, which have been totally shattered and in which nobody believes, but their non-replacement by any alternative discourse — that is, the collapse of *all* radical tradition. But true loyalty to a tradition lies in recognizing in the past its transient and historical character, its difference with the present (a difference that involves continuities and discontinuities at the same time), and not in transforming the past into a model and an origin to which one tries to *reduce* the present through more and more absurd and less credible theoretical manipulations.

Fourthly and finally, there is the question of the relation between the 'superhard' — the transcendentality, the apodicticity, the algorithmic character of decisions — and democracy. An apodictic decision, or, in a more general sense, a decision that claims for itself an incontestable 'rationality', is incompatible with a plurality of points of view. If the decision is based on a reasoning of an apodictic character it is not a decision at all: a rationality that transcends me has *already* decided for me, and my only role is that of *recognizing* that decision and the consequences that unfold from it. This is why all the forms of radical rationalism are just a step away from totalitarianism. But if, on the contrary, it is shown that there is no ultimate rational foundation of the social, what follows is not a total arbitrariness, but the weakened rationality inherent in an argumentative structure grounded on the *verisimilitude* of its conclusions — in what Aristotle called *phronesis*. And this argumentative structure, precisely because it is not based on an apodictic rationality, is eminently pluralistic. Society only possesses the relative rationality — values, forms of calculation, argumentative sequences — that it collectively constructed as *tradition* and that can therefore always be transformed and contested. But in that sense the expansion of the areas of the social that depend less on an ultimate rational foundation, and that are based, therefore, on a communitary construction, is a condition of the radicalization of democracy. Practices such as that of deconstruction, or Wittgenstein's language games, accomplish the function of increasing our awareness of the socially constructed character of our world and open up the possibility of a foundation through collective decisions of what was before conceived as established forever by God, or by Reason, or by Human Nature — all those equivalent names that function by placing the destiny of human beings beyond the reach of their decisions.

Strategies: *In the Marxist tradition, there has been substantial debate concerning the role and place of the intellectual in furthering human liberation. Given your conception of hegemony, it seems clear that the intellectual can play neither the role assigned to it by those theorists of the Second International, nor that which Gramsci signified by the term 'organic intellectual'. What is the role of the intellectual in furthering the project of radical democracy?*

EL: I don't know why you say that our conception is incompatible with the Gramscian idea of the 'organic intellectual'. On the contrary, I think that it is, to a great degree, an extension of the latter. The 'organic intellectual' in Gramscian thought depends on a double extension of the function of intellectual activity, which is perfectly compatible with our approach. In the first place, the 'intellectual' is not for Gramsci a segregated social group but that which establishes the organic unity of a set of activities, which, left to their own resources, would remain fragmented and dispersed. A union organizer, in that sense, would be an intellectual, since s/he welds into an organic whole activities such as the channelling and representation of workers' demands, the forms of negotiation with employer organizations and with the state, the cultural activities of the unions, etc. The intellectual function is, as a consequence, the practice of articulation. And the important thing is to see that this practice is recognized as more and more important insofar as there is a decline of the image of an historical evolution dominated by the necessary movements of the infrastructure. I would like to remind you that Kautsky himself had to admit that socialism does not arise spontaneously from the working class, but has to be introduced into it by the radical intellectuals; that is to say, the unity between *Endziel* and immediate demands depends on the mediation of an organic ideology – that is, on an articulation. And the Gramscian conception of the intellectual is, in that sense, but the extension of this articulatory function to growing areas of social life. Well what, then, is our approach but an anti-essentialist conception of the social whole based on the category of articulation?

In the second place, it is precisely because the 'organic ideologies' in Gramsci play this central role that the intellectual function extends immeasurably with respect to what it had been in the various debates of classical Marxism: if a historical bloc cements its organic unity only through an ideology that founds *the unity* between base and superstructure, then hegemonic articulations are not a secondary or marginal effect but the ontological level itself of the constitution of the social. And please note that there is no 'superstructuralism' or 'idealism' here: economic practices themselves depend on social relations constructed through hegemonic articulations. Well what is this moment of 'intellectual' mediation that gives its relational character to all collective practice and identity, but that which in our works we have called 'discourse'?

In both respects our work can therefore be seen as an extension of Gramsci's work. With this I can answer your last question about the role of the intellectual in furthering the project of radical democracy. The function of the intellectual – or rather, the intellectual function, since the latter does not concentrate on a caste – consists in the invention of languages. If the unity of the historical blocs is given by 'organic ideologies' that articulate into new projects fragmented and dispersed social elements, the production of those ideologies is the intellectual function *par excellence*. Note that those ideologies are not constructed as 'utopias' proposed to society; they are inseparable from the collective practices through which social articulation takes place. They are therefore eminently practical and pragmatic – which does not exclude *certain* utopian or mythical (in the Sorelian sense) aspects, which is given by their dimension of *horizon*.

It is to this latter dimension that I would like to refer, with some final remarks. If intellectuals – now regarded in their traditional restricted sense – are to play a positive role in the construction of the new forms of civilization that we are starting to glimpse, and are not to be responsible for a new *trahison des clercs*, they must construct the conditions of their own dissolution as a caste. That is, we should have fewer 'great intellectuals' and more 'organic intellectuals'. The idea of the 'great intellectual' was linked to a function of *recognition*; the task of the intellectual was inseparably bound to the classical concept of *truth*. Because it was thought that there was an intrinsic truth in things that *revealed itself* to certain particular forms of access that were the private hunting ground of the intellectual. This is why the latter received the set of privileges that established him as a member of a caste. But if we consider today that all truth is relative to a discursive formation, that all choice between discourses is only possible on the basis of constructing new discourses, 'truth' is essentially pragmatic and in that sense becomes democratic. It is because we know today that the social is articulation and discourse that the intellectual dimension cannot be conceived as *recognition* but as construction; but it is for that same reason that intellectual activity cannot be the exclusive hunting ground of an elite of great intellectuals: it arises from all points of the social fabric. If the 'system' was the characteristic expression, the highest point and the ideal of knowledge of the traditional intellectual, the new forms of thought are not only asystematic but essentially *anti*-systematic: they are constructed out of the recognition of their contingency and historicity. But in this general movement of the death of gods, ideologies of salvation and high priests of the intellect, aren't we allowing each man and woman to fully assume the responsibility of their own contingency and their own destiny?

Theory, Democracy and Socialism

1. Intellectual Biography

RB: *You have recently described the approach you have developed with Chantal Mouffe as post-Marxist, that is to say you have emphasized the Marxist background against which your work has developed. Since there are many 'Marxisms' it would be interesting to know which Marxist tradition influenced your initial formation. Were you a militant in any Marxist organization?*

EL: I should first of all tell you that my initial political trajectory was very different from that of Chantal Mouffe. While Chantal's Marxist formation took place in the mid-1960s in Paris – she attended Althusser's seminar for several years and was involved in the seminar which gave birth to *Reading Capital* – I only came to Europe in 1969 and my own Marxist upbringing was in Argentina.

In 1958 I joined the Partido Socialista Argentino (PSA, Argentinian Socialist Party) which split into a number of factions at the start of the 1960s. At that time I was very active in the student movement. I was president of the students' union at the Philosophy and Arts Faculty and was also representative of the left faction of the student movement on the Senate of the University of Buenos Aires. In 1963 I became a member of the Partido Socialista de la Izquierda Nacional (PSIN, Socialist Party of

This interview was organized specially for this volume and was conducted in May 1988 by Robin Blackburn, editor of *New Left Review*; Peter Dews, lecturer in the Department of Philosophy at the University of Essex and a member of the *New Left Review* editorial board; and Anna-Marie Smith, who is preparing a Ph.D. thesis on 'The Politics of Otherness' with the Department of Government at the University of Essex, under the supervision of Ernesto Laclau.

the National Left — one of the splinter groups of the PSA) led by Jorge Abelardo Ramos. The latter was a powerful intellectual and political influence at the time and was irresistibly attractive for young people, like myself, who came from a liberal intellectual background. From 1963–68 I was a member of the PSIN's political leadership and for several years I was editor of *Lucha Obrera* (Workers' Struggle), the party's weekly journal. I also served for a number of periods as editor of the party's theoretical journal, *Izquierda Nacional* (National Left).

It's difficult to explain the cleavages in left-wing politics in Argentina at that time to someone in Britain. Suffice it to say that the crucial dividing line, which was intuitively perceived by all activists, moved away from classical alternatives like reform/revolution and Stalinism/ Trotskyism; it was rather a question of the attitude adopted towards Peronism. In 1946 Perón had been elected president by a heterogeneous coalition of the most diverse kind, ranging from the extreme left to the extreme right and based on the support of the army and the trade unions. This alliance was opposed by another coalition of the traditional parties which went from the Conservatives to the Communists. This situation led to a permanent political division in Argentina, and by the 1960s it had crystallized into two opposite poles on the left: a 'liberal' ('abstract' and 'internationalist') left, on the one hand, and a 'national' left, on the other. Broadly speaking, the latter was 'third worldist' in outlook and its programme was aimed at deepening the national revolution begun by Perón. To make matters even more complicated for a European audience, the Communist Party took the first position and the majority of the Trotskyist groups the second.

The party I belonged to had a clearly nationalist orientation and its strategy was a reformulation of the so-called 'permanent revolution'. The anti-imperialist revolution had started under bourgeois banners with Peronism and this limitation had led to the defeat of 1955 (the fall of Perón): but it was only through a socialist hegemonization of the democratic banners that it could achieve stability and make up for lost ground. Our position was that socialists would only be able to consolidate and advance the anti-imperialist revolution if they could achieve a hegemonic position in the democratic struggles. This was opposed by those who regarded Peronism as fascist and by the small ultra-leftist sects. The former called for a 'popular front' with the liberal oligarchy, while the latter asserted that the collapse of populism meant that democratic struggles had lost all validity, and that an all-out fight for socialism was required.

Our strategy, then, was far from uncommon in that it combined a political sensitivity towards national, democratic and anti-imperialist goals with the continuity of our dependence on class reductionism. As to the first component, I have nothing to add; my point of view continues to a large extent to be similar to what it was then. This experience of the ambiguity of democratic banners — what we would today call 'floating signifiers' — as well as the recognition of the centrality of the categories of 'articulation' and 'hegemony', shaped my conception of politics from then on. When I began to read Gramsci and Althusser systematically in the mid-1960s (especially the Althusser of *For Marx*, the Althusser of overdetermination), my interpretation was essentially political and non-dogmatic because I could relate it directly to my own Argentinian experience.

But there were obviously limits. Our whole strategy was based on a view which drew a rigid connection between political parties and social classes. If, in the national revolution, Peronism represented the national bourgeoisie, our party was to represent working class interests, that is to say a socialist alternative. Behind all this, then, was a Marxism of the most elemental kind, with its class-based conception of social agents and politics as being simply a level of representation of interests. It was therefore not surprising that our party never became anything more than an agitation group with a certain degree of ideological influence.

RB: *Your first published article in English was on Argentina while Latin American variants of populism formed the subject of a key transitional essay published in* Politics and Ideology in Marxist Theory. *Did an experience like that of Peronism lead you to challenge schematic and reductionist accounts of popular ideology?*

EL: Certainly. And it wasn't just my experience but that of a whole generation. Elaborating on what I was saying earlier, let me explain the situation we faced in the 1960s.

Following the oligarchical counter-revolution and the fall of Peronist rule in 1955, the regime which came to power announced the permanent installation of a liberal democratic system (some idea of just how democratic the new regime was can be gained from the fact that it was based on the political proscription of more than 50 per cent of the population). I was almost twenty then and as a typical member of the liberal middle classes I had supported the coup. But disillusionment with the new regime was not long in coming, as its aggressive monetarism, the dismantling of protection for the national economy and the huge transfer of resources to the landowning sector through devaluations, soon became apparent. There was also the regressive nature of the regime's social policies. As a result, in less than a year the whole of the student movement and the middle classes had turned against the new government and this created a propitious climate for the Frondizi alternative in 1958.

At the same time, the Peronist resistance was beginning to organize in the working class districts of Buenos Aires, raising doubts in the minds of radicalized liberal students like ourselves. It was in the following years that I learnt my first lesson in 'hegemony'. The situation was clear. If the liberal oligarchic regime had been successful in absorbing the democratic demands of the masses in a 'transformist' way – in creating what I would call a 'system of differences', to use my current terminology – then Peronism would have receded as a set of anti-establishment symbols to the horizon of the social, as happened with the symbols of Mazzini and Garibaldi in Italy at the beginning of the century. But the very opposite happened: the transformist capacity of the system had as much substance as the 'wild ass's skin' and began to shrink inexorably. As a result, the 'floating signifiers' of Peronist popular-nationalism came to hegemonize an increasing number of social demands and to define the course of the great mass struggles of the 1960s and 1970s. To try and tie those symbols down in class terms was obviously absurd. Instead, the construction of any class identity had to take place on the previous ground that had already been prepared by the circulation of those symbols. Gareth Stedman Jones's comments on the emergence of class identity in the case of British Chartism are something that my experience of the Argentinian working class fully confirms.

That's the reason why I didn't have to wait to read post-structuralist texts to understand what a 'hinge', 'hymen', 'floating signifier' or the 'metaphysics of presence' were: I'd already learnt this through my practical experience as a political activist in Buenos Aires. So when today I read *Of Grammatology*, *S/Z*, or the *Écrits* of Lacan, the examples which always spring to mind are not from philosophical or literary texts; they are from a discussion in an Argentinian trade union, a clash of opposing slogans at a demonstration, or a debate during a party congress. Throughout his life Joyce returned to his native experience in Dublin; for me it is those years of political struggle in the Argentina of the 1960s that come to mind as a point of reference and comparison.

RB: *Do you feel that there is any kinship between your own distinctive intellectual concerns, as they have developed from the mid-1970s, and those of such noted Argentinian sociologists as Gino Germani and Torcuato di Tella? The analysis of populism has, for example, played a key role in their thought too.*

EL: No, I don't think there has been any discernible kinship. Germani was my professor of sociology at the University of Buenos Aires and for a brief period I was his research assistant. But right from the beginning my intellectual orientation was not only different but to a great extent the very opposite. For Germani 'populism' stems from the uneven integration of the masses into the political system and the delays in the transition from a traditional to an industrial society. His whole model of interpretation is based on an extremely simplistic version of the 'modernization and development' theories. For me, on the other hand, 'populism' is the permanent expression of the fact that, in the final instance, a society always fails in its efforts to constitute itself as an objective order. As can be seen, my vision of populism and Germani's are more or less diametrically opposite. Di Tella has advanced a much more complex and nuanced vision of populism than Germani, but his approach is basically taxonomical and thus very distant from my theoretical interests.

RB: *Your influential critique of André Gunder Frank, published in the early 1970s, seems to be couched in orthodox Marxist terms and to chide Frank with a species of revisionism. Do you still identify with this critique? Is it not at odds with the subsequent rejection of the Marxist framework?*

EL: I'd like to make two initial points. In the first place, I do identify myself with all the basic features of my critique of Frank, even though there are a few concepts such as 'mode of production' that I would now formulate differently. In the second place, I haven't rejected Marxism. Something very different has occurred. It's Marxism that has broken up and I believe I'm holding on to its best fragments. Would you see the process of disintegration of the Hegelian school following the death of Hegel as a 'rejection of Hegelianism'? Each of the post-Hegelian currents — including Marx — prolonged certain aspects of Hegelianism and abandoned others. That is what blew up the systematic character of Hegel's philosophy. But it was a question of a rather more subtle process of continuity and discontinuity than is evoked by the idea of simple 'rejection'. We're in a similar position with Marxism now.

Getting to the crux of your question, I never saw my critique of Frank as a defence of Marxist orthodoxy, but as an operation in conceptual precision. In personal conversations and in writing, Frank himself has reproached me for having asserted that he purported to be a Marxist when he had never ever claimed to be one. Frank is probably right on that score, but that does not affect the basic thread of my critique which is that, whether Marxist or not, Frank's conception of capitalism is devoid of any conceptual substance, in spite of the value and interest of many of his insights.

The aim of my critique of Frank, and also of other works, can be characterized as a double movement. The first was to carry through a rigorous recovery of the conceptual content of Marxist categories, avoiding any theoretical inflation or metaphorical application. For example, in the case you refer to, giving a strict definition of capitalism as a mode of production and not simply as production for the market. Having thoroughly defined those categories in conceptual terms, the second movement was to determine the forms of their articulation within wider totalities.

But from the point of view of the nature of these articulatory logics, my position was never an orthodox Marxist one. Orthodox Marxism can be developed on the basis of two strategies. The first is what we could call a 'popular' strategy: through a succession of convenient metonymies, a term like capitalism, which is used to designate a mode of production, is extended to refer to the societies in which capitalism takes place. One thus talks about 'capitalist society', the 'capitalist state' etc. The second strategy is more 'scientific' and consists of presenting forms of the base/ superstructure model of varying degrees of sophistication. Neither of these solutions ever convinced me.

In the same article criticizing Frank, I put forward the idea that articulation between modes of production took place in wider totalities represented by 'economic systems'. This was criticized at the time as being non-Marxist, as I recalled in a recent interview. For me it was clear right from the start that the articulation between 'mode of production' and political and ideological 'levels' could not be seen in terms of the endogenous logic of the mode of production. As you can see, it was the very act of rigorously limiting certain categories to their Marxist content which enabled me to move towards a theory of articulation and thus of social totalities; and it became increasingly clear that this theory was post-Marxist. All these distinctions were not that clear in my mind in the early 1970s, of course. But since then the development of my thought would seem to me to be more a maturation of certain original intuitions than a break with previous work.

RB: *At what point did you conclude that it was unwise to attempt to save the Marxist explanatory system by qualifications and heterodox developments of the sort that you detect in some Western Marxist thinkers? Did directly political developments play an important part in this move beyond Marxist categories?*

EL: Without any doubt. But before answering this question I'd like to re-emphasize the fact that this 'moving beyond' does not involve either a 'rejection' or an 'abandonment', if you mean simply discarding things. Any intellectual tradition worthy of respect can never believe it has reached a definitive settlement of accounts with the past. Have we really finished once and for all with Aristotle, Kant or Hegel? Of course not, and even less so with Marx. Intellectual history is a recurring movement which from time to time reinvents the past, thus giving birth to a continuous process of renewal and rediscovery. In this sense, it is the realm of the 'neo-' and 'post-' '-isms'. To transcend is at the same time to recover.

There are two fundamental reasons why Chantal Mouffe and myself have termed our approach post-Marxist. The first is theoretical. As you can realize, it would have been very easy for us to present our approach as a new interpretation of what Marx 'really wanted to say'. But apart from being an essentially dishonest intellectual practice, this is totally unnecessary today — we're more fortunate than Galileo in that there is no Inquisition there to threaten us. (There are of course a few hacks who set themselves up as an Inquisition, but they are not important.) The danger about passing something off as Marxist when one is clearly going further is that Marxism ends up being totally unrecognizable. It loses all theoretical specificity in that positions and viewpoints become stilted, thus making any kind of dialogue impossible. Marx, Kautsky, Otto Bauer or Rosa Luxemburg mean much more to us if we know ourselves to be different from them, if we can think out the specificity of our situation and our differences when coming to grips with their texts.

The second reason for speaking of 'post-Marxism' is clearly political. Couldn't the same be done with Marxism as with other ideologies such as 'liberalism', 'conservatism' or 'socialism' — in other words, treat it as a vague term of political reference, whose content, boundaries and scope should be redefined at each juncture? Couldn't there just be 'family resemblances' between different 'Marxisms'? I have no objection in principle to this kind of operation which would turn Marxism into a floating signifier and thus give way to completely new language games (on the condition, of course, that this operation is recognized for what it is and does not claim to discover the *real* meaning of Marx's work). But all the reasons for turning Marxism into a frontier with which to determine the limits of our whole political identity seem to me, in the Year of the Lord of 1988, to be essentially reactionary.

Let's just examine a few. The first is to regard Marxism as a theory of social development which is fundamentally different from other radical traditions, based on the gradual simplification of class structure under capitalism and on the increasing centrality of the working class. For reasons you're well aware of, this vision of contemporary society and its conflicts is, in my opinion, totally incorrect. The second is to see the world as fundamentally divided between capitalism and socialism, with Marxism the doctrine of the latter. It should be obvious to everyone at this stage that this fossilized conception of the international world – an ideological by-product of the Cold War – is completely reactionary and hinders any understanding of the nature of both advanced capitalist and Eastern bloc societies. In this era of glasnost and perestroika to insist on Marxism being a 'state truth' can only reinforce the worst, and most profoundly anti-democratic, habits of left-wing thought. The final reason is to create a division between 'ideology' and 'science' and make Marxism coincide with the latter. Can there really be any doubt that such obsolete positivism can only have a retardatory effect on the left's thinking? To repeat, I can't see the slightest *political* use in making Marxism the frontier with which to define a political identity. On the contrary, it can only reinforce theoretical conservatism and encourage political conformity.

2. Theory

A-MS: *In* Hegemony and Socialist Strategy *you and Chantal Mouffe begin by examining the genealogy of the concept of hegemony. Using the genealogical method, you construct a 'history of the present', rather than a supposedly 'objective' history of the Second International. From your perspective, the political thought of Gramsci and that of Sorel constitute a radical break with the paradigm of classical Marxism in so far as the logic of necessity is displaced by the logic of contingency in their work. However, while Gramsci retains a teleological conception of identity, as the hegemonic agent can only be a fundamental class constituted outside political struggles, Sorel asserts that the formation of identity is an entirely contingent process, based solely on social division, frontier and myth. To what extent and in what manner do you believe that these two thinkers 'speak to us' in what might be called our 'postmodern' present?*

EL: The genealogy of what you call our 'postmodern' present consists of showing the discursive surfaces on which the 'metaphysics of presence' was eroding the idea of a ground which is not undermined by negativity or difference. To put it another way: those discursive surfaces on which the political character of the social is revealed. There's an ambiguity here, and I would say it's been there since the very prehistory of Marxism, that is, since Hegelian thought. On the one hand, Hegelianism makes negativity the constitutive element of all identity – the impossibility of any identity to simply 'rest' on itself. But, on the other hand, this movement of the negative does not involve any contingency, since it finds its final identity in the system. This double characteristic is passed on to Marxism, with all its ambiguities and internal possibilities.

In *Hegemony* we presented the dialectics of this internal movement of Marxism: from the social conception of politics dominating the economicism of the Second International to the radical politicization of the social which takes place in the work of Sorel and Gramsci (within the limits that you point out). Our post-modernism, then, is just another step forward in a movement dominating the whole history of Marxism. There are, of course, those for whom Marxism fulfils an edifying function: that of assuring us that the 'inevitable laws of history' do guarantee a promised land, in spite of present misfortunes. For them it is clearly just a question of seeing the indefinite empirical recurrence in the present of the abstract categories of a theory: while for us, the only thing that is absolute is the present, not theory. This means that theory will become contaminated, deformed and eventually destroyed by a reality that transcends it. But it is precisely in this destruction that all thought finds its most dignified form, or, if you like, meets its 'destiny'. As Engels has already said: everything that exists deserves to perish. Sorel and Gramsci were the thinkers who most insisted on bringing down Marxist theories to concrete social contexts. This involves their 'weakening' and historicization at the same time. That way they both 'speak' to our present.

A-MS: *In what I think is a key passage in* Hegemony *Chantal Mouffe and yourself identify an ambiguity in the Leninist conception of hegemony. This conception has, at one and the same time, an authoritarian dimension and a democratic dimension; using Derrida's somewhat problematic terminology, we could say that the logic of the hymen is in operation here. You state that a rigid separation between the leaders and the led emerges where a vanguard clings to the conception of itself as a true embodiment of the 'objective interests of the working class', immune from all political contingencies in terms of its fundamental identity and destiny, while the increasingly divided 'masses' appear to need more and more 'leadership'. The legitimacy of this leadership is based not on its practical capacities but on its supposedly privileged epistemological position; the vanguard 'knows' the underlying movement of history. Would it be overstating the case to say that the logic of necessity constitutes the conditions for the legitimization of authoritarian conceptions of leadership and vanguardist practice, while conversely, the logic of the contingent constitutes the conditions in which increasingly democratic conceptions and practices become conceivable?*

EL: I think you're absolutely right and I'd like to take advantage of your question to clear up a few misunderstandings. In our book we asserted that the authoritarian tendency of Leninist politics can be found in its imbrication between science and politics. But a couple of precisions must be made here. This doesn't mean any kind of irrationalism on our part or that we are advocating an anti-scientific position. Any social practice is the *locus* of specialized knowledge and there's obviously no question of putting that in doubt. But the idea of 'science', as propounded in the vision of 'scientific socialism', is of a very different kind: it postulates a monolithic and unified understanding of the whole of the social process. And if this knowledge of the whole is based on the ontologically privileged position of a single class — which, in turn, is transformed into the epistemologically privileged position of a single political leadership — then all the conditions exist for things to take an authoritarian direction. This idea of a mastery of the social, based on a single nodal point of privileged knowledge, is not exclusive to Leninism, of course: it is also shared by various forms of technocracy, for example.

The second precision is that hegemony, in its Gramscian sense, leads to the opposite result. If the partial forms of unification represented by hegemonic articulations are radically contingent, all partial knowledge will be articulated on the horizon of an essentially open communitary space. As you can see, the 'fundamentalists' constantly confuse the issue. For them, the negation of *the* Science — of the possibility of rationally grasping a supposed foundation of the social — is tantamount to defending an irrationalist position. But that is obviously not the issue. The real issue is to assert the contingent, partial nature of all knowledge.

I think that the swing towards pragmatism that has taken place in several currents of contemporary thought allows a much more consistent defence of democratic alternatives than in the past.

A-MS: *The linguistic conception of identity, in which all identities are relational and there are no positive terms, opens up the possibility of a radical ontology, that is an ontology beyond the classical category of non-relational substance. With the centrality of discourse in your work, it is clear that you have been influenced by the structuralist and post-structuralist developments of this radical ontology. Chantal Mouffe and yourself also make specific use of linguistic terms. For example, you assert that the hegemonic relation is a metonymical relation. Could you discuss the connection between post-structuralist 'ontology' and hegemony, and explain what you mean by this latter assertion?*

EL: How should the specific logic of hegemony be conceived? Think of the working class hegemonization of national-popular symbols and — on the basis of this articulation — constructing a new 'collective will'. If the unity between class identity and national-popular identity is something more than the aggregate of two heterogeneous elements; on the contrary, if this aggregate gives way to a new collective will, formed by the organic unity of both elements, then the condition *sine qua non* is for the identity of both components to be relational (for instance, the identity of the national-popular might change depending on the class component with which it is articulated). Thus, if identities are exclusively relational, then all relation must, by definition, be internal. The concept of an 'external relation' has always seemed inconsistent to me. Indeed, that is exactly what the Saussurian conception of language is about: asserting that linguistic identities are exclusively relational. Moreover, to assert the discursive nature of the social is to show that the merely differential (non-positive) nature of identities is not a feature of the linguistic in the strict sense, but is the very principle involved in the constitution of all social identity. You can see how this is crucial when it comes to under- standing the specific logic of hegemony: if the class and national-popular identities were non-relational positive identities, the idea of an organic unity between them would be senseless; but if they are merely relational identities, then their diverse forms of articulation will transform both. This is what gives the category of 'historic bloc' (the organic unity of what was considered by classical Marxism to be a division between base and superstructure) its primary, ontological character.

Post-structuralism allows the whole gamut of logics stemming from the unclosed nature of relational totalities to be thought out. A 'constitutive outside' exists which both deforms them and is the condition for their constitution at the same time. There is therefore a constant widening of hegemony's limits. All articulation is partial and precarious. That is what gives every collective identity – classes among others – their radically transient and contingent nature. Why is a process of hegemonic relation essentially metonymic? Simply because the contiguous relations between different social elements undergo a process of constant transgression. For example, if a trade union in a certain neighbourhood begins to promote struggles like self-defence against police violence or solidarity with gay rights, or puts forward demands over working class consumption levels, it will become a hegemonic centre. None of these struggles *necessarily* stems from trade union activities in the strict sense of the term; but the fact that it is the trade union movement – rather than other local forces – which becomes the centre around which those struggles can unite means that the latter take on a 'working class' character on the basis of a series of *displacements*. It is because the limits between social identities are not fixed in advance, but are constantly redefined on the basis of hegemonic displacements, that collective wills are radically unstable and contingent. As you can see, post-structuralist categories such as 'floating signifiers', 'deconstruction' and 'hinges', are crucial to understanding the operation of the hegemonic logic – which for me is the very logic of the construction of the social.

A-MS: *With Wittgenstein's critique of the 'hardness of the rule', we have a subversion of the fixity of meaning similar to that in Barthes and Derrida. Wittgenstein points out that because a rule cannot pre-exist the moment of its application (since to follow a rule, I need a rule to apply the rule, and I need another rule to apply this rule, etc.), a rule is only the instance of its use and each instance of its usage modifies the rule as such. Elsewhere you have briefly referred to an analogy between the dissemination of meaning in Wittgenstein and Gramsci's hegemonic conception of the working class. Could you expand on this theme?*

EL: Certainly. The idea of 'applying' a rule assumes a rigid division between the rule as such and the instance of its application. If a rule is merely 'applied', this means that individual instances are of strictly equal value as far as the rule is concerned. In this sense, the notion of 'application', in the strict sense of the term, presupposed a fundamentally repetitive process. But as you point out, if for Wittgenstein every instance of a rule's use *modifies* the rule as such, it cannot be said that a rule is being *ap-*

plied, but that it is being constantly constructed and reconstructed. In other words, between an abstract rule and the instance of its use in a particular context, it is not a relationship of *application* that occurs, but a relationship of *articulation*. And accordingly, if the different instances of an articulated structure have merely differential identities, it can only mean that in two separate instances the rule is in fact a different one, in spite of its 'family resemblances'.

Gramsci's position is similar. If the 'working class' establishes its identity as part of the specific hegemonic articulations forming a concrete historic bloc, the working classes of the different social formations will establish their identity as a set of collective wills of a very different kind, in spite of its 'family resemblances'. Thus, the 'working class' collective identities do not find their point of unity in a 'working class' essence that is common to them all. The link between the different working classes cannot therefore be conceived in terms of a proximate genus/specific difference distinction. In this way you can see the difference between a hegemonic and an essentialist, reductionist conception of politics. In the latter, it's a case of discovering a common foundation behind the diverse range of individual moments, thus reducing them to the repetition of something similar. As the inimitable Tony Benn said in an interview with Bea Campbell, there is no difference between Thatcherism and previous Conservative governments because they're all capitalist. In a hegemonic conception of politics, on the other hand, it's a question of seeing how an individual instance 'transforms' the essence and modifies it by articulating it to a different 'organic' whole. So while the first conception is abstract and metaphysical, the second is radically historical.

PD: *At many points in your work, you reject any notion of the subject as a 'unified and unifying essence', and suggest that the subject is 'constructed through language, as partial and metaphorical incorporation into a symbolic order' (Hegemony, p. 126). There are a number of difficulties with this formulation, however. At one point in Hegemony, you refer to politics as a 'practice of creation, reproduction and transformation of social relations' (Hegemony, p. 153). Yet, who or what is it which creates and transforms in this way? There appears to be a tension in your work between a view of the subject as totally passively constructed, which seems ultimately to derive from Althusser, and your commitment to the democratic and egalitarian components of liberalism, which would surely be nonsensical without some conception of human individuals as — at least potentially — self-determining agents. However, even if one puts most emphasis on the second half of your formulation ('as partial and metaphorical incorporation into a symbolic order'), which is more Lacanian in its resonance, problems are still generated for your commitment to liberal themes. For Lacan's scepticism about modern individualism, and what he sees as the attendant instrumentalization of social relations, is well known. Can one adopt as much of Lacanian theory as you do, yet still remain committed to 'the liberty of the individual to fulfil his or her human capacities' (Hegemony, p. 184)?*

EL: Let's begin with the first part of your question. At no time have I taken the position that the subject is passively constructed by structures, since the very logic of hegemony as the primary terrain for the constitution of subjectivity presupposes a lack at the very heart of structures — that is, the impossibility for them to achieve a full self-identity. The lack is precisely the *locus* of the subject, whose relation with the structures takes place through various processes of *identification* (in the psychoanalytical sense). In the Althusserian theory of interpellation — which I used in my first works — there is without doubt the Spinozan notion of a 'subject effect', which merely stems from the logic of the structures. This leaves out the fact that interpellation is the terrain for the production of discourse, and that in order to 'produce' subjects successfully, the latter must identify with it. The Althusserian emphasis on interpellation as a functional mechanism in social reproduction does not leave enough space to study the construction of subjects from the point of view of the individuals receiving those interpellations. The category of lack is thus absent. But the emphasis in my work, even my first works, is different. Interpellation is conceived as part of an open, contingent, hegemonic-articulatory process which can in no sense be confused with Spinozan 'eternity'.

That's why I'd like to question the exclusive alternatives you put forward — subjectivity as the passive effect of structures or subjectivity as self-determination. This alternative remains entirely within the context of the most traditional conception of identity and fullness: either there is a fullness of the structures — in which case the subject is a passive effect of the latter — or it is one of subjectivity as a positive identity. But I'm making a different point, which is that structures can never acquire the fullness of a closed system *because* the subject is essentially lack. That's why the question of *who* or *what* transforms social relations is not pertinent. It's not a question of 'someone' or 'something' producing an effect of transformation or articulation, as if its identity was somehow previous to this effect. Rather, the production of the effect is part of the construction of the identity of the agent producing it. It is because the lack is constitutive that the production of an effect constructs the identity of the agent generating it. For example, one cannot ask *who* the agent of hegemony is, but *how* someone becomes the subject through hegemonic articulation instead.

Linking this with the political issues you refer to, the affirmation of the egalitarian and democratic dimensions of liberalism does not mean affirming the self-determination of the subject — in other words, his or her full identity as an individual irrespective of any social determination. It means affirming and recognizing the essential indetermination of the social and therefore involves questioning all fullness. When we speak of the 'liberty of the individual to fulfil his or her human capacities', we do not understand that as removing all the barriers preventing the expression of a (potentially) fully constituted identity. Rather, we see it as extending the areas of freedom and creativity by showing the radical contingency of all values and objectivity — and thus of all subjectivity, as well. A free society is not one where a social order has been established that is better adapted to human nature, but one which is more aware of the contingency and historicity of any order. Whether Lacan would have agreed with these formulations or not is a matter for speculation, but I have no doubt whatsoever that they are perfectly compatible with those Lacanian theoretical categories we have incorporated into our work.

PD: *The concept of 'suture', derived from Lacanian theory, plays an important role in your critique of totalizing conceptions of the social. In Lacan's work, it is precisely the subject as 'lack of being' (which is not to say simply nothing) which both demands and prevents the success of suture. What happens to this Lacanian conception of the subject, when the concept of suture is transferred to the social terrain? What is it that both demands and inhibits suture at the social level?*

EL: It is the presence of antagonism as witness to the ultimate impossibility of social objectivity being constituted. But antagonism is only possible because the subject *already* is that 'lack of being' you refer to. As you know, the incorporation of the individual into the symbolic order occurs through *identifications*. The individual is not simply an identity within the structure but is transformed by it into a subject, and this requires acts of identification. It is because the subject is that 'lack of being', which demands and prevents suture, that antagonism is possible. In our book we have shown how antagonism cannot be reduced to either contradiction or to real opposition insofar as neither of the two types involves any 'lack of being' – objectivity is uncontestedly dominant and no 'suture' is required. But because the social never manages to constitute itself as an objective order and the 'symbolic' is always disrupted by the 'real', the dimension of suture cannot be eradicated. Take the hegemonic relation: it would be inconceivable without the 'lack' inherent to it. It is because the bourgeoisie *could not* take up 'its' democratic tasks that Russian social democracy felt they had to become those of the working class, etc. It is this act of 'taking up' a task from the outside, of completing it and filling the gap which has opened up in the 'objectivity' of the structure, that characterizes the hegemonic relation. And it is because that lack is ineradicable that hegemony is, in the final instance, an inherent dimension to all social practice. The myth of the transparent society is simply that of a society devoid of hegemony and suture in which there is nothing 'real' to challenge the objectivity of the symbolic order.

A-MS: *Derrida states that although he is critical of the 'metaphysics of presence' which has its highest point in phenomenology, he retains Husserl's phenomenological reduction because it opens up the possibility of a radical reflection on the 'sense' of the object, moving beyond the empiricist attempt to grasp the thing itself. In your reply to Norman Geras, Chantal Mouffe and yourself indirectly refer to the phenomenological term, 'conditions of possibility'. What is the significance of Husserl's phenomenology in terms of your work? Do you accept Derrida's position vis-à-vis Husserl? To what extent has it been necessary for you to radicalize phenomenological categories such as 'horizon'?*

EL: There have been three main sources of inspiration for our work: phenomenology, post-analytical philosophy and the various currents of thought that can be generally characterized as post-structuralist. As far as phenomenology is concerned, yes, our approach is very close to Derrida's critique of Husserl. Getting to the points you refer to, the transition from the given to its conditions of possibility is a crucial presupposition in our conception of the political nature of the social. Take the dialectic in Husserl between sedimentation and reactivation. It is only when 'the given' is not accepted as such, but referred back to the original act leading to its constitution, that the sense of that 'given' is reactived. It is through the desedimentation of all identity that its prospective being is fully revealed. This dialectic, which is at the very heart of Husserlian thought, has been fundamental to our approach to the question of the nature of the social. Our whole analysis goes against an objectivist conception and presupposes the reduction of 'fact' to 'sense', and of 'the given' to its conditions of possibility. This 'sense' is not a fixed transcendental horizon, but appears as essentially historic and contingent. And this contingency presupposes negativity as its absolute *limit* — that is, a negativity which cannot be dialecticized, and which is not domesticated by the internal movement of the concept. To show the original sense of something, then, is to question its obviousness, to refer it back to the absolute act of its institution. And that act is *absolutely* institutional if the possibilities of other acts existed, if the institutional decision was *ultimately* arbitrary and contingent. Only then can we speak of contingency, since it is at that point alone that we are faced with an essence which does not involve its existence. Thus, the ground on which this absolute act of institution takes place is what we call *politics*, and the desedimentation of the social consists of revealing its political essence. This passage through negativity is not, of course, present in Husserl. Nevertheless, it is only possible by 'radicalizing', as you put it, the Husserlian concept of reactivation. A similar point can be made about the category of 'horizon'. In our approach to the problem, the *visibility* of any horizon presupposes negativity. The coherence of a certain totality, that which separates it from what is beyond it, is not grounded on any positive principle of internal organization, but on the relationship formed by a body of dissimilar elements with something negating them all. You are already aware of the importance this theoretical approach has had for our analysis of the construction of political identities.

PD: *The strong implication of your work is that modern societies are becoming more pluralistic, fluid and open, as the 'democratic revolution' penetrates into ever more areas of social life. There is obviously a convergence between this emphasis, and certain themes of the 'post-modernity' debate — the decline of grand narratives, the multiplication of language games, etc. However, there is another interpretation of postmodernity, perhaps most forcefully stated by Baudrillard, in which the decline of the referent, and the erosion of all authenticity results in a social world of repetition and vacancy, in which antagonism becomes simply another simulation. Are you convinced that this line of thought has nothing to recommend it (Marcuse and Adorno would be antecedents in some respects) and that the pluralism and antagonism which you perceive are genuine? This raises a further question: presumably genuine antagonism must be systematically dysfunctional, yet you reject any attempt to understand the social as a cohesive system as rationalistic. How then is genuine antagonism to be discerned?*

EL: Let me start with the last point. I have never asserted that any attempt to understand the social as a cohesive system is rationalistic. If I had, the very conception of the social as a system of differences — a view that I have always held — would be totally devoid of meaning. My position is very different: it is that the systemic element, its cohesiveness, does not have the status of a ground; that is to say, it does not have the self-transparency of a principle by which the whole of the social, including social antagonisms could be rendered intelligible. But insofar as a social 'order' does exist, there is cohesivity and a system. What happens is that there is always a constitutive outside which deforms and threatens the 'system' and this very fact means that the latter can only have the status of a *hegemonic* attempt at articulation, not of a ground. As we have said repeatedly, if the social fails in its attempt to constitute itself as an objective order, it merely exists as an *effort* to carry out that constitution. While replying to a question by Anna-Marie a moment ago, I remembered that, for Wittgenstein the application of a rule always involves a moment of articulation and that the rule is therefore transformed by its various applications. As you can see, while that doesn't mean depriving social practices of *all* their coherence, it nevertheless does mean denying that this coherence can have the rationalistic status of a superhard 'transcendentality'. Thus, it is precisely antagonism which constitutes the 'outside' inherent to every system of rules. There is therefore nothing inconsistent in my position.

As to Baudrillard, I do not share the view that moving into a certain post-modernity entails the erosion of all authenticity, and thus produces a 'social world of repetition and vacancy'. Contrary to the assumptions of the thinkers of the Frankfurt School, the decline of the 'major actors', such as the working class of classical socialism, has not led to a decrease in social struggles or the predominance of a one-dimensional man, but to a proliferation of new antagonisms. The transformation of the contemporary social scene — with the great mobilizations of 1968 as its epicentre — clearly bears witness to this.

I would go even further: I would say that, far from experiencing a process of depoliticization and uniformization, what we are seeing now is a much deeper politicization of social relations than ever before. Take the ambiguity of the emancipatory discourses as they developed from the eighteenth century onwards. There can be no doubt that they all — Marxism included — enabled the mobilization of immense historical forces in the struggle against traditional forms of subordination. But on the other hand, they advocated the *global* emancipation of humanity, and it was in this totalizing aspiration that the limits of the politicization they made possible lay. For any *human* emancipation must be carried out by the concrete, historical actor with all its limitations; it can therefore only be conceived insofar as this actor is able to transcend its own specificity and embody the objective interests and meaning of the whole of mankind. A radical ontological imbalance thus exists between the demands of the various groups and categories of human beings: while the demands of certain groups are legitimized by the latter's personification of the global objective interests of mankind, there are other demands which, however just, are doomed because they are located outside the universality of the historical process. Think of Kautsky's assertion that social democracy should not represent the interests of all the oppressed but only of the working class, since it was this class that was the incarnation of historical progress. The level of politicization that can be achieved in such emancipatory discourse, then, has a dual limitation: firstly, politics is not a moment of radical *construction*, as it is limited to expressing the objective movement which transcends it; and secondly, this movement determines the legitimacy and objective meaning of the various demands in terms of its own logic. As a result, the various demands have to justify themselves before a historical tribunal that is external to them.

What we're seeing now, I believe, is not the entry into a world of repetition and vacancy, but the disintegration of that dimension of globality inherent to classical emancipatory discourses. It is not the specific demands of the emancipatory projects formulated since the Enlightenment which have gone into crisis; it is the idea that the whole of those demands constituted a unified whole and would be realized in a single foundational act by a privileged agent of historical change. This has a number of important consequences that are worth spelling out.

Firstly, it is not this or that 'privileged agent' which is being questioned, but the category of 'privileged agent' itself. Marcuse offers an alternative between an increasingly one-dimensional society and the emergence of a new privileged agent — students, women, the Third World masses — that would substitute a working class which is increasingly integrated into the system. But this still operates within the classical framework, since the only possibility of change is still considered an act of global emancipation (revolution and its equivalents). Indeed, it is not just that emancipatory demands are diversifying and deepening in today's world but also that the notion of their essential unification around an act of global rupture is fading. This does not mean that the various demands are doomed to isolation and fragmentation, but rather that their forms of overdetermination and partial unification will stem from hegemonic articulations forming part of 'historic blocs' or 'collective wills', and not from the a priori ontological privilege of a particular class or social group.

The second consequence of this growing 'weakening' of the foundationalist pretensions of emancipatory discourses is that it allows a more democratic vision of social demands. People do not now have to justify their demands before a tribunal of history and can directly assert their legitimacy on their own terms. Social struggles can thus be seen as 'wars of interpretations' in which the very meaning of demands is discursively constructed through struggle. The demands of a lesbian group, a neighbours association or a black self-defence group are therefore all situated on the same ontological level as working class demands. In this way the absence of a global emancipation of humanity allows the constant expansion and diversification of concrete 'emancipatory' struggles.

Thirdly, it is precisely this decline in the great myths of emancipation, universality and rationality which is leading to freer societies: where human beings see themselves as the builders and agents of change of their own world, and thus come to realize that they are not tied by the objective necessity of history to any institutions or ways of life – either in the present or in the future. In short, then, I do not believe that the contemporary world can be described in terms of simulation and loss of authenticity, unlike the nostalgics for a 'lost ground'.

PD: *You argue that the concept of 'objective' interests implies 'the idea that social agents have interests of which they are not 'conscious' (see p. 118 above), and conclude that interests are constructed through 'ideological discursive and institutional practices'. But why must interests be either purely constructed or fully conscious? Surely it is possible for individuals and groups to become aware of needs and aspirations of which they were not formerly explicitly aware through a process of self-reflection: how else are we to understand psychoanalysis? This need not imply 'essentialism', since these implicit or unconscious interests can still be socially formed. It is difficulty to see why certain 'constructions' of interests, rather than others, take root, unless they articulate some underlying need. Are you not underestimating the internal complexity of the concept of interests, and indeed of the relation between the conscious and the unconscious?*

EL: I think your question is based on a misunderstanding. When we speak of the 'conscious' in the passage you refer to, it is not in opposition to the 'unconscious' in the psychoanalytical sense, but to an unawareness characterizing 'non-rational' behaviour. What we are criticizing is an attitude laying down what people should do in certain circumstances or what they should prefer on the basis of general, abstract reasoning; the kind of attitude that constructs an 'interest' and then concludes that it is a case of 'non-rational' behaviour or 'false conscience' when people do not fall into line. The psychoanalytical 'unconscious' has no role here. If someone does not make a correct reasoning, this does not mean that it is in their unconscious.

On the other hand, if we take 'conscious' to mean what is understood in the several Freudian topographies, I agree with you entirely that interests are not completely conscious. But for Freud, the 'unconscious' is anything but a 'rational interest' that must be uncovered. As to the complexity of the notion of 'interest', I think we stress this in the paragraph you quote: that the forms of calculation by which an interest is constructed are not automatic and transparent, but occur through a complicated range of discursive, ideological and institutional processes, which give them a rationality that can only be relative.

PD: *In your reply to Norman Geras you clarify your position on idealism and materialism by distinguishing between the 'being' and the 'existence' of an object. However, this very distinction raises a further problem for your attempt to transcend the distinction between the linguistic and the extra-linguistic. For it is clear from your own account that material objects do possess an identity outside of any differential context whereas the same cannot be said for the elements of a linguistic system. How do you account for this discrepancy? A further question follows from this. If the system of physical objects — in the more general sense, nature — exists outside of all discursive contexts why can't it exert a general pressure on human society, for example in terms of the need for material reproduction, which is independent of any specific discursive construal of nature? Why, in general, must all ontological effects be epistemologically mediated? To insist on this seems simply to repeat one of the most characteristic elisions of modern philosophy. Certainly Heidegger, whom you invoke, would not be sympathetic to it.*

EL: As far as the first point is concerned, I don't feel the inconsistency you seem to detect in what I put forward exists. At no time have we asserted that 'material objects do possess an identity outside of any differential context'. For us, 'identity' is equivalent to a 'differential position in a system of relations'; in other words, all identity is discursive. What we have said — and this is very different — is that material objects have an existence independent of any differential context. That's why we have insisted on the historicity of the being of objects, and have deliberately distinguished that being from their mere existence. There is also no inconsistency in sustaining that a discursive structure is composed of some elements which do have material *existence* and others which don't.

As to the second point, we must be clear about what is meant by an ontological effect that is not epistemologically mediated. In the first place, the status of the discursive is not that of an epistemological mediation; its *primary* reference point is not knowledge as a contemplative activity. Its status is like that of Wittgenstein's language games which embrace the whole of social practices, as you know. The primary level of discursive constitution is the practical interrelation with objects. But for reasons we have explained *in extenso*, nature is also as discursive as a poem by Mallarmé, and the pressure it exerts on us always takes place in the discursive field. There's a problem worth clarifying here. Let's suppose that someone sustains that men are obliged to materially reproduce their existence. There is no doubt about that. But does it then follow that such a necessity is independent of any discursive structure? Of course not, because it will always be provided for by means of specific (and thus discursive) relations of production. The supposed 'need' of all societies is always the result of an act of abstraction on our part. This act can be justified on analytical or scientific grounds, but that does not authorize us to hypostasize an abstract identity and endow it with a concrete existence. To do so is to slip into a similar practice to the abstractions of classical political economy which Marx rightly criticized. The 'abstract conditions of any society' are simply that: abstractions. They only exist in the scientific or other discourses creating them: they do not constitute mysterious metaphysical entities that underlie every social relation, dividing it permanently between an abstract essence and a concrete empiricity. However abstract and general 'needs' may be, their articulation will always occur within specific discursive practices. As you can see, this is very different from an 'epistemological mediation'. I merely want to add that if by 'ontological effect' which is not discursively mediated you mean the action of an 'outside' on a specific discursive field, it is not just something I agree with, but is a central feature of our problematic, which is based on asserting the impossibility of a symbolic closure of the social.

PD: *You argue that 'the idea of truth outside all context is simply nonsensical' (see* *p. 105 above**). Yet how does one define a context? Given your own account of the constant re-articulation of elements within a 'general field of discursivity', it would* *appear impossible to define a self-enclosed context (Derrida's work certainly also points in the same direction). This raises the question of your reference to Rorty and American neo-pragmatism, since Rorty notoriously invokes, as the basis of his hermeneutics, a bland homogeneous 'we', whose reference seems to oscillate between, at one extreme, the Western liberal democracies, and at the other, North American professional philosophers. Do you accept this kind of parochialism, as the necessary cost of overcoming foundationalism, or do you believe there is some third alternative?*

EL: What I believe without any doubt is that one thinks from a tradition and that traditions are the context of any truth. How can a context be defined? I know very well that contexts do not have fixed limits and are in a constant process of change and redefinition. But that does not mean that a *certain* structural context does not exist; that one historical bloc, for example, cannot be differentiated from another, with all the limitations that this entails. The argument over the difficulty of defining contexts is one against an essentialist closure of them, but it does not constitute a denial of the category of context as such, and even less a defence of foundationalism. For example, in our book we have tried to define hegemonic formations by emphasizing two moments: on the one hand, the constitution of such formations through the construction of stable systems of differences; and on the other, the moment of instability resulting from the presence of a constitutive outside which constantly transgresses and subverts those systems. What my studies – and those of my students – have shown me is that there is always an element of negativity in the constitution of a discursive field (theoretical fields included). A formation will assume coherence through its opposition to that which denies it.

As to the question of pragmatism, I think it is useful to link it to the logic of hegemony. I have always thought that, in many respects, the Gramscian conception of the hegemonic construction of collective identities comes very close to several positions of American pragmatism. The choice is certainly not between a relativist parochialism and a foundationalist universalism. It is a question of pragmatically constructing a hegemonic centre which articulates a growing range of social discourses and logics around it, and thus gives rise to a relative 'universalism'. The relativity of this universalism breaks with the parochialism vs. foundationalism alternative. Indeed, foundationalism *is* the extreme form of parochialism, since it dogmatically attributes to its point of view the condition of a transparent means through which reality would speak without mediation. Moreover, as you can see, to assert the pragmatic construction of a tradition, of a 'we', is not in any way to determine the *direction* it is to move in. While I generally sympathize with Rorty's epistemological stance, I personally disagree with his political positions to a large extent.

PD: *In your reply to Geras, you define discourse as the 'horizon of the constitution of the being of every object' (p. 105). But this is in fact to attribute to discourse a transcendental status. At the same time, your position would not make sense, unless discourses were empirical processes, susceptible to transformation through political practice, and therefore having conditions of possibility. Which is the basic status of discourse in your work, or is it possible that there is equivocation here?*

EL: No, there isn't any equivocation. The definition you quote is not of 'discourse', but of the 'discursive'. The complete sentence is: 'The discursive is not therefore an object among other objects (although, of course, concrete discourses are), but rather a theoretical horizon.' In other words, the same sentence introduces a distinction which dispels the equivocation you refer to. What is being asserted is that 'the discursive', as the horizon of any object's constitution, cannot generally possess conditions of possibility, whereas the concrete discourses built within that horizon certainly do possess them. Such conditions of possibility are themselves discursive.

PD: *You argue that the working class cannot be considered to have any privileged role in the struggle against capitalism. But this raises the question of your definition of capitalism. If we understand by capitalism a system of production based on wage labour, then surely those who are obliged to sell their labour power may play some distinctive role in its abolition. If this is not the case, then what would your definition of capitalism be?*

EL: To begin with, let's clarify that we have never said that the working class does not have a privileged role in the struggle against capitalism because that role corresponds to some other social agent. What we have said are two things: first, that a privileged role cannot be attributed to the workers a priori in terms of a general theory of transition; and second, that the very concept of 'privileged agent of change' must be questioned. There are many social struggles, the processes of overdetermination are complex, and the identity of the agents of a fundamental political change cannot be read directly from the data of the social structure.

It's nevertheless interesting to note the logical gap that has slipped into your argument. My definition of capitalism is exactly the same as yours: it is a system of production based on wage labour. But as I think I have repeatedly shown, this definition does not necessarily mean that antagonism is *inherent to the relations of production*, which is what you assume in your argument. At several points in this volume, I have backed up the thesis that antagonism is not established *within* capitalist relations of production, but *between* the latter and the identity of the social agents — workers included — outside of them. Thus, if we are dealing with a relationship of exteriority, there are no grounds at all for the role of workers to be privileged a priori over that of other sectors in the anti-capitalist struggle. The dislocations generated by capitalism's uneven and combined development do not only affect workers, but many other sectors of the population as well. This does not mean that workers' organizations cannot play an important hegemonic role in the direction of popular struggles in certain circumstances; but it does mean that this depends on concrete historical conditions and cannot be logically deduced from the mode of production. The Marxism of the Second International was deeply aware of the dislocatory effects of capitalist development; but it believed at the same time that the endogenous logic of capitalism was leading to the simplification of the class structure through proletarianization, the multiplication of dislocatory effects could only increase the political centrality of the proletariat. The dislocatory effects continue today, but the increasing proletarianization has not taken place. A much more complex theory of anti-capitalist struggles than that offered by traditional Marxism is therefore required.

PD: *Would you agree that the distinction, pointed out by Mouzelis, between a 'conceptual framework' and a 'substantive theory', goes a long way towards allaying your suspicions that any comprehensive approach to the understanding of history and society must necessarily be aprioristic and rationalistic?*

EL: Apriorism and rationalism are not linked to a holistic approach out of opposition to one that is atomistic, but to the conception of social identities which perceives full and sutured identities in the latter. An atomistic approach to the social is as essentialist as a holistic one; the first has merely transferred the fullness of the totality's social identities to the elements. That is why we distinguished in *Hegemony* between an essentialism of the totality and an essentialism of the elements. Besides, our vision is to a large extent holistic, since it presupposes that any identity is differential — and thus, any relationship internal — and that the systems of differences are articulated in totalities which are 'historical blocs' or 'hegemonic formations'. But unlike classical sociological holism — Durkheim's, for example, or that of Parsons, to which Mouzelis refers *in extenso* — we do not feel these configurations or social totalities to be self-regulating totalities, but precarious articulations that are always threatened by a 'constitutive outside'. Neither the totality nor the elements therefore ever manage to constitute full identities. It is in this way that a break is made with apriorism and rationalism, not through the unilateralization of any of the terms of an alternative in which both sides share the same logic of the identity.

Moving to Mouzelis's criticism of our book, the problem with his position is that he wants to have his cake and eat it at the same time. He presents what is a theoretical obstacle as the solution to the problem. Take his denial of the presence of a theoretical dualism in Marx's work. Mouzelis recognizes that it contains many mechanistic and deterministic texts, but sustains that there are others — especially his historical writings — in which classes are presented as actors instead of puppets in the process of social change. He concludes: 'What is more important is that Marx's work as a whole provides the *conceptual means* for looking in a theoretically coherent manner at social formations and their overall reproduction/transformation from both an agency and a structural/institutional point of view.' (*New Left Review* 167, p. 122) But this is an entirely dogmatic statement, as Mouzelis does not give a single example from Marx's work of the 'conceptual means' that might enable a logical coherence to be established between these two dimensions. Instead, he limits himself to quoting cases in which either approach predominates. I am fully prepared to admit that both approaches coexist and that is precisely why I speak of dualism in Marxism — including Marx. In order to demonstrate that there is no dualism, something very different from showing the coexistence side by side of the two approaches is needed: it would have to be shown that both are logically articulated in a coherent whole. But Mouzelis does not even make a start at this in his essay. The closest he comes is when he states that 'the prominence of the relations of production in Marx's conceptual scheme is a strong guarantee against technicist-neutralist views of the social' (Mouzelis p. 122). This proves nothing, however, since the relations of production appear *totally* subordinated to the forces of production in Marx's mechanistic writings. As a result, dualism remains unchanged.

I think the real reason Mouzelis does not see the dualism in Marx's work is because the very same dualism underlies the distinction that is central to his own approach — between a subject's practices and institutional structures. Adding heterogeneous elements and concepts is not enough to build a unified theoretical framework; it is the logical articulation between them that must be shown. But if the practices cannot be explained in terms of the structures, or the structures in terms of the practices, what is that if not dualism in the strictest sense of the term? Parsons and Durkheim, on the one hand, and the symbolic interactionists and other related tendencies, on the other, do at least have the virtue of being coherent in their unilateralism. Mouzelis, by contrast, does not wish to give up either side of the alternative, with the result that his discourse is based in no man's land and on the incoherency inherent to all dualism. Our attempt to deal with this alternative has not been based on the unilateralization of the agency at the cost of the structure, as Mouzelis states, but on the elaboration of a unified theoretical framework and language which allow both the agency and the institutions to be conceived within them. It is completely untrue that we have ever stated that social practices occur in an institutional vacuum. Indeed, institutions are fully present in our approach: they are what we have called *systems of differences*. Faced with the affirmation that there are structures on one side and practices on the other, we have asserted that social agents are *partially* internal to the institutions, thus forcing both the notion of 'agency' and 'institution' to be deconstructed. Regarding agency, our conception of the decentred subject means that there is a plurality of subject positions — or differential positions — which are thus internal to institutions. To assert that social practices take place in an institutional vacuum would be to deny the institutional nature of subject positions and to refer their unity back to the subjectivity of the agent itself. That goes right against our whole approach. On the other hand, the agents are not just blind instruments or bearers of structures for the simple reason that the latter do not constitute a closed system, but are riven with antagonisms, threatened by a constitutive outside and merely have a weak or relative form of integration. All this requires constant acts of recreation of the institutional complexes by the agents: that is what constitutes the practice of articulation. It is not the practice of subjects constituted outside any system of differences (institutions), but of subjects constituted by those differences and the fissures or gaps they reveal. In opposition to the postulation of two *separate* metaphysical entities — agents and structures — we suggest the following: (a) that there are merely relative *degrees* of institutionalization of the social, which penetrate and define the subjectivity of the agents themselves; and (b) that the institutions do not constitute closed structural frameworks, but loosely integrated complexes requiring the constant intervention of articulatory practices. As can be seen, what we wish to say by asserting the contingent nature of the social is that there is no institutional structure which is not *ultimately* vulnerable; and not, as Mouzelis has understood, that everything in the field of the social is in a state of permanent flux.

Mouzelis's stance does not help us move a single inch towards the elimination of the dualism between agent and structure. It is also worth adding that, for him, dualism is always resolved by leaning on the side of structures, albeit with a few cosmetic concessions to the agent. Consider the following paragraph: 'It is not difficult to see that the working class movement, however fragmented or disorganized, has greater transformative capacities and therefore better *chances* of playing a leading role in a hegemonic context than, say, the sexual liberation movement. The reason for this has to do less with political initiatives and articulatory practices than with the more central structural position of the working class in capitalist society'. (Mouzelis pp. 115–16) Apart from suggesting that Mouzelis would have a few surprises if he visited San Francisco, we can only conclude that we are back to the crudest form of economism: the classes constituted at the economic level *determine* the hegemonic roles in the political field. Mouzelis's statement regarding working class hegemony is of course false in ninety-nine per cent of cases; but at a theoretical level one could ask: if the structure of the capitalist mode of production *generally* determines things as specific as who is going to constitute a hegemonic sector in particular societies and situations, what role is played by the 'agents' who, according to Mouzelis, are different entities from the structures?

I cannot accept the distinction between 'conceptual framework' and 'substantive theory' either, at least in the way it is formulated by Mouzelis. This is largely for the reasons we gave earlier when discussing Wittgenstein and his conception of 'applying a rule'. Here again, the relevant question is: to what extent do the 'substantive findings' modify the framework – so that a relation of articulation occurs between both – and to what extent is substantive theory an *application sensu stricto* of the conceptual framework? Those who maximize the structural effects of a conceptual framework will be inclined towards the second alternative, of course; but for reasons that are no doubt clear to you, I am inclined towards the first.

3. Politics

RB: *In the classical tradition the goals of the socialist movement have included the bringing about of a classless society, ending exploitation and oppression, asserting human control of anarchic economic forces, ensuring that the 'free development of all is the pre-condition for the free development of each', aiming at an economic reorganization guided by the principle 'to each according to their needs, from each according to their abilities' and so forth. Do such goals remain valid within a post-Marxist perspective? What in your view are the distinctive features of the emancipatory project at the end of the twentieth century? Do they necessitate revisions of fundamental goals or simply to express them in a new form?*

EL: Things certainly have changed and it's important to specify in what ways. In my view, there are three dimensions drastically differentiating a late twentieth century emancipatory socialism from those formulated only a few decades ago. The first is that we would today speak of 'emancipations' rather than 'Emancipation'. While the socialist project was presented as the global emancipation of humanity and the result of a single revolutionary act of institution, such a 'fundamentalist' perspective has today gone into crisis. Any struggle is, by definition, a *partial* struggle — even the violent overthrow of an authoritarian regime — and none can claim to embody the 'global liberation of man'. The second dimension is partly related with the first: if struggles are partial, they nevertheless tend to extend to more and more subject positions, and the articulation between the latter — insofar as it is necessary or convenient, which is not always the case — tends to be more complex. The third dimension could be called the 'de-universalization' of the socialist project. If socialism is part of what we have called the 'democratic revolution', socialist demands can only be articulated to other democratic demands of the masses, and these will vary from country to country. For example, demands in a country subject to colonialist or racist subordination will not be the same as in a West European-style liberal democracy. Classical socialism was essentially universalistic and, in that sense, abstract. I believe its decomposition will lead to a variety of local 'socialisms'.

The initial reaction of many to these transformations has been a disillusion that can easily lead to depoliticization. What Pierre Rosanvallon has termed a 'crisis of representations of the future' has taken place. It will without doubt take a few years to forge new representations of the future and a new perspective on which emancipatory political imaginaries can be reconstructed. Even so, a number of opportunities can already be glimpsed in the current crisis that a new left could take advantage of. Let us mention just a few. The plurality of emancipations obviously opens up the possibility of a more democratic socialism. The notion of the 'global emancipation of humanity' involved a duality between the entity embodying that universality and universality itself. As you know, this leads to the possibility — or reality, in many cases — of all kinds of totalitarian deviations. In contrast, a democratic socialism must construct through its own action the limits and partial character of any power. Let us suppose a revolutionary power has violently overthrown a repressive regime. (I give this example so as not to reduce 'the democratic' to 'reformist politics in a liberal parliamentary regime' not because I disagree with the latter, but because there are historical situations in which it simply does not exist and is not contained in the organizational forms from which the democratization process must start.) There is a whole world of difference as to how the new revolutionary government will be conceived: either it will be total power, embodying the global emancipation of the nation *in all spheres*, or it will be the starting point of a democratization process, in which the different social sectors forge their own forms of organization and representation in order to advance their demands. If it is this second path that is wanted, then the crisis of the globalistic emancipatory project clearly represents a decisive step forward in terms of a political imaginary for the left. It should not be forgotten that a democratic socialism is one which raises the awareness of *all* human beings that they must be the exclusive architects of their own destiny, and that there are no 'laws of history' guaranteeing certain actors privileged functions a priori.

The second dimension is that we are clearly witnessing a proliferation of democratic demands today. This did not occur in the classical socialist project and thus represents an obvious step forward. Finally, the socialist project's loss of universality has a positive dual effect. On the one hand, it has allowed the greatest possible convergence between a plurality of separate democratic demands that a class-based universalism might have aprioristically kept apart. On the other, it has meant that any progress towards a universalization of values does not stem from a rootless cosmopolitanism, but is based on a plurality of national and local emancipatory projects. This is without doubt a slower and more complex process than the one envisaged by the classical 'Internationals', but starts from a broader foundation and is undoubtedly much more democratic in its respect for specificity.

A-MS: *Would you not agree that the categories 'right-wing' and 'left-wing' have become increasingly less productive in terms of political analysis and strategies? That is, have not the meanings of these categories been taken for granted to the extent that they no longer automatically produce distinctions which are basic to the emancipatory project? In HSS Chantal Mouffe and yourself argue that an authoritarian tendency can be found in what are commonly considered 'leftist' movements, parties and governments, as well as on the right. Are you not suggesting that the distinction between authoritarianism versus radical democracy is more productive? Clearly, the point here is not to adopt an agnostic position vis-à-vis the right, but to submit the category 'left' to an interrogation and, indeed, to redefine that category radically as a result of contemporary experience.*

EL: I agree completely. Like any other social reality, the discursive complexes called 'right' and 'left' — and the opposition between them — are historical precipitates of experiences with precise conditions of possibility. In European historical experience, the right-left opposition was the name of a political boundary. The 'productivity' of such a classification, to which you refer, is in direct proportion to the ability of its two poles to become the nucleus around which a great number of social demands revolve. Let us quote two examples of our research group in Essex. Rastafarian discourse, which you are studying, has been shown to be a benchmark of increasing social and political usefulness in Britain over the last decade, while apartheid in South Africa, studied by Aletta Norval, is currently being demonstrated to be of declining productiveness; it is increasingly unable to articulate a coherent discourse of social division.

As far as the European experience is concerned, the left–right distinction — which, as you know, comes from the French Revolution — was a clear political frontier in the first half of the nineteenth century and was, in one way or another, reconstituted on new grounds throughout the whole of the following century. But you are right to state that its political usefulness has done nothing but decline since the period of anti-fascist struggle and Cold War. The reason for this decline is clear. The usefulness of political categories can only be maintained if they manage to constitute polar political imaginaries, and that depends on whether they are seen as the natural surface on which *every* new social and political demand can be inscribed. Their erosion begins when this agglutinative capacity declines and when a range of inscription surfaces emerge that often contradict each other. In the age of Chartist mobilization in Britain or the Commune of Paris, it was not difficult to know where the left was, but with the experience of the new social movements in the contemporary world, the situation is much more complicated. To cite just a few examples. In San Francisco, anyone would think that the presence of strong gay, chicano and black communities would offer all the conditions for the construction of a popular pole. Yet as they all have contradictory demands, that agglutination does not occur. Moving on to the second example, what happens if a factory polluting the environment stirs the local residents into mobilization and the workers side with the factory owners to defend their jobs? The examples could be multiplied *ad nauseam*. Social conflictiveness is so widespread and has taken on such new forms in today's world, that it has more than surpassed the hegemonic capacity of the old left. Hence the decline in Europe of both social democracy and communism as forces able to galvanize the political imaginary. If the Italian Communist Party, the most intelligent and articulate force of the old left, finds such difficulty in adapting to the new times, what is happening to political fossils like the French and Portuguese communist parties comes as no surprise. Their fate is sealed.

But if the old left – with its inveterate class-based politics, its productivism and antiquated statism – is dying everywhere, the creation of a fresh political frontier whose productivity might be the source of a new imaginary, is only in its initial stages. I have little doubt that the popular pole of this new imaginary will revolve around the themes implicit in the concepts of 'democratic revolution' and 'radical and plural democracy'. Such formulas have several virtues, I believe. Firstly, they create a horizon – which is what the imaginary consists of at the end of the day – that enables a whole multitude of social and political demands, including many of the old left, to be equated; demands that have hitherto belonged to separate discursive universes. Secondly, they enable this discourse to be extended to the countries of the Eastern bloc and the efforts of their peoples to free themselves from the yoke of the bureaucratic regimes ruling there. Without a democratic political imaginary to rally the pressure of the masses, all attempts at liberalization will be reduced to timid forms of modernization and rationalization by a bureaucracy that is slightly more broadly based. Finally, the rights of the peoples of the Third World to self-determination and a more just distribution of global wealth can only be strengthened if they are seen as part of a chain of democratic equivalences, linked to the demands of the oppressed in the rest of the world. And in turn, an awareness of such rights will be enriched in democratic content if it is lived out in a way that places equal value on the demands of other peoples and sectors, thus further distancing the possibility of a merely xenophobic discourse. In this way the democratic chain of equivalences in the countries of the Third World can be expanded. This will at least provide a basis on which the struggle can begin against the bureaucratic or simply despotic forms of power that have succeeded the decolonization of many of those countries.

RB: *What are the implications of 'radical democracy' for the socialist project? While 'radical democracy' as a concept has relevance to some new social movements, is this really the appropriate concept for specifying the goals of the green movement or the peace movement?*

EL: As we have often sustained, socialism is an integral part of the project of radical democracy. The latter changes the way in which the 'universality' characterizing democracy is conceived. Classical socialism saw the elimination of different forms of oppression and inequality as a result of the seizure of power by the proletariat, and also as a series of staggered steps to abolish the private ownership of the means of production. In other words, the 'universality' peculiar to a classless society was to flow from the proletariat's historical function as the 'universal class'. It is in the conception of this moment of universality that the difference with our present project lies. Our project no longer assumes this moment to be a structural effect grounded on an eschatology of history; it is a process of *universalization* of demands, based on their articulation with increasingly extensive chains of equivalences. It is thus always an incomplete universality. 'Humanity' is no longer seen as a ground but as a perspective. As universality is no longer the privilege of an 'unlimited' social actor — like the working class in Marxism — it can only be pragmatically constructed through the 'equivalential' effects of struggles carried out by actors that are always limited. In this sense, socialist demands simply take their place alongside other democratic demands, and the possibility of a democratic socialism is based on this articulation.

For that very reason I can only give a positive reply to your question as to whether the concept of 'radical democracy' adequately characterizes the peace or green movements. A different articulation of those demands is of course — and in fact has always been — possible, making them compatible with certain kinds of conservative or even authoritarian discourse. But this merely means that the democratic articulation of those demands is the result of a hegemonic struggle like everything else. As you know, even feminist discourses can be perfectly articulated with fundamentally reactionary ones. Social struggles do not have definite goals right from the start, but build and transform them in the course of struggle itself. Moreover, since these struggles do not take place in compartmentalized social spaces, but on complex terrains in which the demands of the various social actors are constantly interwoven, articulation is not a process external to individual demands; rather it is the very terrain on which the latter are specified and defined. If they are not articulated with other demands of the radical democratic project, they will be articulated in some other way; but the element of articulation will *always* be there. Politically, it makes all the difference if ecological discourse, for example, is conceived as the need for authoritarian state intervention to protect the environment, or as part of a radical critique of the irrationality of the political and economic systems in which we live, in which case it establishes a relationship of equivalence with the emancipatory projects of other social movements.

A-MS: *In discussions on the conception of radical hegemony, you have made references to the actual political movements, such as Jesse Jackson's 'Rainbow Coalition', as an illustration of your argument. Is it necessary, or even desirable, for the advance of radical democracy that political movements actually unite to form an identifiable movement? Wouldn't an articulated ensemble of elements in a radical democratic hegemony constitute a movement in a metaphorical rather than an actual sense? Given the proliferation of antagonisms and the criss-crossing of frontiers in the social, does not the advance of radical democracy entail shifts in frontiers, identities and 'interests' which are so local that no party machinery could create them? The achievements of the women's movement are interesting in this respect. Speaking generally, the various elements of this movement have had, in collective terms, highly ambiguous relations with formal political parties and state institutions. These elements are so heterogeneous, local and informally articulated, that it is almost impossible to speak of a 'women's movement'. And yet, without the structures, resources and programmes traditionally thought to be necessary for the achievement of political goals, the women's movement has achieved an extensive transformation in gender relations in a very short period.*

EL: The problem has many facets and I began to refer to some of them a moment ago in my answer to Robin. You are obviously right to assert that it is neither necessary nor desirable for the project of radical democracy that social and political movements come together in unified political structures. The plurality and proliferation of the various social movements conspires against forms of organization depending on the 'party' in its classical sense. That whole tidy image of politics, in which agents constituted in one area of the social are 'represented' by parties constituted at another, has for a long time been completely obsolete. But as we stated a moment ago, if, on the one hand, we do not have clear-cut forms of political organization, on the other, we do not have social movements with clear-cut identities as such either. The latter *always* occur on terrains in which many other things also take place — antagonisms, power strategies, etc. — things that are external to the problems and goals around which those movements have constituted themselves. In other words, articulation will be posed as a central problem right from the beginning, or at least from the moment the movements gain a certain level of political relevance. There is no reason why this articulation should adopt the party political form; on the contrary, it will be the result of a complex overdetermination of instances and levels. You have just mentioned Jackson's 'Rainbow Coalition', which is far from being a case of radical hegemony by the way. In a society where the different components of a *possible* national and popular collective will appear fragmented, dispersed and even in conflict among themselves, cannot they perhaps find, as in a mirror, the imaginary representation of a possible unity and identity in the rhetoric of the Rainbow Coalition? And can't this imaginary, constituted at the level of national politics, exert influence over the social practice of the individual movements? In turn, the separate existence of these movements will apply pressure in the opposite direction, determining the limits and forms of what is politically representable.

I'm saying all this, not to question your criticism of traditional forms of political intervention, but to place it on the complex terrain in which it is legitimate, which is that of the ambiguity and opaqueness of the processes of representation. The notion of representation as the transparency of the identity between representer and represented identity was always incorrect, of course: but it is even more so when applied to contemporary societies in which the instability of social identities makes the constitution of the latter around solid and permanent interests much more ill-defined. A complete theory of the role of representation in the production of social and political identities in late capitalism remains to be elaborated. This theory — which would have to make extensive use of the contribution that psychoanalysis has made to the progress in our understanding of relations of representation — will shed considerable light on the mechanisms of construction and distribution of power in those societies.

A-MS: *Is there any legitimate role left for a utopia in the radical democratic project? A classical utopia is a vision of the social as society, and as beyond antagonisms. You have demonstrated that the discursive effects of such a vision, even if taken as a 'regulative idea', are such that it can no longer be incorporated into the radical democratic discourse. In Hegemony, Chantal Mouffe and yourself suggest that the radical democratic project should institutionalize the impossibility of constituting the social as a closed society. Are you not suggesting, then, that a utopia be retained, but one which is, in a suitable post-modern sense, anti-utopian.*

EL: I think there are two differences between utopian thought and that of a radical democracy. They are so crucial that radical democracy could be conceived as a formally anti-utopian thought.

The first difference can be spotted easily through the comparison that Sorel made between 'utopia' and 'myth'. Utopia, as you point out, is the blueprint of a society in which the dream of the social's positivity, of the absence of antagonisms, has been fully realized. That is why it is regarded by Sorel as a mere intellectualistic construction that is incapable of shaping the consciousness of the masses. Utopia is essentially asceptic, since it is a 'model' of society conceived independently of the struggles needed to impose it. Negativity has been banished from it. In the case of myth, on the other hand, we have an ensemble of images and objectives which make up the identity of the masses as communities in struggle; the emphasis is on the formation of identities, not on the outlining of the concrete forms of society towards which struggles would tend as their term *ad quem*. If utopia presents us a social order from which power has been radically eliminated, myth, on the other hand, tends to constitute a will to power. Myth therefore sets *tasks* and in this sense comes close to the Kantian idea of a 'regulative idea'. But if radical democracy is anti-utopian in that it does not advocate any blueprint for society, it can also only live and assert itself through the constant production of social myths. Today we no longer believe, as Sorel did, in the necessity of a single myth — the general strike — around which a working class would be reconstituted, but in a range of myths that correspond to the plurality of social spaces on which a radical democracy is built. But the structure of mythical identity as described by Sorel remains essentially valid. In this sense, it is worth pointing out that the distinction between utopia and myth, and between utopian and scientific socialism, are of a very different nature. Scientific socialism's criticism of utopia is based on the divorce between the model of society advocated and the historical processes required to lead to it: and when scientific socialism does incorporate those processes to its analysis it does so by means of a causalist and objectivist approach. It is precisely this causality and objectivism that the Sorelian conception of social myths questions: identities are constituted mythically because the intrinsic negativity of antagonism is ontologically primary and constitutive.

The second difference between utopia and radical democracy is that utopia, as a model of society, is essentially a closed space of differences, while radical democracy is built through chains of equivalences that are always open and incomplete. What is more, radical democracy makes this openness and incompletion the very horizon on which all social identity is constituted. I thus think you are right to sustain that anti-utopia is the only utopia compatible with a radical democracy.

A-MS: *Many of your critics have criticized you for the complexity of your argument; they disagree with the necessity of a fundamental move beyond Marxism. From my experience as a feminist and a gay activist, I would say that the hegemony project is a step on a long and difficult road towards the construction of the theoretical and political conditions in which the 'Marxist left' can begin to understand, and possibly intervene creatively in the terrain of the struggles of the 'new social movements'. The project is not about constituting new privileged social agents; it aims instead to constitute the conditions in which new forms of politicization of the social can be thought. Not only are the agents and the location of the antagonisms 'new', the strategies are novel as well. In the women's and gay movements, for example, there are many strategies based on unfixed identities. On the one hand, there are the assertions of who we essentially 'are' as women, gays, etc., accompanying our demands for rights and the social space for the construction of those identities. On the other hand, there are strategies which entail the constant subversion of these identities, the proliferation of new identities and antagonisms and the asking of the impossible question of who we could be. Do you agree with this characterization of the hegemonic project? What is your sense of this double game of identities?*

EL: The relation between identities and strategies is undoubtedly changing. Or rather, we could say that the conditions in which the new social movements are struggling make visible something that has always been the case: namely, that strategies create identities, not the opposite. The traditional conception of the relation between identity and strategy assumed (1) that identity was given right from the beginning and was therefore stable; and (2) that social agents could, on the basis of these identities, establish relations of strategic calculation with a milieu that was essentially external to them. All the strategic speculations of the

Second International assumed the fixity of the social agents' class identity, for example. In contrast, the hegemonic approach can only prove intelligible insofar as there is an inversion of the way in which relations between identities and strategies are conceived. A 'corporate' class and a 'hegemonic' class are not the same class following two different strategies, but two strictly separate social identities, since the way in which their different strategies constitute their identities varies. It is for that very reason that hegemony endows social agents with a new identity and constitutes them as 'collective wills'. If identity was a mere structural datum acquired right from the start, then relations between social agents and their strategies could only be relations of exteriority.

What is happening today is that this construction of identities is more visible than in the past. In more stable societies there is what might be called a 'fetishism of identities'. Merely relational identities, whose constitution thus depends on the whole of the discursive-strategic field in which they are inserted, are presented as if they belonged to the agents' very individuality and had established relations of mere exteriority with that field. But we are forced by the speed and multiplicity of social change in our societies to constantly redefine identities, thus laying bare the 'language games' or strategies on which their constitution depends. In order to understand the specificity of these movements, an important study, or series of studies, would be to determine and classify the different kinds of language games they practise and use to build their strategy. Ethnomethodology has made certain progress in this direction, but I think a more comprehensive and operational version of the theory of hegemony would provide a more extensive and productive background with which to deal with this task.

A-MS: *In* Hegemony, *Chantal Mouffe and yourself distinguish between relations of subordination and relations of oppression, the former being relations in which an agent is subject to the decisions of another, and the latter being relations of subordination which have transformed themselves into sites of antagonisms. In my research on the logic of racism in post-war Britain, the construction of the black identity and the resistance of blacks against racism, I find that it is useful to make a further distinction between different types of resistance expressed within the broad category of a relation of oppression. There is, for example, evidence of antagonism, the division of the social into the two camps of the white racists versus the black oppressed in many different discourses of black resistance. Without imposing a hierarchy or teleology, it could nevertheless be said that not all of these discourses are equally subversive of the logic of racism. Some pose a central challenge to the racist exclusion of blacks as un-British in their 'blackness' by calling into question the conception of nation and the entire logic of articulating 'whiteness' to true citizenship, while other discourses do not do so. Will you be making further efforts to offer methodological tools for research along these lines? Have you developed your original conception of antagonism further than the formulation in* Hegemony?

EL: As you know, the development and perfection of the theory of antagonisms is absolutely central to our own theoretical and political project. At an exclusively theoretical level, conceiving the specificity of the antagonistic relationship involves getting into the analysis of the category of 'contingency' – as opposed to that of 'accident' – and demonstrating how the constitution of all identity is based on the presence of a constitutive 'outside' which affirms and denies such identity at the same time. In several of his works Slavoj Žižek has recently tried to link our category of 'antagonism' to the Lacanian 'real' in a way that I find convincing and worthy of further expansion. I also believe that the various theses being prepared on these problems under our Ph.D. programme at Essex will enable us to move towards an increasingly refined typology of situations of social conflict.

I believe in any case that the opposition between logic of difference and logic of equivalence, as presented in *Hegemony* does provide – through the possible articulation between both – the conceptual framework for that typology to be outlined, at least initially. For the radicality of a conflict can depend entirely on the extent to which the differences are re-articulated in chains of equivalence. For example, in the case of racism in Britain that you are studying it seems clear that while the Asian communities have managed to constitute themselves as legitimate 'differences' within the British social space, the West Indian communities have been much less able to do so, thus expanding (radicalizing) the chains of equivalence in certain discourses of total confrontation, such as that of the Rastafarians, for instance. To see, in a particular society, the whole complex game through which systems of differences are re-articulated in chains of equivalence that construct social polarity; to see, in another direction, how transformist policies reabsorb discourses of polarity into a system of 'legitimate' differences; this is to understand, at a microscopic level, how hegemony is constructed. As I was saying to you before, it is only through a multitude of concrete studies that we will be able to move towards an increasingly sophisticated theory of hegemony and social antagonisms.

RB: *In* Hegemony *what value you find in the work of such Marxists as Gramsci or Luxemburg is systematically counterposed to the Marxist allegiance of their thought. Would it not be entirely possible to construct a different Marxism from the one which is the object of your attack in this book, one which synthesizes the most adequate and creative strands in the work of Marx and the various Marxists you discuss, and feeling free to discard or develop all that was found inadequate or inappropriate to contemporary conditions and the project of human emancipation?*

EL: I partly agree with you. The operation you have just described to be performed in relation to Marxist tradition is one of the dimensions of the project in *Hegemony.* I say just one of the dimensions of our project, because a post-Marxist radical democracy must feed off a variety of theoretical and political traditions, many of which are external to the Marxist one. Neither feminism, ecology nor any of the wide range of current antisystemic movements have based their discourse and social imaginary on Marxism, yet they are essential components of the radical democracy project. This 'purification' of the Marxist tradition you refer to is just one part of a much vaster intellectual and political project. But as your question refers to Marxism, let us concentrate on that. The different Marxism you refer to — one which synthesizes the most adequate and creative strands in the work of Marx and his successors — is an essential component of post-Marxism. As I have pointed out repeatedly in this interview, the reason for the term 'post-Marxism' is that the ambiguity of Marxism — which runs through its whole history — is not a *deviation* from an untainted source, but dominates the entire work of Marx himself. In dealing with authors like Gramsci and Luxemburg, then, our book has not separated what is valuable from that which you characterize as the 'Marxist allegiance of their thought', since the tension between both aspects is already there in Marx's writings. It is because Marxism has been nothing but the historical locus of such ambivalence, because its history has largely been an attempt to resolve that ambivalence by a movement away from its essentialist features — a process that our book describes in detail — that a final settlement of scores with that essentialism must be termed post-Marxism, not simply Marxism. But the act of constitution of post-Marxism is not different from its genealogy: that is, from the complex discourses through which it has been gradually gestating, including the Marxist tradition. In this sense, post-Marxism restores to Marxism the only thing that can keep it alive: its relation with the present and its historicity.

In order to understand the specificity of our project, it is worth comparing it with two approaches that are quite common. The first is the classical sectarian approach which presents the Marxist tradition in terms of an eschatology. It is a quite subtle and pervasive approach that could be called the 'myth of the origins'. After a supposedly golden age of original purity, everything that followed was a process of slow or rapid — but in any case inexorable — decline. The ills of Soviet society could be corrected by returning to the uncontaminated spirit of October 1917. The antidote for the degeneration of Marxism is to go back to the original spirit inspiring Marx's work. Trotskyists are the clearest example of this attitude: that is why they are the last Stalinists, continuing as they do to perceive reality from the straitjacket of the discursive universe of the Comintern. As in all eschatologies, the myth of the origins is accompanied by the promise of a restoration: the consummation of times will involve the restoration of original purity. That is why their approach to the political world involves a search for the signs of annunciation of the second coming: the miners' strike in Britain would be the sign of the revolutionary reconstruction of the working class; the crisis in Wall Street in autumn 1987 would be that of world capitalism. The more remote from reality the eschatological promises get, the more they are inclined to take a magic turn. In the final months of the Third Reich, Goebbels sought a sign announcing the restoration of its fortunes, and thought he had found it in Roosevelt's death. This approach to Marxism has its counterpart in another attitude which is apparently its opposite, but in fact connives secretly with it. It is to abandon Marxism plain and simple. As the eschatological promises are no longer believed in, but continue to be respected with a certain religious reverence, the whole tradition can be dropped en bloc: that way the irreverence of engaging in an internal criticism is avoided.

But such an engagement is decisive if one wants to keep a tradition alive. And as we are talking of our work, I challenge you to tell me how many authors, apart from us, have attempted to deal with the political problems of post-modern societies by dredging the genealogy of the present. We have thus proceeded, among other things, to carry out a meticulous rereading of the works of Otto Bauer and Rosa Luxemburg, Sorel and Gramsci, Trotsky and Kautsky. But this rereading can only be done if the dialectic between mythical origins and eschatological restoration is left to one side. The problems facing present Soviet society, including its possible liberalization and democratization, will not be solved by a return to 1917, but by the construction of new forms that will take into account the huge changes that society has undergone in three-quarters of a century. To this end, a criticism will have to be made of what it was in 1917 and in Leninism, *inter alia*, that made possible all that came after. The 'spirit' of original Marxism is no less impure, imperfect and insufficient than the discourses with which our contemporaries attempt to construct and interpret the world. This is not to say that a return to the past has no meaning or political importance; but that this can only be the case if one seeks comparisons revealing the specificity of the present, not if one attempts to anchor the latter to an origin that would reveal its essence.

RB: *In your book you appear to regard the experience of the countries which have broken with capitalism as generally negative. Surely the Communist world is now gripped by a new wave of reform movements. Do you see any prospects that more authentic socialist societies will develop in the East?*

EL: If you are asking for a prediction, I do not know enough about those societies to make one. Like everyone else I am merely following the developments related to the process begun by Gorbachev with interest and concern. But if you are asking a general question as to how I envisage a possible pattern of change in the Communist world, as well as its implications for a project of radical democracy in the West, I am prepared to venture a few reflections.

Firstly, it is clear that any democratic transformation in the Soviet Union and similar societies will lead to the de-ideologization of those systems. The form it will take will not be a change in state ideology, but a decline in the state's ability to impose any kind of uniform ideology on the rest of society. This is a hugely positive phenomenon. It means that civil society will be increasingly capable of self-regulation; that it will have the possibility of greater pluralism; and also that the hegemonic capacity of the totalitarian forms assumed by state ideology will decline.

Secondly, at this stage it is clear that, whatever the future development of economic management in the countries of the Communist bloc, the total centralization of the production process in the hands of the state has ceased to be a positive value, let alone a *sine qua non* or the dividing line between a democratic and socialist society, on the one hand, and a capitalist society, on the other. On the contrary, it is clear for everyone that the most bureaucratic, inefficient and retrogressive forms of economic management in the Communist world have been linked to the super-statism of the Stalinist years. The disastrous results of that experience are more than visible. An enormous concentration of wealth and economic power in a few multinational companies is, of course, equally incompatible with a democratic society; but it is becoming more and more clear that the alternative does not lie in total state management. I think that the issue of democratic control of economic management is beginning to raise similar problems in both East and West and that the solutions — if a democratic development is to take place — will be found in a set of pragmatic measures. These will combine private and public ownership of the means of production; avoid the concentration of economic power, whether in the hands of the state or of monopolies; and, above all, create the institutional mechanisms, which will vary from country to country, that enable the different sectors of the population to participate in the economic decisions affecting society as a whole.

Finally, let me return to a point I was referring to before. The societies of East and West no longer seem separated by a deep trench in terms of the dominant mode of production in both. If socialist demands now seem to us to be part of a vaster process we have called the democratic revolution, the old Marxist vision of uneven and combined development sheds new light on the current world situation. In many respects, the West has progressed much further down the road to radical democracy than communist societies — among other reasons because their political regimes are infinitely more compatible with a profound democratization of society. But in terms of economic inequalities, job security, access to education, etc., it cannot be denied that communist societies have achieved something that must be preserved and generalized. The point I wish to emphasize is that the project of radical democracy must unite both aspects and reject the absurd choice between an elimination of economic power that is incompatible with freedom, and the preservation of a freedom that is incompatible with equality. If, for historical reasons that are precisely related to uneven and combined development, there has been a separation and polarization of demands — thus creating the impression of a radical incompatibility between them - the project of radical democracy must break with that incompatibility, presenting itself as a universalistic movement with much deeper roots than the polarization we have inherited from East and West.

RB: *The construction of the first post-capitalist states represented a formidable advance in the power of human social organization, one that could be compared with the rise of capitalism in Western Europe or the consolidation of a variety of Eastern empires. Such previous advances in social power have yielded terrible abuse and it has taken hard-fought struggles and innovatory social movements to curb their excesses. Are we not today witnessing an attempt to recuperate the socialist potential of anti-capitalist and anti-imperialist revolutions?*

EL: Forgive me if I mock a little, but I think you are giving a totally disproportionate version of the 'universal' importance of the Russian Revolution and the processes which followed it. The state which emerged from the October Revolution was certainly not 'post-capitalist', if by 'post-capitalism' we mean a form of socio-economic organization that is at a higher stage than capitalism. What happened was very different. The combination of dislocations produced by the world imperialist chain and the First World War led to a revolutionary crisis that made the seizure of power by the Bolsheviks possible. The ideology of that seizure of power was socialist, but what came after was not 'post-capitalism' in any sense of the term. It was a desperate effort by the state to develop, at any human price, the economic and military potential to catch up with the West and resist its aggression. This path produced all kind of tensions. It led, without any doubt, to great technological and economic progress; but it also led to terrible imbalances that are still visible today, thus showing the price that was paid for that forced development. The Russian Revolution was the first of the revolutions in the peripheral world, not a higher point in the 'universal' development of the forces of production. If it has universal significance, it is that it meant the beginning of this process of crisis in the West's economic and political hegemony, which was later accentuated with the Chinese Revolution and others in the Third World. But in this sense it does not have an anti-capitalist potential to '*recover*'. What it does have is a set of antagonisms generated by bureaucratic power; and they might be the starting point for social struggles that could lead to the democratization of the Soviet Union and similar societies.

RB: *In different ways Poland, South Africa and Brazil have all witnessed remarkable popular movements against dictatorship in the 1980s. Yet in each case, it could be argued, these movements were critically strengthened by the fact that they found support among the working class and adopted class forms of organization, such as the trade union. Do not these experiences call into question your rejection of class as a necessary category for understanding radical, antisystemic potential?*

EL: Let us agree on exactly what we are talking about. We have never denied that trade union organizations can play an important role of hegemonic condensation in particular social and political contexts. What we have denied is very different. It is that that centrality is a necessary structural effect of the evolutionary laws of capitalism, and therefore, that the *political* centrality of the working class could stem from supposed economic trends leading to growing proletarianization. The centrality of the working class in classical Marxist discourse was not any kind of centrality; it was strictly linked to a structural analysis, which was largely erroneous, of the laws of operation of capitalism. In none of the cases you quote is the political centrality achieved by the trade union movement linked to the kind of economic centrality of the working class postulated by classical Marxism. In the case of Poland, *Solidarnosc* managed to galvanize and condense around a democratic imaginary all the potential forms of protest that an authoritarian state was repressing, thus transforming itself into the nodal point of the people-power confrontation. But this has little to do with socialism in its classical sense, and absolutely nothing to do with Marxism's postulation that the centrality of the working class arises from the simplification of class structure under capitalism. In the case of South Africa that political centrality of the trade union movement has never existed and the struggle within the trade unions themselves between a 'workerist' tendency and a 'populist' tendency shows that the construction of an antisystemic popular pole does not depend on 'class' as its nodal point. As to the case of Brazil – I think you are referring to the Workers' Party (PT) led by Lula - anyone who knows anything about recent Brazilian politics is aware that the trade unions played a clearly marginal role in the process of removing the military regime; and also that the working class lacks any centrality in Brazilian social structure. Moreover, the PT – which undoubtedly began not just as a working class, but even as a workerist party – has increasingly lost such a character as it has become integrated into the political system at a national level.

   In other words, there is little relation between the examples you give, and above all, they do not represent a generalizable trend. To be frank, I do not think our understanding of contemporary social struggles is greatly helped by abstracting isolated empirical data from the specific structural contexts that explain them, and by considering them 'proof' that the trend towards working class centrality, determined by Marx in the nineteenth century, is still valid. To proceed in that way is just typical of the attitude I characterized earlier as the 'search for the signs of restoration'. It is to view the contemporary political scene with the same anxious look that one imagines Columbus, on his first voyage of discovery, gazing at the horizon in the hope of glimpsing firm ground.

RB: *In your book you insist on the pluralism of the socialist project. Yet you also allude to the need for different movements to achieve effective forms of alliance against the established order. Is not some knowing 'subject' reintroduced here as arbiter of what would constitute an effective alliance?*

EL: No. There's no question of a 'knowing subject' at all, since articulation is not the discovery of a profound and necessary unity existing between different movements and forms of struggle, but the creation and construction of something new. It is therefore not an exercise of 'knowledge', but one that is eminently practical. I have already given the reason why the aprioristic unity of different struggles, or their absolute separation, do not prove possible, earlier on in this interview: struggles always take place in highly overdetermined social and political spaces, and the choice is thus between their different forms of articulation, and never between articulation and non-articulation. As I have pointed out, this means that the articulating force transforms its identity in the process of articulation, which does not therefore have the external character of an arbiter.

RB: *In Marx's view the historical ground of the socialist project was based on some combination of (1) human species being; (2) the proletarian condition and capacity (this latter sometimes taken to include the realm of reproduction as well as production). These linked identities furnished the socialist programme with a unifying principle that aimed to be rooted in social reality. If this historically and socially rooted perspective is abandoned, is there not a risk of opening the way to validating arbitrarily constructed, and even quite fanciful, identities such as might be proposed by religious fundamentalists?*

EL: The danger exists. But it exists in reality, not in my theoretical approach, since those identities that you call 'fanciful' are constantly created and recreated in the world in which we live. Thus, if your question is 'ontological' in character, my reply is that there is nothing to be gained by constructing the myth of a human 'nature' that would correspond to what human beings *are* outside of any form of social organization. Let us leave that empty idle talk about 'human nature' to the builders of ideal societies. In this respect, I believe I belong to the best of the Marxist tradition in sustaining that human beings have no other nature than the one they give themselves in the social production of their own existence. From an ultimate ontological and epistemological point of view, religious fundamentalism and the most 'refined' of Western socialisms are on an equal footing.

Let it be on the record, however, that I have said that this is only the case on the basis of an *ultimately* ontological and epistemological point of view. But human beings do not exist at that 'ultimate' level, and always work in concrete historical situations; and in terms of those situations, it is certainly not the case that all alternatives have a similar value. Having said that I will now go on to the second, and most probable, sense of your question: that it is a normative question. As in the other cases, the Cartesian illusion of an absolute starting point must also be given up, since the person making ethical judgements is never an abstract individual, but a member of a certain community that already believes in a number of principles and values. It is because you and I believe in the right of human beings to determine their own sexual orientation that we will condemn discrimination against homosexuals or the legal punishment of adultery. And in turn, we will base that right on more general ethical values. But at some point, this justification will be interrupted in a relatively arbitrary way. As with anything else, the limits of moral opinions are essentially open and no final closure can be granted by any kind of ethical discourse.

Yet again we are faced with the issue of hegemony. If a set of moral principles constituted a complete and closed system based on apodictic certainties, a norm or conduct could be evaluated more or less automatically. But that system does not exist; it is merely a rationalistic myth. What we find is a plurality and dispersion of moral principles which govern the conduct of human beings in their different spheres of activity, and maintain a merely relative coherence between themselves that is always negotiated. That is why ethical decision-making principles must be based on open processes of constant debate; it is only that way that a 'common sense' emerges. Let us imagine that a choice must be made between a religious fundamentalism and a socialist humanism as the abstract principles on which the community is to be organized. Outside of any concrete social situation it is impossible to choose for the simple reason that no common assumptions can be made about them that would lead to a decision either way. And it is clear that if those assumptions existed, the choice would not really be a choice, since one of the two positions would be inconsistent and the other would therefore simply be its 'truth'. We would therefore not be dealing with a choice but with the clarification of the only decision possible. Imagine a society dominated by religious fundamentalism which establishes women's subordination as a basic principle of the social order. Let us also suppose that the prevalent socio-economic conditions of the society in question lead to the growing participation of women in a range of economic and professional activities. In such circumstances a tension is likely to emerge between the daily experience of both sexes' equality at the intellectual and professional level and the sexual inequality prescribed by religion. This tension constitutes the fissure in the hegemony of religious discourse and is the basis on which an egalitarian critique of fundamentalism will build its conditions of credibility. But in turn, the fundamentalist discourse will operate likewise, seeking to work on the hegemonic fissures that the egalitarian discourse reveals.

All this seems to me to be essential to understanding the intimate unity that exists between ethical decisions, processes of debate and hegemony. A line of argument rarely proceeds by showing the internal incoherence, in the logical sense, of a certain discourse. On the contrary, it generally attempts to demonstrate the implications of that discourse for something *outside* it. In other words, any argument is articulatory and hegemonic. The centrality and credibility gained by a discourse in a particular society depends on its ability to extend its argumentative fabric in a number of directions, all of which converge in a hegemonic configuration. Only within this configuration does a decision — ethical or otherwise — acquire meaning. The structure of any decision has a discursive *outside* as its intrinsic point of reference.

At this point, the question could perhaps be asked: is it not possible to point out situations that are the source of ethical values and arise from the human *species* itself, regardless of any sense of community? Finally, facts such as all humans need to eat, reproduce, protect themselves from the inclemency of the weather, etc., could also be named. You are as aware as I am of this kind of argument, based as it is on listing the conditions without which human life on earth would be impossible, and then deducing that those conditions constitute human 'nature' and that that nature is the source of moral imperatives. But this kind of argument is not worth a dried-up fig. Firstly, because the notion that humans constitute a 'species' is relatively new and has been slowly gaining ground over the last 2,500 years. Secondly, because the notion that to be a member of the community is to be the bearer of certain rights is an even newer idea. It is also one that is not wholly acclimatized with the societies in which we live: we do not have to go back to the Roman slave owners — it is enough to recall Auschwitz as an extreme case, as well as all the other situations and discourses in which social division prevails over equality between human beings considered as a species. The extent to which 'human' discourses will hegemonize differences, or to which differences will constitute a frontier that will transform 'human' identities into an empty and obsolete myth, is something which is not decided and depends in any case on struggle. 'Humanity' is a project of political construction, not something that has always been there, waiting to be recognized.

I think that makes my position clear. I certainly believe that there are no values or ethics that are not community-based. But communities consist of discursive spaces, rather than geographical locations. Feminism, the gay movement or anti-nuclear struggles are communities whose boundaries do not coincide with the 'national' community in its traditional sense. But for that very reason 'humanity' – in the sense of the unity of the species – is just another community: one to which the social struggles of the last two hundred and fifty years have given an increasingly hegemonic role, basing its constitution on a plurality of rights. It is by recognizing the discursive nature of this hegemonic construction that we will be able to advance to a *real* humanism; a humanism that acknowledges its radical historicity, and does not take any of the conditions for its arrival for granted.

APPENDIX

In October 1987 I participated, together with Chantal Mouffe, in a conference in Ljubljana, organized by the Institute for Marxist Studies of the Slovenian Academy of Arts and Sciences, on 'New Social Movements as a Political Dimension of Metaphor'. As the conference coincided with the publication of the Slovenian edition of *Hegemony and Socialist Strategy*, it was partly devoted to the discussion of the latter. Among the various contributions there was a remarkable piece by Slavoj Žižek which touches on central aspects of the issues discussed in the present volume. We reproduce it as an appendix, with the kind permission of its author.

E.L.

Beyond Discourse-Analysis

Slavoj Žižek

Hegemony and Socialist Strategy is usually read as an essay in 'post-structuralist' politics, an essay in translating into a political project the basic 'post-structuralist' ideas: there is no transcendental Signified; so-called 'reality' is a discursive construct; every given identity, including that of a subject, is an effect of the contingent differential relations, etc. This reading also provokes the usual criticism: language serves primarily as a medium of extra-linguistic power-relations; we cannot dissolve all reality into a language-game, etc. It is our claim that such a reading misses the fundamental dimension of *Hegemony*, the dimension through which this book presents perhaps the most radical breakthrough in modern social theory.

It is no accident that the basic proposition of *Hegemony* – 'Society doesn't exist' – evokes the Lacanian proposition 'la Femme n'existe pas' ('Woman doesn't exist'). The real achievement of *Hegemony* is crystallized in the concept of 'social antagonism': far from reducing all reality to a kind of language-game, the socio-symbolic field is conceived as structured around a certain traumatic impossibility, around a certain fissure which *cannot* be symbolized. In short, Laclau and Mouffe have, so to speak, reinvented the Lacanian notion of the Real as impossible, they have made it useful as a tool for social and ideological analysis. Simple as it may sound, this breakthrough is of such a novelty that it was usually not even perceived in most responses to *Hegemony*.[1]

The Subject of Antagonism

Why this stress on the homology between the Laclau–Mouffe concept of antagonism and the Lacanian concept of the Real? Because it is our thesis that the reference to Lacan allows us to draw some further conclusions from the concept of social antagonism, above all those that concern the status of the subject corresponding to the social field structured around a central impossibility.

As to the question of the subject, *Hegemony* presents even a certain regression from Laclau's previous book *Politics and Ideology in Marxist Theory*[2]: in this book we find a finely elaborated Althusserian theory of interpellation, while in *Hegemony*, Laclau and Mouffe are basically still conceiving the subject in a way that characterizes 'post-structuralism', from the perspective of assuming different 'subject-positions'. Why this regression? My optimistic reading of it is that it is — to use the good old Stalinist expression — 'a dizziness from too much success', an effect of the fact that Laclau and Mouffe had progressed too quickly, i.e. that, with the elaboration of their concept of antagonism, they have accomplished such a radical breakthrough that it was not possible for them to follow it immediately with a corresponding concept of subject — hence the uncertainty regarding the subject in *Hegemony*.

The main thrust of its argumentation is directed against the classical notion of the *subject* as a substantial, essential entity, given in advance, dominating the social process and not being produced by the contingency of the discursive process itself: against this notion, they affirm that what we have is a series of particular subject-positions (feminist, ecologist, democratic ...) the signification of which is not fixed in advance: it changes according to the way they are articulated in a series of equivalences through the metaphoric surplus which defines the identity of every one of them. Let us take, for example, the series feminism — democracy — peace movement — ecologism: insofar as the participant in the struggle for democracy 'finds out by experience' that there is no real democracy without the emancipation of women, insofar as the participant in the ecological struggle 'finds out by experience' that there is no real reconciliation with nature without abandoning the aggressive-masculine attitude towards nature, insofar as the participant in the peace-movement 'finds out by experience' that there is no real peace without radical democratization, etc., that is to say, insofar as the identity of each of the four abovementioned positions is marked with the metaphoric surplus of the other three positions, we can say that something like a unified subject-position is being constructed: to be a democrat means at the same time to be a feminist, etc. What we must not overlook is, of course, that such a unity is always radically contingent, the result of a symbolic condensation, and not an expression of some kind of internal necessity according to which the interests of all the above-mentioned positions would in the long run 'objectively convene'. It is quite possible, for example, to imagine an ecological position which sees the only solution in a strong anti-democratic, authoritarian state resuming control over the exploitation of natural resources, etc.

Now, it is clear that such a notion of the subject-positions still enters the frame of the Althusserian ideological interpellation as constitutive of the subject: the subject-position is a mode of how we recognize our position of an (interested) agent of the social process, of how we experience our commitment to a certain ideological cause. But, as soon as we constitute ourselves as ideological subjects, as soon as we respond to the interpellation and assume a certain subject-position, we are a priori, *per definitionem* deluded, we are overlooking the radical dimension of the social antagonism, that is to say, the traumatic kernel the symbolization of which always fails; and – this is our hypothesis – it is precisely the Lacanian notion of the subject as 'the empty place of the structure' which describes the subject in its confrontation with the antagonism, the subject which isn't covering up the traumatic dimension of social antagonism.

To explain this distinction between subject and subject-positions, let us take again the case of class antagonism. The relationship between the classes is antagonistic in the Laclau/Mouffe sense of the term, i.e. it is neither contradiction nor opposition but the 'impossible' relationship between the two terms: each of them is preventing the other from achieving its identity with itself, to become what it really is. As soon as I recognize myself, in an ideological interpellation, as a 'proletarian', I am engaged in the social reality, fighting against the 'capitalist' who is preventing me from realizing fully my human potential, blocking my full development. Where here is the ideological illusion proper to the subject-position? It lies precisely in the fact that it is the 'capitalist', this external enemy, who is preventing me from achieving an identity with myself: the illusion is that after the eventual annihilation of the antagonistic enemy, I will finally abolish the antagonism and arrive at an identity with myself. And it is the same with sexual antagonism: the feminist struggle against patriarchal, male chauvinist oppression is necessarily filled out by the illusion that afterwards, when patriarchal oppression is abolished, women will finally achieve their full identity with themselves, realize their human potentials, etc.

However, to grasp the notion of antagonism in its most radical dimension, we should *invert* the relationship between the two terms: it is not the external enemy who is preventing me from achieving identity with myself, but every identity is already in itself blocked, marked by an impossibility, and the external enemy is simply the small piece, the rest of reality upon which we 'project' or 'externalize' this intrinsic, immanent impossibility. That would be the last lesson of the famous Hegelian dialectics of the Lord and the Bondsman[3], the lesson usually overlooked by Marxist reading: the Lord is ultimately an invention of the Bondsman, a way for the Bondsman to 'give way as to his desire', to evade the blockade of his own desire by projecting its reason into the external repression of the Lord. This is also the real ground for Freud's insistence that the *Verdrängung* cannot be reduced to an internalization of the *Unterdrückung* (the external repression): there is a certain fundamental, radical, constitutive, self-inflicted impediment, a hindrance of the drive, and the role of the fascinating figure of external Authority, of its repressive force, is to make us blind to this self-impediment of the drive. That is why we could say that it is precisely in the moment when we achieve victory over the enemy in the antagonistic struggle in social reality that we experience the antagonism in its most radical dimension, as a self-hindrance: far from enabling us finally to achieve full identity with ourselves, the moment of victory is the moment of greatest loss. The Bondsman frees himself from the Lord only when he experiences how the Lord was only embodying the auto-blockage of his own desire: what the Lord through his external repression was supposed to deprive him of, to prevent him from realizing, he — the Bondsman — never possessed. This is the moment called by Hegel 'the loss of the loss': the experience that we *never had* what we were supposed to have lost. We can also determine this experience of the 'loss of the loss' as the experience of the 'negation of the negation', i.e. of pure antagonism where the negation is brought to the point of self-reference.

This reference to Hegel might seem strange: isn't Hegel the 'absolute idealist' *par excellence*, the philosopher reducing all antagonism to a subordinate moment of the self-mediating identity? But perhaps such a reading of Hegel is itself victim of the 'metaphysics of presence': perhaps another reading is possible where the reference to Hegel enables us to distinguish the pure antagonism from the antagonistic fight in reality. What is at stake in pure antagonism is no longer the fact that — as in an antagonistic fight with the external adversary — all the positivity, all the consistency of our position lies in the negation of the adversary's position and *vice versa*; what is at stake is the fact that the negativity of the other which is preventing me from achieving my full identity with myself is just an externalization of my own auto-negativity, of my self-hindering. The point is here how exactly to read, which accent to give to the crucial thesis of Laclau and Mouffe that in the antagonism, the negativity as such assumes a positive existence. We can read this thesis as asserting that in an antagonistic relationship, the positivity of 'our' position consists only in the positivation of our negative relation to the other, to the anta- gonist adversary: the whole consistency of our position is in the fact that we are negating the other, 'we' are nothing but this drive to abolish, to annihilate our adversary. In this case, the antagonistic relationship is in a way symmetrical: each position is only its negative relation to the other (the Lord prevents the Bondsman from achieving full identity with himself and *vice versa*). But if we radicalize the antagonistic fight in reality to the point of pure antagonism, the thesis that, in the antagonism, the negativity as such assumes a positive existence, must be read in another way: the other itself (the Lord, let's say) is, in his positivity, in his fasci- nating presence, just the positivation of our own — Bondsman's — nega- tive relationship towards ourselves, the positive embodiment of our own self-blockage. The point is that here, the relationship is no longer symmetrical: we cannot say that the Bondsman is also in the same way just the positivation of the negative relationship of the Lord. What we can perhaps say is that he is the Lord's symptom. When we radicalize the antagonistic fight to a point of pure antagonism, it is always one of the two moments which, through the positivity of the other, maintains a negative self-relationship: to use a Hegelian term, this other element functions as a 'reflexive determination' ('*Reflexionsbestimmung*') of the first — the Lord, for example, is just a reflexive determination of the Bondsman. Or, to take the sexual difference/antagonism: man is a reflexive determination of woman's impossibility of achieving an identity with herself (which is why woman is a symptom of man).

We must then distinguish the experience of antagonism in its radical form, as a limit of the social, as the impossibility around which the social field is structured, from antagonism as the relation between antagonistic subject-positions: in Lacanian terms, we must distinguish antagonism as *real* from the social *reality* of the antagonistic fight. And the Lacanian notion of the subject aims precisely at the experience of 'pure' anta- gonism as self-hindering, self-blockage, this internal limit preventing the symbolic field from realizing its full identity: the stake of the entire process of subjectivation, of assuming different subject-positions, is ulti- mately to enable us to avoid this traumatic experience. The limit of the social as it is defined by Laclau and Mouffe, this paradoxical limit which means that 'Society doesn't exist', isn't just something that subverts each subject-position, each defined identity of the subject; on the contrary, it is at the same time what sustains the subject in its most radical dimension: 'the subject' in the Lacanian sense is the name for this internal limit, this internal impossibility of the Other, of the 'substance'. The subject is a paradoxical entity which is so to speak its own negative, i.e. which persists only insofar as its full realization is blocked — the fully realized subject would be no longer subject but substance. In this precise sense, subject is beyond or before subjectivation: subjectivation designs the movement through which the subject integrates what is given him/her into the universe of meaning — this integration always ultimately fails, there is a certain left-over which cannot be integrated into the symbolic universe, an object which resists subjectivation, and the subject is precisely correlative to this object. In other words, the subject is correlative to its own limit, to the element which cannot be subjectified, it is the name of the void which cannot be filled out with subjectivation: the subject is the point of failure of subjectivation (that's why the Lacanian mark for it is $).

The Dimension of Social Fantasy

The 'impossible' relationship of the subject to this object the loss of which constitutes the subject is marked by the Lacanian formula of fantasy: $◇a. Fantasy is then to be conceived as an imaginary scenario the function of which is to provide a kind of positive support filling out the subject's constitutive void. And the same goes, *mutatis mutandis*, for the social fantasy: it is a necessary counterpart to the concept of antagonism, a scenario filling out the voids of the social structure, masking its constitutive antagonism by the fullness of enjoyment (racist enjoyment, for example).[4] This is the dimension overlooked in the Althusserian account of interpellation: before being caught in the identification, in the symbolic (mis)recognition, the subject is trapped by the *Other* through a paradoxical object-cause of desire in the midst of it, embodying enjoyment, through this secret supposed to be hidden in the Other, as exemplified by the position of the man from the country in the famous apologue about the door of the Law in Kafka's *The Trial*[5], this small history told to K. by the priest to explain to him his situation *vis-à-vis* the Law. The patent failure of all main interpretations of this apologue seems only to confirm the priest's thesis that 'the comments often enough merely express the commentator's bewilderment' (p. 240). But there is another way to penetrate the mystery of this apologue: instead of seeking directly its meaning, it would be preferable to treat it the way Claude Lévi-Strauss treats a given myth: to establish its relations to a series of other myths and to elaborate the rule of their transformation. Where can we find, then in *The Trial* another 'myth' which functions as a variation, as an inversion of the apologue concerning the door of the Law?

We don't have to look far: at the beginning of the second chapter ('First Interrogation'), Josef K. finds himself in front of another door of the Law (the entrance to the interrogation chamber); here also, the door-keeper lets him know that this door is intended only for him — the washerwoman says to him: 'I must shut this door after you, nobody else must come in', which is clearly a variation of the last words of the door-keeper to the man from the country in the priest's apologue: 'No one but you could gain admittance through this door, since this door was intended only for you. I am now going to shut it.' At the same time, the apologue concerning the door of the Law (let's call him, in the style of Lèvi-Strauss, m^1) and the first interrogation (m^2) can be opposed through a whole series of distinctive features: in m^1, we are in front of the entrance to a magnificent court of justice, in m^2, we are in a block of workers' flats, full of filth and obscene crawling; in m^1, the door-keeper is an employee of the court, in m^2, it is an ordinary woman washing children's clothes; in m^1 it is a man, in m^2 a woman; in m^1, the door-keeper prevents the man from the country from passing the door and entering the court, in m^2, the washerwoman pushes him into the interrogation chamber half against his will, i.e. the frontier separating the everyday life from the sacred place of the Law cannot be crossed in m^1, but in m^2, it is easy to cross.

The crucial feature of m^2 is already indicated with its localization: the court is situated in the middle of the vital promiscuity of workers' lodgings — Reiner Stach is quite justified in recognizing in this detail a distinctive trait of Kafka's universe, 'the trespass of the frontier which separates the vital domain from the judicial domain'[6]. The structure is here that of the band of Moebius: if we progress far enough in our descent to the social underground, we find ourselves suddenly on the other side, i.e. in the middle of the sublime and noble Law. The place of transition from one domain to the other is a door guarded by an ordinary washerwoman of a provocative sensuality. In m^1, the door-keeper doesn't know anything, whereas here, the woman possesses a kind of advance knowledge: she simply ignores the naive cunning of K., his excuse that he is looking for a joiner called Lanz, and gives him to understand that they have been waiting for him a long time, although K. chose to enter her room quite by chance, as a last desperate essay after a long and useless ramble:

> The first thing he saw in the little room was a great pendulum clock which already pointed to ten. 'Does a joiner called Lanz live here?' he asked. 'Please go through,' said a young woman with sparkling black eyes, who was washing children's clothes in a tub, and she pointed her damp hand to the open door of the next room.... 'I asked for a joiner, a man called Lanz.' 'I know,' said the woman, 'just go right in.' K. might not have obeyed if she had not come up to him, grasped the handle of the door, and said: 'I must shut this door after you, nobody else must come in.' (pp. 45–6)

The situation here is the same as in the well-known accident from *The Arabian Nights*: the hero, lost in the desert, enters quite by chance a cave where he finds three old wise men awakened by his entry who say to him: 'Finally, you have arrived! We have waited for you for the last three hundred years!' This mystery of the necessity behind the contingent encounter is again that of the transference: knowledge that we seek to produce is presupposed to exist already in the other. The washerwoman's paradoxical advance knowledge has nothing whatsoever to do with a so-called 'feminine intuition': it is based on a simple fact that she is connected with the Law. Her position regarding the Law is far more crucial than that of a small functionary; K. discovers it soon afterwards when his passionate argumentation before the tribunal is interrupted by an obscene intrusion:

> Here K. was interrupted by a shriek from the end of the hall; he peered from beneath his hand to see what was happening, for the reek of the room and the dim light together made a whitish dazzle of fog. It was the washer-woman, whom K. had recognized as a potential cause of disturbance from the moment of her entrance. Whether she was at fault now or not, one could not tell. All K. could see was that a man had drawn her into a corner by the door and was clasping her in his arms. Yet it was not she who had uttered the shriek but the man; his mouth was wide open and he was gazing up at the ceiling. (p. 55)

What is then the relation between the woman and the court of Law? In Kafka's work, the woman as a 'psychological type' is wholly consistent with the anti-feminist ideology of an Otto Weininger: a being without a proper self, incapable of assuming an ethical attitude (even when she appears to act on ethical grounds, there is a hidden calculation of enjoyments behind it), a being which hasn't got an access to the dimension of truth (even when what she is saying is literally true, she is lying with her subjective position), a being about which it is not sufficient to say that she is feigning her affections to seduce a man – the problem is that there is nothing behind this mask of simulation, nothing but a certain gluttonous enjoyment which is her only substance. Confronted with such an image of woman, Kafka doesn't succumb to the usual critical-feminist temptation (of demonstrating how this figure is the product of certain social-discursive conditions, of opposing to it the outlines of another type of femininity, etc.). His gesture is much more subversive – he wholly accepts this Weiningerian portrait of woman as a 'psychological type', but he makes it occupy an unheard of, unprecedented place, the place of the Law. This is perhaps, as was already pointed out by Stach, the elementary operation of Kafka: this short-circuit between the feminine 'substance' ('psychological type') and the place of the Law. Smeared over by an obscene vitality, the Law itself – in a traditional perspective a pure, neutral universality – assumes the features of a heterogeneous, inconsistent *bricolage* penetrated with enjoyment.

In Kafka's universe, the court is above all *lawless* in a formal sense: as if the chain of 'normal' connections between causes and effects is suspended, put in parentheses. Every attempt to establish the mode of functioning of the court by means of logical reasoning is doomed in advance to fail: all the oppositions noted by K. (between the anger of the judges and the laughter of the public in the gallery; between the merry right side and the severe left side of the public) prove themselves false as soon as he tries to base his tactics on them; after an ordinary answer by K., the public bursts out in laughter.

The other, positive side of this inconsistency is of course the enjoyment: it erupts openly when K's presentation of his case is interrupted by a public act of sexual intercourse. This act, difficult to perceive because of its over-exposure itself (K. had to 'peer beneath his hands to see what was happening'), marks the moment of the eruption of the traumatic real, and the error of K. consists in overlooking the *solidarity* between this obscene perturbation and the court. He thinks that everybody would be anxious to have order restored and the offending couple at least ejected from the meeting, but when he tries to rush across the room, the crowd obstructs him, someone seizes him from behind by the collar ... at this point, the game is over: puzzled and confused, K. loses the thread of his argument; filled with impotent rage, he soon leaves the room. The fatal error of K. was to address the court, the Other of the Law, as a homogeneous entity, attainable by means of consistent argument, whereas the court can only return him an obscene smile mixed with signs of perplexity – in short, K. expects from the court *acts* (legal deeds, decisions), but what he gets is an *act* (a public copulation). Kafka's sensitiveness to this 'trespass of the frontier which separates the vital domain from the judicial domain' depends upon his Judaism: the Jewish religion marks the moment of their most radical separation. In all previous religions, we always run into a place, a domain of sacred enjoyment (in the form of ritual orgies, for example), whereas Judaism evacuates from the sacred domain all traces of vitality and subordinates the living substance to the dead letter of the Father's Law. With Kafka, on the contrary, the judicial domain is again flooded with enjoyment, we have a short-circuit between the *Other* of the Law and the *Thing*, the substance of enjoyment.

That is why his universe is eminently one of *super-ego*: the Other as the Other of the symbolic Law is not only dead, it does not even know that it is dead (like the terrible figure from Freud's dream) – it could not know it insofar as it is totally insensible to the living substance of enjoyment. The super-ego embodies on the contrary the paradox of a Law which 'proceeds from the time when the Other wasn't yet dead. The super-ego is a surviving remainder' (Jacques-Alain Miller). The super-ego imperative 'Enjoy!', the turning round of the dead Law into the obscene figure of super-ego implies a disquieting experience: suddenly, we become aware of the fact that what a minute ago appeared to us a dead letter is really alive, respiring, palpitating. Let us remind ourselves of a scene from the movie *Aliens 2*: the group of heroes is advancing along a long tunnel, the stone walls of which are twisted like interlaced plaits of hair; suddenly, the plaits start to move and to secrete a glutinous mucus, the petrified corpses come to life again.

We should then reverse the usual metaphorics of 'alienation' where the dead, formal letter sucks out, as a kind of parasite or vampire, the living present force, i.e. where the living subjects are prisoners of a dead cobweb. This dead, formal character of the Law is a *sine qua non* of our freedom: the real totalitarian danger arises when the Law no longer wants to stay dead. The result of m¹ is then that there isn't any truth about *truth*: every warrant of the Law has the status of a semblance, the Law doesn't have any support in the truth, it is necessary without being true; the meeting of K. with the washerwoman adds to this the reverse side usually passed by in silence: insofar as the Law isn't grounded in truth, it is impregnated with enjoyment.

Towards an Ethic of the Real

Now, it should be clear how the two notions with which we tried to supplement the theoretical apparatus of *Hegemony* — the *subject* as an empty place correlative to the antagonism; social *fantasy* as the elementary ideological mode to mask the antagonism — proceed simply from taking into account the consequences of the breakthrough accomplished by this book.

The main achievement of *Hegemony*, the achievement because of which this book — far from being just one in the series of 'post-'works (post-Marxist, post-structuralist, etc.) — occupies in relation to this series a position of *extimité*, is that, perhaps for the first time, it articulates the contours of a political project based on an ethics of the real, of the 'going through the fantasy (*la traversée du fantasme*)', an ethics of confrontation with an impossible, traumatic kernel not covered by any *ideal* (of the unbroken communication, of the invention of the self). That's why we can effectively say that *Hegemony* is the only real answer to Habermas, to his project based on the ethics of the ideal of communication without constraint. The way Habermas formulates the 'ideal speech situation' already betrays its status as fetish: 'ideal speech situation' is something which, as soon as we engage in communication, is 'simultaneously denied and laid claim to'[7], i.e. we must presuppose the ideal of an unbroken communication to be already realized, even though we know simultaneously that this cannot be the case. To the examples of the fetishist logic *je sais bien, mais quand même*, we must then add the formula of the 'ideal speech situation': 'I know very well that communication is broken and perverted, but still … (I believe and act as if the ideal speech situation is already realized)'.

What this fetishist logic of the ideal is masking, is of course, the limitation proper to the symbolic field as such: the fact that the signifying field is always structured around a certain fundamental deadlock. This deadlock doesn't entail any kind of resignation — or, if there is a resignation, it is a paradox of the *enthusiastic resignation*: we are using here the term 'enthusiasm' in its strict Kantian meaning, as indicating an experience of the object through the very failure of its adequate representation. Enthusiasm and resignation are not then two opposed moments: it is the 'resignation' itself, i.e. the experience of a certain impossibility, which incites enthusiasm.

Notes

1. For an explication of the paradoxes of the Lacanian Real, see Slavoj Žižek, *The Sublime Object of Ideology*, London 1989, pp. 161—73.

2. Ernesto Laclau, *Politics and Ideology in Marxist Theory: Capitalism – Fascism – Populism*, London 1977 (2nd impression 1987).

3. G.W.F. Hegel, *Phenomenology of Spirit*, translated by A.V. Miller, Oxford 1977, pp. 111—19.

4. For an explication of the notion of social fantasy, see Žižek, pp. 124—8.

5. Franz Kafka, *The Trial*, Harmondsworth 1985. (Page numbers in brackets are for this edition).

6. Reiner Stach, *Kafkas erotischer Mythos*, Frankfurt 1987, p. 35.

7. Jürgen Habermas, *Der philosophische Diskurs der Moderne*, Frankfurt 1985, p. 378.

Index

Staten, H. 84, 131, 137
Sweezy, P. M. 182
Szankay, Z. xiv

Taylor, C. 106, 131
Tocqueville, A. de 54, 126, 128
Trotsky, L. 46–51, 85, 122, 123, 132, 166, 237

Urry, J. 58, 85

Verwoerd, H. T. 139, 140, 142

Vorster, J. 140, 142, 143

Weber, M. 53
Weininger, O. 256
Wittgenstein, L. 5, 22, 29, 62, 84, 101, 104, 107, 109, 111, 119, 130, 191, 194, 208, 214, 218, 224
Wolin, S. 28
Wright, E. O. 13, 14, 15, 84

Zasulich, V. 46
Žižek, S. xiv, 98, 130, 235, 247–60 *passim*